PA
3621
.V6

Von HILDEBRAND

Greek culture

10435

GREEK CULTURE

The Adventure of the Human Spirit

The Cultures of Mankind

Greek Culture

The Adventure of the Human Spirit

Edited by Alice von Hildebrand

George Braziller · New York

DESIGN BY JULIUS PERLMUTTER

ACKNOWLEDGMENTS

The editor and publisher have made every effort to determine and credit the holders of copyrights of the selections in this book. Any errors or omissions may be rectified in future editions. The editor and publisher wish to thank the following for permission to reprint the material included in this anthology:

George Allen & Unwin Ltd.—for selections from *The Birds* by Aristophanes, translated by Gilbert Murray, 1950.

Clarendon Press, Oxford—for selections from *Metaphysics* by Aristotle, translated by W. D. Ross; for selections from *Nicomachean Ethics* by Aristotle, translated by W. D. Ross; for selections from *Politics* by Aristotle, translated by Benjamin Jowett; and for selections from *The Oxford Book of Greek Verse in Translation,* edited by T. F. Higham and C. M. Bowra.

Dodd, Mead & Co. and The Bodley Head Ltd.—for a selection from *Orthodoxy* by G. K. Chesterton. Copyright 1908 by Dodd, Mead & Co.; renewed 1935 by Gilbert K. Chesterton. Reprinted by permission of the publishers.

Harvard University Press and William Heinemann, London—for selections from *Xenophon* and *Plutarch's Lives.* Loeb Classical Library. Reprinted by permission of the publishers and the Loeb Classical Library.

David Higham Associates, Ltd.—for selections from *Histories* by Herodotus, translated by Aubrey de Selincourt. Copyright 1960 by Aubrey de Selincourt. Reprinted by permission.

Washington Square Press—for selections from *The Peloponnesian Wars* by Thucydides, translated by Benjamin Jowett and edited by P. A. Brunt. Copyright ©, 1963 by Washington Square Press, Inc. Reprinted by permission of the publisher.

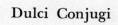

Dulci Conjugi

PREFACE

The history of Greece relates one of the most extraordinary adventures of the human mind. If ever the awesome greatness of man's spirit appeared in all its splendor, untarnished and undistorted, it was in Greece. This is why the impressive literature which has been devoted to its greatness cannot discourage one from trying to make one's own humble contribution: the praise of Greece can never be quite adequate, can never exhaust its merits.

So rich and varied is the literature on Greece that any new publication should begin with an apology, or rather a justification of its existence. *Cantare amantis est* says St. Augustine. He who has been granted to taste the flavor of Greek culture, he who has understood how it can enrich and deepen the human mind, will be filled with both admiration and gratitude and will sing the praises of Greece just because they deserve to be sung. Quite apart from any pragmatic consideration, it is right and proper to proclaim what Greece has been, is, and will remain in the history of man's achievements and man's conquests.

This due response which is essentially knitted to a deep enthusiasm, may then become contagious and attract some young mind to discover by itself the world of Greece, a world so rich that one is bound to keep its imprint; one will not be quite the same after having passed the threshold of the Greek world.

Finally, the very fact that Greece's attraction for the human mind, far from decreasing, seems to be gaining new impetus, testifies to the fertility of the Greek genius: in its depth and universality lies the secret of this attraction—eloquent testimony that true greatness transcends any particular culture, or any particular epoch: its message is directed to man himself.

A note on the texts: The titles given to many of the selections are mine; the original sources in such cases are indicated at the end of the selections. Because of space restrictions, it has unfortunately been necessary to abridge many of the selections; I have preferred this to sacrificing variety among the texts. Omitted passages are indicated either by ellipses or three dots centered on the page; where necessary I have inserted transitional notes to assist the reader.

Contents

I THE SPIRIT OF ADVENTURE

II THE ADVENTURE OF THE SPIRIT

1. The Birth of Philosophy

2. The Birth of History

3. The Birth of Literature

4. The Birth and Glory of Drama

5. The Glory of Philosophy

6. The Rise of Theology

CONTENTS

III FATE AND FREEDOM

1. Fate, Suffering and Crime

2. The Responsibility of Men

IV INDIVIDUAL AND POLIS

1. The Rise of the Polis

2. Man and His Conscience

3. Love and Friendship

GREEK CULTURE

List of Illustrations

INTRODUCTION

As the legend goes, when Oedipus arrived at Corinth, the city was plagued by a Sphinx that pitilessly slaughtered those incapable of solving the following riddle: Who is the animal that is first four footed, then two footed, then three footed? Oedipus recognized man; the Sphinx was vanquished and the victor became king of Corinth.

This story is magnificently symbolic of Greece. For in Greece man himself seems to awaken to what it means to be a person in the deepest sense of this term, that is to be a being called upon to take a position toward himself and toward the world. Man is not only in the world; he can emerge from it, question it, face it, enter into dialogue with it. In Greece man conquers this kingly position; he gains a novel dimension of consciousness of himself and of the world he is in. To identify oneself is the precondition for conquering the world.

We are far from wishing to underrate the remarkable achievements that have preceded Greek culture; rather, it is against the background of these accomplishments that the matchless greatness of the Greek mind detaches itself.

We shall see throughout this anthology that the spiritual awakening just mentioned has enabled the Greeks to penetrate into the world of art, science and philosophy and to conquer it, and has made them the shapers of occidental culture.

This is why the history of Greece is the history of one great adventure of the human mind; it is the history of a people whose genius has boldly conquered the Promethean fire and has illumined the world by its light and beauty. This spiritual awakening, this emergence of man from his surroundings, manifests itself in the predominant role granted to sight in the Greek world. Sight, Plato tells us, is the most noble of our senses; in seeing, a distance separates us from the object, and this very distance is the presupposition for gaining knowledge. Greek wisdom has always advocated self-knowledge, a knowledge so hard to attain precisely because this distance instead of being pre-given, must be attained.

There is a strict analogy between sight and intellectual knowledge, analogy that finds its expression in the term "see" used equally for perceiving and for understanding. Whereas the Jewish people were above all "hearers" of the word of God, the Greeks are essentially seers, and this characteristic manifests itself both in their artistic achievements and in the role art played in Greek life.

> The characteristic Greek method of constructing and looking at a work of art was first and foremost an aesthetic instinct, based on the simple act of sight.
>
> Werner Jaeger, *Paideia*

The distance to the world conquered by the Greeks is coupled with a deep feeling for objects, an espousing of their nature; they steer clear of the danger of seeing things unlovingly, "from without" with a coolness that freezes objects and prevents them from revealing themselves. To the Greek mind, to win a distance from objects does not warrant a non-committal attitude toward them.

This spiritual awakening runs parallel to a new attitude toward the sense world, which benefits from this emergence of the spirit. Far from relegating sense experience to the background, the victory of the spirit in Greece sheds a keener light on our senses; it seems to enhance colors, smells, sounds, and to reveal their meaningful character. The Greek world knows no artificial separation between the world of the spirit and the world of the senses; its basic tendency is to create a harmony between them.

The emergence of man from his surroundings gloriously manifests itself in the birth of philosophy. Greece is the cradle of philosophy, and the Greeks are the philosophers of the world par excellence. Whereas subtle theological explanations of the world, and wise teachings as to how suffering can be overcome abound in India and China, philosophy in the strict sense, i.e., the passionate search after truth *for its own sake,* starts with the Greeks. The question *ti esti,* what is it, rooted in wondering, freed from any pragmatic approach, and the systematic search after truth, begin with the pre-Socratics and reach a climax in Plato and Aristotle. In spite of the gigantic development of philosophy through the centuries, one is always tempted to go back to the Greeks when one wishes to explain to others the nature of philosophy, for "philosophy had its word" in Greece, to borrow an expression dear to Aristotle.

He who has taught the history of philosophy knows the delight of introducing young minds to the study of the pre-Socratics; in them we

1. *The Calf-bearer,* or *Moschophoros.*

2. Treasury of the Athenians. Delphi.

can witness philosophy itself at work. The depth of the questions raised (where do things come from?), is often at odds with the helplessness of the answers given. But these answers are then put to the test, examined, rejected, while the question is kept as a valuable gift from the past, and is then re-examined. And yet the healthy intellectual dynamism of the Greeks—so far removed from movement for movement's sake—springing from a vigorous and alert relationship to objects, carries them closer to a true answer. Once again this new answer can prove to be unsatisfactory and incomplete, but yet, it can contain a grain of truth that deserves to be carefully kept and protected. Early Greek philosophy presents a luminous pattern hard to duplicate in the history of philosophy.

In Socrates the development of philosophy is connected with another dimension of the awakening typical of Greece, one that surpasses the purely philosophical quest. For in him we witness a breakthrough to the predominant role of morality; an awakening to the voice of conscience, a discovery of the specific nature of morality, a discovery which has almost the character of something miraculous. The greatness of Socrates and of socratic teaching appears in the proper light as soon as we examine his position against the background of the oriental conception of morality. In the latter, moral good and evil tend to be replaced by the categories of high and low, and morality itself is more or less identified with asceticism. If we prescind from the notion of morality prevalent in Israel, indissolubly connected as it was with revelation, the following words put in Socrates' mouth by Plato display their revolutionary character:

. . . to do is a greater evil than to suffer injustice . . .

Plato, *Gorgias*

Not only did Socrates discover the primacy of moral values; over and above it, his very personality testified to this new conception of morality. One could see him on the streets of Athens neglecting his personal interests, trying to awaken his hearers to moral maturity, radiating justice, selflessness, sobriety, kindness. He was possessed of a zeal free from fanaticism, respectful of the individual soul, arrogating only the role of a midwife helping to give birth to truth in the souls of his disciples. He had to pay the price that prophets often must pay, but he was ready for it all along, and when his hour came, he greeted it peacefully, with neither resentment nor anguish. He never expected his message to be heard by all men; "For this opinion [that we should not retaliate] has never been held and never will be held by any considerable number of persons"

(Plato, *Crito*). He knew it had been heard by some and will continue to be so throughout the history of the world by men of good will.

The resonance of this teaching came in Plato who not only immortalized his master, but also gave Socratic teaching a metaphysical basis. No doubt, Plato's own genius carried him above and beyond the Socratic doctrine of learned ignorance, but one should not forget that Socrates left an indelible imprint on his disciple and remained the inspiration and the model for the latter's ethical teaching.

In Plato, philosophy reaches a climax; not only does he discuss the cardinal philosophical themes (as Jacques Chevalier has put it: those man raises when facing death), the themes we share with the Athenians of the fifth and fourth centuries; but above everything else, Plato teaches the spirit in which one should philosophize, a spirit of absolute devotion to truth: "I am one of those very willing to be refuted if I say anything which is not true . . . for I hold that this is the greater gain of the two . . ." (Plato, *Gorgias*) and of reverence in front of the mystery of the cosmos: "Let parents bequeath to their children not a heap of riches, but the spirit of reverence" (Plato, *Laws*).

Rare are the philosophers who can steer clear of error throughout their careers, but the important point is to examine the ground from which these errors spring. Platonic mistakes can never be traced back to a spirit of irreverence; he considers reverence to be an indispensable presupposition for fruitful philosophical investigation. At times, the errors he makes are the tribute he has to pay for a profound intuition unduly extended; at times, Plato remained the prisoner of sociological conditions prevalent in his time. Nevertheless Platonic philosophy often contains self correctives which, at least, place distortions and mistakes in the proper perspective. Platonic philosophy has the ring of truth; errors on his tongue are more dissonances than bad music. However one stands toward him, he is and will remain one of the great lights shed by reason in a universe plagued by uncertainty and doubt. Maybe Gabriel Marcel uttered a profound truth when he wrote: "What the world needs today is a cure of Platonism" (*Les Hommes contre l'Humain*).

It is said of Schubert that he doubted of ever being able to write good music, for, he reasoned, what can one say after Beethoven? Was Aristotle's position any easier for coming after Plato? And yet, far from being crushed by his predecessor's greatness, Aristotle succeeded in finding his own way to philosophy, certain as he was that he was called upon to give something Plato had not given, could not give. In him, philosophy as "scientific knowledge" takes a fresh start. Jaeger claims that Plato's genius surpassed Aristotle's but that the latter can lay claim to superiority when scientific and methodical presentation are in order. The gamut of Aristotle's interests is overwhelming; he left us works on logic, metaphysics, ethics, aesthetics, epistemology, which are classics, and opened broad new avenues in the field of history and of the sciences. Aristotle's interest is universal; his erudition and inquisitiveness of mind are unparalleled. To do justice to his greatness, one must for a moment forget Plato and open one's mind to a different philosophical approach, coupled with the same devotion to truth.

It is, I believe, a great mistake to pit Plato against Aristotle, and present them as irreconcilable enemies. Granted that their thoughts are often at variance, granted that on many issues, one must choose between them, the fact remains that in the light of the history of philosophy, or rather *thanks* to the further development of philosophy, these two giants of thought strike us as basically close to one another: both accept God's existence, both believe in the possibility of attaining objective knowledge, both saw philosophy in the most beautiful and deepest light.

We would however fail to understand the Greek mind if upon contemplating this unique awakening of the intellect, this victory of the *logos* in philosophy, we overlooked the deeply religious character of the Greeks, and the role the *mythos* played in Greece. Although the *mythos* preceded the *logos*, both are interwoven in the Greek world. The firm grip the *logos* began to have over the Greek mind from the sixth century on, did not sound a warning for the disappearance of religion; throughout their history, the Greeks remained a deeply religious people.

The rejection of the anthropomorphism immanent in Greek mythology should not lead one to overlooking this deep religiosity. Essential as the truth of theological formulations may be, the religiosity of a people should not be judged exclusively on that count, but should also include a reverent examination of the lived religious attitude of people and of the importance of religion in their lives. *Religio* means a bond toward a being above one, and the Greeks were deeply conscious of their dependence upon the gods; we might even say, of their creaturehood. Their fear of *hybris*—one of the most typical attitudes of the Greeks—evidences the awe they felt toward the gods. Hybris, which originally meant an illegal action (Jaeger, *Paideia*), takes more and more the meaning of "metaphysical impertinence," of irreverent self-assurance in which man breaks the bond of *religio* and feels himself to be his own master. An epitome of hybris is to be found in the words of Ajax in Sophocles' tragedy:

3. *Two Goddesses,* from the east pediment of the Parthenon.

> Father, with heaven's help a mere man of nought
> Might win victory: but I, albeit without
> Their aid, trust to achieve a victor's glory.
>
> *Ajax*

This hybris is primarily responsible for the downfall of the hero.

It is also deeply meaningful for the Greek religious sense that their progressive criticism of mythology and anthropomorphism started by Xenophanes did not lead them to scientific atheism, but much rather to a deepening of their conception of God, as evidenced in the teaching of Socrates, Plato, and Aristotle.

The overwhelming role of religion in Greek life is also shown by the fact that nothing great was undertaken without cultic sacrifice, and that even daily life was pervaded by cultic acts. The part played by oracles is well known. Consequently Greek life cannot be understood if one overlooks this dialogue with the Gods, this pious, reverent looking up to the Gods.

The Greeks had a deep sense of sacredness, they lived in a world pervaded by a sacred atmosphere; this fact is brought into sharp focus if we turn to *The Iliad* and *The Odyssey* and remember that these two works formed the Greek consciousness.

The key function of mythology in Greece becomes manifest as soon as we realize that these people viewed the sea, lightning, thunder, the seasons, rivers, trees, animals as things sacred, and personalized them as gods and demigods. Seen in this light, Greek mythology gains its true meaning. Its anthropomorphism cannot be denied, and yet, over and above these errors, there lurks a great metaphysical depth. Apart from the enchanting poetic elements Greek mythology incarnates, we find personified in each divinity an element of the physical or spiritual world viewed in the most beautiful light. Greek mythology is not the product of a fertile imagination that has run wild, but much rather a poetic formulation of a metaphysical insight, and an objectivation of a religious attitude.

It is the classical character of Greek mythology that led Joseph de Maistre to say that the Greek deities were *"des vérités renversées."* This is so true that when Thales predicted an eclipse of the sun, and thereby gave a first blow to mythology, the Greeks, far from becoming atheists, were slowly led to deepening their own ideas about the gods. In Plato, many *vérités renversées* have been put straight; he kept the Homeric idea of the closeness of gods to men, while purifying it of its human, all too human elements. "Now God ought to be to us the measure of all things" wrote Plato in the *Laws*.

The key role of religion in Greek life manifests itself also in one of the greatest glories of Greece: their fine arts and literature. The timeless beauty of Greek sculpture and architecture has been praised perhaps even more than the Greek accomplishments in philosophy. This art was indissolubly linked to religion; it organically grew out of it and was a fruit of the Greek cult of the gods. Here again we can witness the harmonious cooperation between Greek humanism and religion. Greek art testifies to man's spiritual emancipation, to his becoming a conscious creator; and simultaneously it reflects the religious attitude of the Greeks and thus should never be severed from its cultic background. Though beauty assumed in Greek art a full thematicity, it never was uprooted from its cultic soil.

Greek sculptures display the lived harmony that existed between man and nature. The poise so typical of Greek art, the gracefulness of movement, the naturalness of positions testify to the fact that the Greeks were at home in their own bodies. Their art shows no trace of strain and artificiality. It reflects the extraordinary sense of proportion the Greeks intuitively possessed in their relation to nature, to the gods, and in the relationship they created between architecture and nature. These traits give witness to the Greek victory over chaos and to the harmony they established between man's bondage to the gods and to the cosmos on the one hand, and the freedom of the human person on the other.

Apart from having produced writings whose depth and beauty have hardly ever been surpassed and rarely ever paralleled, the Greeks gave birth to literature in the modern sense of the term. From them we have inherited a new conception of literature as a work of art whose locus is beauty. Their originality in this sphere can be best illustrated by comparing the Greek accomplishments in this domain with the Old Testament. The Bible is no doubt incredibly beautiful; it is replete with passages of ultimate dramatic power, such as the stories of Joseph and of David; it has lines of the greatest poetic charm in the *Canticle of Canticles,* but the "theme" of the Old Testament is not the creation of a work of art. Its concern is to communicate to man the divine message and to establish a living dialogue between the Creator and his creature. Whereas beauty of style essentially belongs to the greatness of this sacred work, nevertheless the primary intention of the Bible is to communicate Truth. It claims to be the Divine Word addressed to man, and lays no claim whatever to being a work of art. To approach the Bible exclusively as if it were such is equivalent to misunderstanding its essence.

Greek literature, on the other hand, while deeply embedded in cultic and educational trends, puts a new stress on beauty *for its own sake.* The world of the Old Testament is theocentric par excellence; Greece is humanistic, so much so, that the gods themselves were seen in a human light and were given human proportions.

The part played by the drama in Greek life should retain our attention. Poets were, for Athenians, something of spiritual leaders (see Jaeger, *Paideia,* Vol. I, p. 247), whose task was not exhausted by the creation of works of art. They were also called upon to fulfill an educational function, and were held responsible for shedding light on the dark recesses of human conscience, on the mysterious and tragic side of human destiny. They showed that man whose greatness is so undeniable, can be the prey of circumstances so tragic, of situations so heartrending, that he seems predestined to fall. This unpredictable element in human life that can bring the most noble men to crime, never lost its sway over the Greek mind:

> There is a saying among men, put forth of old, that thou canst not rightly judge whether a mortal's lot is good or evil, ere he die.
>
> Sophocles, *Trachiniae*

The pitiless criticisms Aristophanes leveled at Euripides (let us remember *The Frogs* and the *Thesmophoriazusae*) become intelligible as soon as we realize that the former was convinced that the latter failed his uplifting educational mission.

The Greek fascination over educational problems was born out of a double awareness: the greatness of man, and the consciousness that this greatness, far from developing immanently, can be marred. How is man to be educated so that the rich possibilities lying dormant in him will find their fulfillment? The Greek sense of proportion manifests itself in the efforts they made to create a well-rounded education, taking into account man's body as well as man's mind. Nothing human was to be neglected, for the beauty of the whole depends upon the harmonious development of all its parts. Gymnastics was as important for the body as mathematics was for the mind. The Greek conception of education sheds the brightest light on its humanism. Jaeger wrote: "The greatest work of art they had to create was Man" (*Paideia*, I, XXII).

One has interpreted Greece as the land of gaiety and joy, as opposed to the dark and severe medieval outlook on existence. No doubt the Greeks steered free from the pessimistic interpretation of human existence the Orient has inherited from Buddha. The equation of life and suffering is not Greek. "I tell myself that we are a long time underground, and that life is short but sweet" is the argument used by Pheres to account for his refusal to die in place of his own son (Euripides, *Alcestis*).

As inborn artists, the Greeks were much too conscious of the radiance and beauty of created goods, of the glow of "the wine dark sea," of the "rose-fingered dawn," to see existence in a pessimistic light. Like artists they appreciated anything beautiful and poetic. They conceived life as a gift, joy as a "duty." Let us recall the striking lines of Euripides:

> Only on them that spurn
> Joy, may his anger burn.
> *Bacchae*

Chesterton claims, however, that there was another side to Greek life:

> It is said that Paganism is a religion of joy and Christianity of sorrow; it would be just as easy to prove that Paganism is pure sorrow and Christianity pure joy. . . . there was more cosmic contentment in the narrow and bloody streets of Florence than in the theater of Athens or the open garden of

4. *"François vase,"* crater by Ergotimos and Klitias.

Epicurus. Giotto lived in a gloomier town than Euripides, but he lived in a gayer universe. . . .

Orthodoxy

Much as the Greeks enjoyed living, never did they shut their eyes to the dark, unexplained, fearful side of human existence, constantly threatened, insecure and fleeting as the moment itself:

> . . . to the gods alone comes never old age or death, but all else is confounded by all-mastering time. . . .

Sophocles, *Oedipus at Colonus*

It was a common saying among the Greeks that it was better to be a beggar in the kingdom of light than a king in Hades. In one of the most pathetic dramas of Euripides (*The Trojan Women*), as the heroine wishes herself dead, she is reminded of the fearful character of death:

> Death cannot be what life is, child; the cup
> Of death is empty, and life has always hope.

The matchless sense of proportion which overwhelms one in Greek art pervaded the entire Greek life. We encounter it in literature, in the role granted to temperance and justice, sophrosyne and wisdom, in the part played by the laws in communal life. It appears as metaphysical principle in Anaximander's cosmic justice as well as in the Pythagorean notion of harmony. We find it again in the often repeated exhortation that men should not transcend certain boundaries:

> But if any man walks haughtily in deed or words, with no fear of Justice, no reverence for the images of gods, may an evil doom seize him for his ill-starred pride.
>
> Sophocles, *Oedipus the King*

Men are called upon by the gods to respect the proportions of the cosmos and woe to him who forgets this elementary metaphysical principle:

> For lo, swift ruin worketh sure judgment on hearts
> With pride puffed up and high presumption,
> On all stored wealth that overpasseth
> The bound of due measure.
>
> Aeschylus, *Agamemnon*

This sense of proportion lies at the antipodes of mediocrity; not only does it not exclude a fruitful tension between opposites but it is essentially linked to it; for "the hidden harmony is better than that which is obvious," says Heraclitus. This fruitful polarity, so typical of the richness of the Greek approach to life, finds again a striking expression in Heraclitus' "War is the father of all things"; it manifests itself again in the interpenetration of the Apollonian and Dionysian elements which, according to Nietzsche, form the two decisive poles of Greek culture.

In the historical consciousness of the Greeks, we find another facet of their spiritual awakening; the relationship to the past had in Greece a special flavor which distinguishes it from the sense for traditions typical of other countries. The cult of ancestors was at the very core of many pre-Hellenic cultures; moreover, all religions necessarily imply an element of tradition and a vivid consciousness of the past. But Herodotus gains an awareness of the value of history proper, and he is keen upon acquiring historical knowledge for its own sake. In perusing his *History of the Per-*

31

5. *Herakles and Athena,* detail of cup by Douris.

sian Wars, one is amazed about his objectivity in presenting "what has been" (to use a definition of history by Ranke), by his sense of historic responsibility coupled with a feeling for characteristic anecdotes, and a deep moral sense. In Thucydides, full-fledged historical research is constituted.

The emancipation of the human mind in Greece comes again strikingly to the fore when we examine the Greek city-state and compare it to prior achievements in the domain of politics. To the already existing forms of government the Greeks added a new dimension of consciousness with respect to man's character as a social being. The logical structure of the polis, the dignity of the law, the pivotal importance of justice, the magnitude of the polis in the individual's life: all these notions display the maturity acquired by the Greeks in this domain.

Werner Jaeger remarks that in Greece, the individual gained a profound recognition; he emerged from the anonymity typical of the Orient; and simultaneously the immense value of organized communal life stepped into the foreground. For the Athenians of the fifth and sixth centuries, the polis was more than a well-organized body indispensable for leading an ordered life; it was such an essential part of man's personal existence that Socrates, though unjustly condemned, refused to escape for fear of injuring the state (Plato, *Crito*).

The Greek conception of the polis is a manifestation of man's awakening; it must be sharply distinguished from collectivism which dissolves the character of man as person. Much rather the Greek conception of the polis presupposes a full evaluation of the individual.

In this respect it is once again very illustrative to compare the Greek mind with the Oriental one, as expressed, for instance, in Buddhism or Hinduism. In the latter, the very fact of man's individuality is considered to be a limitation; a-personality is an ideal. But the state as such has no vital importance. The Yogi completely retires into his self and advocates thereby a peculiar withdrawal from all community life and *a fortiori* from the state. This introversion aims not, however, at a full personal life but rather at the evanescence of the individual in cosmic experience. In Hellas, on the contrary, a full awakening to individual existence is interwoven with a profound awareness of the central importance of communal life, and of the fact that the authentic development of the city-state required the recognition of man's individual value. The totalitarian danger which does lurk in Greece stems not from a blindness for the individual, but rather from the wish to find an absolute shelteredness that individual life cannot offer. Jaeger says:

6. Temple of Poseidon, southwest view. Paestum.

His [Aristotle's] definition can be understood only by studying
the structure of the early polis; for its citizens held their communal existence to be the sum of all the higher things of life
—in fact to be something divine.

Paideia

Moreover the Greek emphasis on the city-state essentially differs from
statolatries of modern times. The significance of the polis for the Greeks
cannot be understood in the light of the medieval or modern conceptions
of the state. For them, it was the community that incorporated all cultural goods and represented the moral order. Its orbit was not limited to
the *res publica*, i.e., to the organization of public life and to the sphere
of jurisdiction. Apart from essential differences, their relation to the
city-state is rather to be viewed in the light of what Jerusalem meant for
the Jewish people and the Church for Catholics.

It is well nigh impossible to make global statements about the mind of
a people whose history covered a period of more than one thousand years.
The time of Homer and Hesiod obviously differs in many respects from
the fifth century B.C. in Athens. But as long as we limit ourselves to the
basic characteristics of the Greek mind—namely the full awakening of

34

man and a rich humanism in all domains of human activity—these hold true for all periods of Greek history, notwithstanding important modifications within each period. These traits grow and develop until they reach a height in the fifth century and, in a certain way, in Plato. More detailed queries about Greek history must be answered individually for each period has its particular flavor.

Questions such as: "What was the position of women in Greece?" or "What was the Greek conception of marriage?" have often been raised and one is tempted to answer them by taking the fifth century as pattern; this leads to a one-sided answer. The complexity of Greece is such that next to the phenomenon of homosexuality, one finds glowing praises of marriage and of the love between man and woman. Let us recall the legend of *Orpheus and Euridice* and two dramas of Euripides, *Alcestis* and *Helen,* devoted to the praise of conjugal love. True as it is that the role assigned to women is at times insignificant, female personalities such as Homer's *Andromache* and *Penelope* and above all Sophocles' *Antigone* are also typically Greek. It is interesting to note that most of Euripides' dramas are named after women.

Our praise of Greece would be incomplete if we failed to mention the transition of Hellas into Hellenism. At the very moment that Alexander the Great's conquests put an end to Greek political independence, the Greek spirit achieved its greatest victory, for it was the same Alexander who penetrated the entire orbit of antiquity with Greek culture and whose triumphant military conquests brought about a penetration of the world by this culture. In the very act of dying Hellas gave birth to Hellenism. During this late period the spiritual fertility of Athens cannot be matched against its former achievements. But Greece continued nevertheless to make notable contributions to the world of the spirit. The encounter of the Greek genius with Egypt, Syria, Asia Minor, Persia, and finally Rome, gave birth to a new type of culture having a value and a charm of its own. Granted that the world of Alexandria differs radically from the one of Athens in the fifth or fourth century B.C., nevertheless it is a manifestation of Greece's indomitable spiritual power and fertility.

During the long epoch of Hellenism we find impressive figures such as Epicurus, Polybius, Plutarch, Epictetus. Last but not least two late blossoms of the Greek genius should retain our attention. On the one hand we find Plotinus and his grandiose attempts at building a metaphysics in the framework of a pagan synthesis of Greek and Oriental trends. On the other hand we encounter Justinus, Origenes, Gregory of

7. *Nike of Samothrace.*

Nyssa, who, as Werner Jaeger has shown, have put the Greek tradition at the service of Christianity.

Much as the Christian era differs from Hellenism, nevertheless it is indebted to the spirit of Greece, for great Christian theologians ingrafted shoots of Greek thought on the spiritual tree of Christian theology. Apart from the spirit of Hellenism and of the early Greek Fathers of the Church, mention should be made of the unparalleled influence the Greek mind exercised over the cultural history of Europe. In Hellenism we are still confronted with an evolution of the Greek spirit itself, stemming from the original Greek tradition; this applies analogously to the entire Byzantine culture. In later times, however, though continuity with the past had been broken, the Greek spirit radiated in other ways. The influence Neo-Platonism exercised over Saint Augustine and through him on the early Middle Ages, as well as the Aristotelian penetration of Arabic and Jewish thought, hardly needs mentioning. In Saint Thomas Aquinas, Aristotle achieved his greatest victory and made deep inroads into Christian philosophy. The humanism of the fifteenth century and the renaissance of Greek art in Italy are spectacular instances of the influence exercised by the Greek spirit. One glance thrown at occidental culture as a whole confirms always again the unique role which Greek culture and the Greek genius played and are still playing in the history of Europe.

I

The Spirit of Adventure

Now it is time for you to fall
in love with evil war.

Homer, *Iliad*

It is typical of great minds to thirst for great things, and the spiritual alertness of the Greeks made them long to transcend the scope of everyday life, to uproot habits and to face the unknown. For the early Greeks areté *was identified with courage; it was this virtue that above all else deserved praise and allowed one to achieve a sort of immortality.*

It is quite essential to realize that this courage was not the expression of mere vitality, but much rather of an audacity flowing out of the awareness of spiritual superiority. The Greek feeling of superiority over what they called the Barbarians, sprang from their deeply rooted conviction that it is the intellect that conquers the earth.

The adventures of the Greeks were not conditioned by necessities that often forced entire populations to move forward in the hope of finding skies more clement and soils more fertile; nor are they to be compared to the Persian thirst for aggrandizement. The Greeks have proved to the world that devotion to an ideal and thirst for fame can be the driving forces leading to great deeds. Let us recall the famous words quoted by Herodotus: "Good heavens, Mardonius, what kind of men are these that you brought us to fight against, men who compete with one another for no material reward, but only for honor."

Herodotus (484-?) was caught by the spirit of adventure when he decided to visit foreign countries, and to study their customs. For the first time in history, we have records of someone who undertook tiresome journeys, driven by spiritual curiosity.

In the Anabasis *of Xenophon (430-?), we witness a military adventure, motivated primarily by thirst for fame, mixed with an idealistic devotion to Cyrus. The Greek spirit of endurance is here described at its best.*

HOMER

THE ADVENTURES OF ULYSSES

"Onward we sailed with sorrowing hearts, and reached
The country of the Cyclops, an untamed
And lawless race, who, trusting to the gods,
Plant not, nor plough the fields, but all things spring
For them untended,—barley, wheat, and vines
Yielding large clusters filled with wine, and nursed
By showers from Jove. No laws have they; they hold
No councils. On the mountain heights they dwell
In vaulted caves, where each one rules his wives
And children as he pleases; none give heed
To what the others do. Before the port
Of that Cyclopean land there is an isle,
Low-lying, neither near nor yet remote,—
A woodland region, where the wild goats breed
Innumerable; for the foot of man
Disturbs them not, and huntsmen toiling through
Thick woods, or wandering over mountain heights,
Enter not here. The fields are never grazed
By sheep, nor furrowed by the plough, but lie
Untilled, unsown, and uninhabited
By man, and only feed the bleating goats.
The Cyclops have no barks with crimson prows,
Nor shipwrights skilled to frame a galley's deck
With benches for the rowers, and equipped
For any service, voyaging by turns
To all the cities, as is often done
By men who cross the deep from place to place,
And make a prosperous region of an isle.
No meagre soil is there; it well might bear
All fruits in their due time. Along the shore
Of the gray deep are meadows smooth and moist.
The vine would flourish long; the ploughman's task
Is easy, and the husbandman would reap
Large harvests, for the mould is rich below.
And there is a safe haven, where no need
Of cable is; no anchor there is cast,

8. Naxian Sphinx.

Nor hawsers fastened to the strand, but they
Who enter there remain until it please
The mariners, with favorable wind,
To put to sea again. A limpid stream
Flows from a fount beneath a hollow rock
Into that harbor at its further end,
And poplars grow around it. Thither went
Our fleet; some deity had guided us
Through the dark night, for nothing had we seen.
Thick was the gloom around our barks; the moon
Shone not in heaven, the clouds had quenched her light.
No eye discerned the isle, nor the long waves
That rolled against the shore, till our good ships
Touched land, and, disembarking there, we gave
Ourselves to sleep upon the water-side
And waited for the holy Morn to rise.
   "And when at length the daughter of the Dawn,
The rosy-fingered Morn, appeared, we walked
Around the isle, admiring as we went.
Meanwhile the nymphs, the daughters of the God
Who bears the aegis, roused the mountain goats,
That so our crews might make their morning meal.
And straightway from our ships we took in hand
Our crooked bows and our long-bladed spears.
   " 'Let all the rest of my beloved friends
Remain, while I, with my own bark and crew,
Go forth to learn what race of men are these,
Whether ill-mannered, savage, and unjust,
Or kind to guests and reverent toward the gods.'
   "I spake, and, having ordered all my crew
To go on board and cast the hawsers loose,
Embarked on my own ship. They all obeyed,
And manned the benches, sitting there in rows,
And smote the hoary ocean with their oars.
But when we came upon that neighboring coast,
We saw upon its verge beside the sea
A cave high vaulted, overbrowed with shrubs
Of laurel. There much cattle lay at rest,
Both sheep and goats. Around it was a court,
A high enclosure of hewn stone, and pines

Tall stemmed, and towering oaks. Here dwelt a man
Of giant bulk, who by himself, alone,
Was wont to tend his flocks. He never held
Converse with others, but devised apart
His wicked deeds. A frightful prodigy
Was he, and like no man who lives by bread,
But more like a huge mountain summit, rough
With woods, that towers alone above the rest.
    "Then, bidding all the others stay and guard
The ship, I chose among my bravest men
Twelve whom I took with me. I had on board
A goatskin of dark wine,—a pleasant sort,
Which Maron late, Evanthes' son, a priest
Of Phoebus, guardian god of Ismarus,
Gave me, when, moved with reverence, we saved
Him and his children and his wife from death.
For his abode was in the thick-grown grove
Of Phoebus. Costly were the gifts he gave,—
Seven talents of wrought gold; a chalice all
Of silver; and he drew for me, besides,
Into twelve jars, a choice rich wine, unspoiled
By mixtures, and a beverage for gods.
No one within his dwellings, maids or men,
Knew of it, save the master and his wife,
And matron of the household. Whensoe'er
They drank this rich red wine, he only filled
A single cup with wine, and tempered that
With twenty more of water. From the cup
Arose a fragrance that might please the gods,
And hard it was to put the draught aside.
Of this I took a skin well filled, besides
Food in a hamper,—for my thoughtful mind
Misgave me, lest I should encounter one
Of formidable strength and savage mood,
And with no sense of justice or of right.
    "Soon were we at the cave, but found not him
Within it; he was in the fertile meads,
Tending his flocks. We entered, wondering much
At all we saw. Around were baskets heaped
With cheeses; pens were thronged with lambs and kids,

Each in a separate fold; the elder ones,
The younger, and the newly weaned, had each
Their place apart. The vessels swam with whey,—
Pails smoothly wrought, and buckets into which
He milked the cattle. My companions then
Begged me with many pressing words to take
Part of the cheeses, and, returning, drive
With speed to our good galley lambs and kids
From where they stabled, and set sail again
On the salt sea. I granted not their wish;
Far better if I had. 'T was my intent
To see the owner of the flocks and prove
His hospitality. No pleasant sight
Was that to be for those with whom I came.
    "And then we lit a fire, and sacrificed,
And ate the cheeses, and within the cave
Sat waiting, till from pasturing his flocks
He came; a heavy load of well-dried wood
He bore, to make a blaze at supper-time.
Without the den he flung his burden down
With such a crash that we in terror slunk
Into a corner of the cave. He drove
His well-fed flock, all those whose milk he drew,
Under that spacious vault of rock, but left
The males, both goats and rams, without the court.
And then he lifted a huge barrier up,
A mighty weight; not two-and-twenty wains,
Four-wheeled and strong, could move it from the ground:
Such was the enormous rock he raised, and placed
Against the entrance. Then he sat and milked
The ewes and bleating goats, each one in turn,
And gave to each its young. Next, half the milk
He caused to curdle, and disposed the curd
In woven baskets; and the other half
He kept in bowls to be his evening drink.
His tasks all ended thus, he lit a fire,
And saw us where we lurked, and questioned us:—
    " 'Who are ye, strangers? Tell me whence ye came
Across the ocean. Are ye men of trade,
Or wanderers at will, like those who roam

9. Archaic head.

The sea for plunder, and, with their own lives
In peril, carry death to distant shores?'
　　"He spake, and we who heard with sinking hearts
Trembled at that deep voice and frightful form,
And thus I answered: 'We are Greeks who come
From Ilium, driven across the mighty deep
By changing winds, and while we sought our home
Have made a different voyage, and been forced
Upon another course; such was the will
Of Jupiter. We boast ourselves to be
Soldiers of Agamemnon, Atreus' son,
Whose fame is now the greatest under heaven,
So mighty was the city which he sacked,
So many were the warriors whom he slew;
And now we come as suppliants to thy knees,

47

And ask thee to receive us as thy guests,
Or else bestow the gifts which custom makes
The stranger's due. Great as thou art, revere
The gods; for suitors to thy grace are we,
And hospitable Jove, whose presence goes
With every worthy stranger, will avenge
Suppliants and strangers when they suffer wrong.'
   "I spake, and savagely he answered me:—
'Thou art a fool, O stranger, or art come
From some far country,—thou who biddest me
Fear or regard the gods. We little care—
We Cyclops—for the Aegis-bearer, Jove,
Or any other of the blessed gods;
We are their betters. Think not I would spare
Thee or thy comrades to avoid the wrath
Of Jupiter, unless it were my choice;
But say,—for I would know,—where hast thou left
Thy gallant bark in landing? was it near,
Or in some distant corner of the isle?'
   "He spake to tempt me, but I well perceived
His craft, and answered with dissembling words:—
   " 'Neptune, who shakes the shores, hath wrecked my bark
On rocks that edge thine island, hurling it
Against the headland. From the open sea
The tempest swept it hitherward, and I,
With these, escaped the bitter doom of death.'
   "I spake; the savage answered not, but sprang,
And, laying hands on my companions, seized
Two, whom he dashed like whelps against the ground.
Their brains flowed out, and weltered where they fell.
He hewed them limb from limb for his repast,
And, like a lion of the mountain wilds,
Devoured them as they were, and left no part,—
Entrails nor flesh nor marrowy bones. We wept
To see his cruelties, and raised our hands
To Jove, and hopeless misery filled our hearts.
And when the Cyclops now had filled himself,
Devouring human flesh, and drinking milk
Unmingled, in his cave he laid him down,
Stretched out amid his flocks. The thought arose

In my courageous heart to go to him,
And draw the trenchant sword upon my thigh,
And where the midriff joins the liver deal
A stroke to pierce his breast. A second thought
Restrained me,—that a miserable death
Would overtake us, since we had no power
To move the mighty rock which he had laid
At the high opening. So all night we grieved,
Waiting the holy Morn; and when at length
That rosy-fingered daughter of the Dawn
Appeared, the Cyclops lit a fire, and milked
His fair flock one by one, and brought their young
Each to its mother's side. When he had thus
Performed his household tasks, he seized again
Two of our number for his morning meal.
These he devoured, and then he moved away
With ease the massive rock that closed the cave,
And, driving forth his well-fed flock, he laid
The massive barrier back, as one would fit
The lid upon a quiver. With loud noise
The Cyclops drove that well-fed flock afield,
While I was left to think of many a plan
To do him mischief and avenge our wrongs,
If haply Pallas should confer on me
That glory. To my mind, as I revolved
The plans, this seemed the wisest of them all.
    "Beside the stalls there lay a massive club
Of olive-wood, yet green, which from its stock
The Cyclops hewed, that he might carry it
When seasoned. As it lay it seemed to us
The mast of some black galley, broad of beam,
With twenty oarsmen, built to carry freight
Across the mighty deep,—such was its length
And thickness. Standing by it, I cut off
A fathom's length, and gave it to my men,
And bade them smooth its sides, and they obeyed
While I made sharp the smaller end, and brought
The point to hardness in the glowing fire;
And then I hid the weapon in a heap
Of litter, which lay thick about the cave.

I bade my comrades now decide by lot
Which of them all should dare, along with me,
To lift the stake, and with its point bore out
Our enemy's eye, when softly wrapped in sleep.
The lot was cast, and fell on those whom most
I wished with me,—four men, and I the fifth.

　"At eve the keeper of these fair-woolled flocks
Returned, and brought his well-fed sheep and goats
Into the spacious cavern, leaving none
Without it, whether through some doubt of us
Or through the ordering of some god. He raised
The massive rock again, and laid it close
Against the opening. Then he sat and milked
The ewes and bleating goats, each one in turn,
And gave to each her young. When he had thus
Performed his household tasks, he seized again
Two of our number for his evening meal.
Then drew I near, and bearing in my hand
A wooden cup of dark red wine I said:—

　"'Take this, O Cyclops, after thy repast
Of human flesh, and drink, that thou mayst know
What liquor was concealed within our ship.
I brought it as an offering to thee,
For I had hope that thou wouldst pity us,
And send us home. Yet are thy cruelties
Beyond all limit. Wicked as thou art,
Hereafter who, of all the human race,
Will dare approach thee, guilty of such wrong?'

　"As thus I spake, he took the cup and drank.
The luscious wine delighted mightily
His palate, and he asked a second draught.

　"'Give me to drink again, and generously,
And tell thy name, that I may make a gift
Such as becomes a host. The fertile land
In which the Cyclops dwell yields wine, 't is true,
And the large grapes are nursed by rains from Jove,
But nectar and ambrosia are in this.'

　"He spake; I gave him of the generous juice
Again, and thrice I filled and brought the cup,
And thrice the Cyclops in his folly drank.

But when I saw the wine begin to cloud
His senses, I bespake him blandly thus:—
  " 'Thou hast inquired, O Cyclops, by what name
Men know me. I will tell thee, but do thou
Bestow in turn some hospitable gift,
As thou hast promised. Noman is my name,
My father and my mother gave it me,
And Noman am I called by all my friends.'
  "I ended, and he answered savagely:—
'Noman shall be the last of all his band
Whom I will eat, the rest will I devour
Before him. Let that respite be my gift.'
  "He spake, and, sinking backward at full length,
Lay on the ground, with his huge neck aside;
All-powerful sleep had overtaken him.
Then from his mouth came bits of human flesh
Mingled with wine, and from his drunken throat
Rejected noisily. I put the stake
Among the glowing coals to gather heat,
And uttered cheerful words, encouraging
My men, that none might fail me through their fears.
And when the olive-wood began to blaze,—
For though yet green it freely took the fire,—
I drew it from the embers. Round me stood
My comrades, whom some deity inspired
With calm, high courage. In their hands they took
And thrust into his eye the pointed bar,
While perched upon a higher stand than they
I twirled it round. As when a workman bores
Some timber of a ship, the men who stand
Below him with a strap, on either side
Twirl it, and round it spins unceasingly,
So, thrusting in his eye that pointed bar,
We made it turn. The blood came streaming forth
On the hot wood; the eyelids and the brow
Were scalded by the vapor, and the roots
Of the scorched eyeball crackled with the fire.
As when a smith, in forging axe or adze,
Plunges, to temper it, the hissing blade
Into cold water, strengthening thus the steel,

So hissed the eyeball of the Cyclops round
That olive stake. He raised a fearful howl;
The rocks rang with it, and we fled from him
In terror. Plucking from his eye the stake
All foul and dripping with the abundant blood,
He flung it madly from him with both hands.
Then called he to the Cyclops who in grots
Dwelt on that breezy height. They heard his voice
And came by various ways, and stood beside
The cave, and asked the occasion of his grief.

 " 'What hurts thee, Polyphemus, that thou thus
Dost break our slumbers in the ambrosial night
With cries? Hath any of the sons of men
Driven off thy flocks in spite of thee, or tried
By treachery or force to take thy life?'

 "Huge Polyphemus answered from his den:—
'O friends! 't is Noman who is killing me;
By treachery Noman kills me; none by force.'

 "Then thus with winged words they spake again:—
'If no man does thee violence, and thou
Art quite alone, reflect that none escape
Diseases; they are sent by Jove. But make
Thy prayer to Father Neptune, ocean's king.'

 "So spake they and departed. In my heart
I laughed to think that by the name I took,
And by my shrewd device, I had deceived
The Cyclops. Meantime, groaning and in pain,
And groping with his hands, he moved away
The rock that barred the entrance. There he sat,
With arms outstretched, to seize whoever sought
To issue from the cavern with the flock,
So dull of thought he deemed me. Then I planned
How best to save my comrades and myself
From death. I framed a thousand stratagems
And arts,—for here was life at stake, and great
The danger was. At last I fixed on this.

 "The rams were plump and beautiful, and large
With thick dark fleeces. These I silently
Bound to each other, three and three, with twigs

Of which that prodigy of lawless guilt,
The Cyclops, made his bed. The middle ram
Of every three conveyed a man; the two,
One on each side, were there to make him safe.
Thus each of us was borne by three; but I
Chose for myself the finest one of all,
And seized him by the back, and, slipping down
Beneath his shaggy belly, stretched myself
At length, and clung with resolute heart, and hands
That firmly clenched the rich abundant fleece.
Then sighed we for the holy Morn to rise.
    "And when again the daughter of the Dawn,
The rosy-fingered Morn, looked forth, the males
Went forth to pasture, while the ewes remained
Within the stables, bleating, yet unmilked,
For heavy were their udders. Carefully
The master handled, though in grievous pain,
The back of every one that rose and passed,
Yet, slow of thought, perceived not that my men
Were clinging hid beneath their woolly breasts.
As the last ram of all the flock went out,
His thick fleece heavy with my weight, and I
In agitated thought, he felt his back,
And thus the giant Polyphemus spake:—
    " 'My favorite ram, how art thou now the last
To leave the cave? It hath not been thy wont
To let the sheep go first, but thou didst come
Earliest to feed among the flowery grass,
Walking with stately strides, and thou wert first
At the fresh stream, and first at eve to seek
The stable; now thou art the last of all.
Grievest thou for thy master, who has lost
His eye, put out by a deceitful wretch
And his vile crew, who stupefied me first
With wine,—this Noman,—who, if right I deem,
Has not escaped from death. O, didst thou think
As I do, and hadst but the power of speech
To tell me where he hides from my strong arm,
Then should his brains, dashed out against the ground,

Be scattered here and there; then should my heart
Be somewhat lighter, even amid the woes
Which Noman, worthless wretch, has brought on me!'
    "He spake, and sent him forth among the rest;
And when we were a little way beyond
The cavern and the court, I loosed my hold
Upon the animal and unbound my men.
Then quickly we surrounded and drove off,
Fat sheep and stately paced, a numerous flock,
And brought them to our ship, where joyfully
Our friends received us, though with grief and tears
For those who perished. Yet I suffered not
That they should weep, but, frowning, gave command
By signs to lift with speed the fair-woolled sheep
On board, and launch our ship on the salt sea.
They went on board, where each one took his place
Upon the benches, and with diligent oars
Smote the gray deep; and when we were as far
As one upon the shore could hear a shout,
Thus to the Cyclops tauntingly I called:—
    " 'Ha! Cyclops! those whom in thy rocky cave
Thou, in thy brutal fury, hast devoured,
Were friends of one not unexpert in war;
Amply have thy own guilty deeds returned
Upon thee. Cruel one! who didst not fear
To eat the strangers sheltered by thy roof,
Jove and the other gods avenge them thus.'
    "I spake; the anger in his bosom raged
More fiercely. From a mountain peak he wrenched
Its summit, hurling it to fall beside
Our galley, where it almost touched the helm.
The rock dashed high the water where it fell,
And the returning billow swept us back
And toward the shore. I seized a long-stemmed pike
And pushed it from the shore, encouraging
The men to bend with vigor to their oars
And so escape. With nods I gave the sign.
Forward to vigorous strokes the oarsmen leaned . . ."

.   .   .

"Onward we sailed, with sorrow in our hearts
For our lost friends, though glad to be reprieved
From death. And now we landed at an isle,—
Aeaea, where the fair-haired Circè dwelt,
A goddess high in rank and skilled song,
Own sister of the wise Aeaetes. Both
Were children of the source of light, the Sun,
And Persè, Ocean's daughter, brought them forth.
We found a haven here, where ships might lie;
And guided by some deity we brought
Our galley silently against the shore,
And disembarked, and gave two days and nights
To rest, unmanned with hardship and with grief.
    "When bright-haired Morning brought the third day round,
I took my spear and my good sword, and left
The ship, and climbed a height, in hope to spy
Some trace of human toil, or hear some voice.
On a steep precipice I stood, and saw
From the broad earth below a rising smoke,
Where midst the thickets and the forest-ground
Stood Circè's palace. Seeing that dark smoke
The thought arose within my mind that there
I should inquire. I pondered till at last
This seemed the wisest,—to return at once
To my good ship upon the ocean-side,
And give my crew their meal, and send them forth
To view the region.

                    .   .   .

    "They found the fair abode where Circè dwelt,
A palace of hewn stone within the vale,
Yet nobly seated. There were mountain wolves
And lions round it, which herself had tamed
With powerful drugs; yet these assaulted not
The visitors, but, wagging their long tails,
Stood on their hinder feet, and fawned on them,
Like mastiffs on their master when he comes
From banqueting and brings them food. So fawned

10. *Poseidon (Zeus ?)*.

The strong-clawed wolves and lions on my men.
With fear my men beheld those beasts of prey,
Yet went, and, standing in the portico
Of the bright-haired divinity, they heard
Her sweet voice singing, as within she threw
The shuttle through the wide immortal web,
Such as is woven by the goddesses,—
Delicate, bright of hue, and beautiful.
　　"Polites then, a chief the most beloved
And most discreet of all my comrades, spake:—
　　" 'Some one is here, my friends, who sweetly sings,
Weaving an ample web, and all the floor
Rings to her voice. Whoever she may be,
Woman or goddess, let us call to her.'
　　"He spake; aloud they called, and forth she came
And threw at once the shining doors apart,
And bade my comrades enter. Without thought
They followed her. Eurylochus alone
Remained without, for he suspected guile.
She led them in and seated them on thrones.
Then mingling for them Pramnian wine with cheese,
Meal, and fresh honey, and infusing drugs
Into the mixture,—drugs which made them lose
The memory of their home,—she handed them
The beverage and they drank. Then instantly
She touched them with a wand, and shut them up
In sties, transformed to swine in head and voice,
Bristles and shape, though still the human mind
Remained to them. Thus sorrowing they were driven
Into their cells, where Circè flung to them
Acorns of oak and ilex, and the fruit
Of cornel, such as nourish wallowing swine.
　　"Back came Eurylochus to our good ship
With news of our poor comrades and their fate,
He strove to speak, but could not; he was stunned
By that calamity; his eyes were filled
With tears, and his whole soul was given to grief.
We marvelled greatly; long we questioned him,
And thus he spake of our lost friends at last:—
　　" 'Through yonder thickets, as thou gav'st command,

Illustrious chief! we went, until we reached
A stately palace of hewn stones, within
A vale, yet nobly seated. Some one there,
Goddess or woman, weaving busily
An ample web, sang sweetly as she wrought.
My comrades called aloud, and forth she came,
And threw at once the shining doors apart,
And bade us enter. Without thought the rest
Followed, while I alone, suspecting guile,
Remained without. My comrades, from that hour,
Were seen no more; not one of them again
Came forth, though long I sat and watched for them.'

"He spake; I slung my silver-studded sword
Upon my shoulders,—a huge blade of brass,—
And my bow with it, and commanded him
To lead the way. He seized and clasped my knees
With both his hands in attitude of prayer,
And sorrowfully said these winged words:—

" 'Take me not thither; force me not to go,
O foster-child of Jove! but leave me here;
For thou wilt not return, I know, nor yet
Deliver one of our lost friends. Our part
Is to betake ourselves to instant flight
With these who yet remain, and so escape.'

"He spake, and I replied: 'Eurylochus,
Remain thou here, beside our roomy ship,
Eating and drinking. I shall surely go.
A strong necessity is laid on me.'

"I spake, and from the ship and shore went up
Into the isle; and when I found myself
Within that awful valley, and not far
From the great palace in which Circè dwelt,
The sorceress, there met me on my way
A youth; he seemed in manhood's early prime,
When youth has most of grace. He took my hand
And held it, and, accosting me, began:—

" 'Rash mortal! whither art thou wandering thus
Alone among the hills, where every place
Is strange to thee? Thy comrades are shut up
In Circè's palace in close cells like swine.

Com'st thou to set them free? Nay, thou like them
Wilt rather find thyself constrained to stay.
Let me bestow the means to make thee safe
Against that mischief. Take this potent herb,
And bear it with thee to the palace-halls
Of Circè, and it shall avert from thee
The threatened evil. I will now reveal
The treacherous arts of Circè. She will bring
A mingled draught to thee, and drug the bowl,
But will not harm thee thus; the virtuous plant
I gave thee will prevent it. Hear yet more:
When she shall smite thee with her wand, draw forth
Thy good sword from thy thigh and rush at her
As if to take her life, and she will crouch
In fear, and will solicit thine embrace.
Refuse her not, that so she may release
Thy comrades, and may send thee also back
To thine own land; but first exact of her
The solemn oath which binds the blessed gods,
That she will meditate no other harm
To thee, nor strip thee of thy manly strength.'
    "The Argus-queller spake, and plucked from earth
The potent plant and handed it to me,
And taught me all its powers. The root is black,
The blossom white as milk. Among the gods
Its name is Moly; hard it is for men
To dig it up; the gods find nothing hard.
    "Back through the woody island Hermes went
Toward high Olympus, while I took my way
To Circè's halls, yet with a beating heart.
There, as I stood beneath the portico
Of that bright-haired divinity, I called
Aloud; the goddess heard my voice and came,
And threw at once the shining doors apart,
And prayed me to come in. I followed her,
Yet grieving still. She led me in and gave
A seat upon a silver-studded throne,
Beautiful, nobly wrought, and placed beneath
A footstool, and prepared a mingled draught
Within a golden chalice, and infused

A drug with mischievous intent. She gave
The cup; I drank it off; the charm wrought not,
And then she smote me with her wand and said:—
'Go to the sty, and with thy fellows sprawl.'

"She spake; but drawing forth the trusty sword
Upon my thigh, I rushed at her as if
To take her life. She shrieked and, stooping low,
Ran underneath my arm and clasped my knees,
And uttered piteously these winged words:—

" 'Who art thou? of what race and of what land,
And who thy parents? I am wonder-struck
To see that thou couldst drink that magic juice
And yield not to its power. No living man,
Whoever he might be, that tasted once
Those drugs, or passed them o'er his lips, has yet
Withstood them. In thy breast a spirit dwells
Not to be thus subdued. Art thou not then
Ulysses, master of wise stratagems,
Whose coming hither, on his way from Troy,
In his black galley, oft has been foretold
By Hermes of the golden wand? But sheathe
Thy sword and share my couch, that, joined in love,
Each may hereafter trust the other's faith.'

"She spake, and I replied: 'How canst thou ask,
O Circè, that I gently deal with thee,
Since thou, in thine own palace, hast transformed
My friends to swine, and plottest even now
To keep me with thee, luring me to pass
Into thy chamber and to share thy couch,
That thou mayst strip me of my manly strength
I come not to thy couch till thou engage,
O goddess, by a solemn oath, that thou
Wilt never seek to do me further harm.'

"I spake; she straightway took the oath required,
And, after it was uttered and confirmed,
Up to her sumptuous couch I went.

.   .   .

She came to me and spake these winged words:—
" 'Why sittest thou like one who has no power

Of speech, Ulysses, wrapt in thoughts that gnaw
Thy heart, and tasting neither food nor wine?
Still dost thou dream of fraud? It is not well
That thou shouldst fear it longer, since I pledged
Myself against it with a mighty oath.'

  "She spake, and I replied: 'What man whose heart
Is faithful could endure to taste of food
Or wine till he should see his captive friends
Once more at large? If with a kind intent
Thou bidst me eat and drink, let me behold
With mine own eyes my dear companions free.'

  "I spake; and Circè took her wand and went
Forth from her halls, and, opening the gate
That closed the sty, drove forth what seemed a herd
Of swine in their ninth year. They ranged themselves
Before her, and she went from each to each
And shed on them another drug. Forthwith
Fell from their limbs the bristles which had grown
All over them, when mighty Circè gave
At first the baleful potion. Now again
My friends were men, and younger than before,
And of a nobler mien and statelier growth.
They knew me all; and each one pressed my hand
In his, and there were tears and sobs of joy
That sounded through the palace. Circè too
Was moved, the mighty goddess. . . ."

·   ·   ·

                          ". . . All that day
Till set of sun we sat and banqueted
Upon the abundant meats and generous wines;
And when the Sun went down, and darkness came,
The crew beside the fastenings of our bark
Lay down to sleep, while Circè took my hand,
Led me apart, and made me sit, and took
Her seat before me, and inquired of all
That I had seen. I told her faithfully,
And then the mighty goddess Circè said:—

  " 'Thus far is well; now heedfully attend

To what I say, and may some deity
Help thee remember it! Thou first wilt come
To where the Sirens haunt. They throw a spell
O'er all who pass that way. If unawares
One finds himself so nigh that he can hear
Their voices, round him nevermore shall wife
And lisping children gather, welcoming
His safe return with joy. The Sirens sit
In a green field, and charm with mellow notes
The comer, while beside them lie in heaps
The bones of men decaying underneath
The shrivelled skins. Take heed and pass them by.
First fill with wax well kneaded in the palm
The ears of thy companions, that no sound
May enter. Hear the music, if thou wilt,
But let thy people bind thee, hand and foot,
To the good ship, upright against the mast,
And round it wind the cord, that thou mayst hear
The ravishing notes. But shouldst thou then entreat
Thy men, commanding them to set thee free,
Let them be charged to bind thee yet more fast
With added bands. And when they shall have passed
The Sirens by, I will not judge for thee
Which way to take; consider for thyself;
I tell thee of two ways. There is a pile
Of beetling rocks, where roars the mighty surge
Of dark-eyed Amphitritè; these are called
The Wanderers by the blessed gods. No birds
Can pass them safe, not even the timid doves,
Which bear ambrosia to our father Jove,
But ever doth the slippery rock take off
Some one, whose loss the God at once supplies,
To keep their number full. To these no bark
Guided by man has ever come, and left
The spot unwrecked; the billows of the deep
And storms of fire in air have scattered wide
Timbers of ships and bodies of drowned men.
One only of the barks that plough the deep
Has passed them safely,—Argo, known to all

By fame, when coming from Aeaeta home,—
And her the billows would have dashed against
The enormous rocks, if Juno, for the sake
Of Jason, had not come to guide it through.

.   .   .

"She spake; the Morning on her golden throne
Looked forth; the glorious goddess went her way
Into the isle, I to my ship, and bade
The men embark and cast the hawsers loose.
And straight they went on board, and duly manned
The benches, smiting as they sat with oars
The hoary waters. Circè, amber-haired,
The mighty goddess of the musical voice,
Sent a fair wind behind our dark-prowed ship
That gayly bore us company, and filled
The sails. When we had fairly ordered all
On board our galley, we sat down, and left
The favoring wind and helm to bear us on,
And thus in sadness I bespake the crew:—
   " 'My friends! it were not well that one or two
Alone should know the oracles I heard
From Circè, great among the goddesses;
And now will I disclose them, that ye all,
Whether we are to die or to escape
The doom of death, may be forewarned. And first
Against the wicked Sirens and their song
And flowery bank she warns us. I alone
May hear their voice, but ye must bind me first
With bands too strong to break, that I may stand
Upright against the mast; and let the cords
Be fastened round it. If I then entreat
And bid you loose me, make the bands more strong.'
   "Thus to my crew I spake, and told them all
That they should know, while our good ship drew near
The island of the Sirens, prosperous gales
Wafting it gently onward. Then the breeze
Sank to a breathless calm; some deity

Had hushed the winds to slumber. Straightway rose
The men and furled the sails and laid them down
Within the ship, and sat and made the sea
White with the beating of their polished blades,
Made of the fir-tree. Then I took a mass
Of wax and cut it into many parts,
And kneaded each with a strong hand. It grew
Warm with the pressure, and the beams of him
Who journeys round the earth, the monarch Sun.
With this I filled the ears of all my men
From first to last. They bound me, in their turn,
Upright against the mast-tree, hand and foot,
And tied the cords around it. Then again
They sat and threshed with oars the hoary deep.
And when, in running rapidly, we came
So near the Sirens as to hear a voice
From where they sat, our galley flew not by
Unseen by them, and sweetly thus they sang:—
   " 'O world-renowned Ulysses! thou who art
The glory of the Achaians, turn thy bark
Landward, that thou mayst listen to our lay
No man has passed us in his galley yet,
Ere he has heard our warbled melodies.
He goes delighted hence a wiser man;
For all that in the spacious realm of Troy
The Greeks and Trojans by the will of Heaven
Endured we know, and all that comes to pass
In all the nations of the fruitful earth.'
   " 'T was thus they sang, and sweet the strain. I longed
To listen, and with nods I gave the sign
To set me free; they only plied their oars
The faster. Then upsprang Eurylochus
And Perimedes, and with added cords
Bound me, and drew the others still more tight.
And when we now had passed the spot, and heard
No more the melody the Sirens sang,
My comrades hastened from their ears to take
The wax, and loosed the cords and set me free."

(from *The Odyssey,* Books IX, X, XII)

HERODOTUS

EGYPTIAN CUSTOMS

It was the Egyptians who first made it an offence against piety to have intercourse with women in temples, or to enter temples after intercourse without having previously washed. Hardly any nation except the Egyptians and Greeks has any such scruple, but nearly all consider men and women to be, in this respect, no different from animals, which, whether they are beasts or birds, they constantly see coupling in temples and sacred places—and if the god concerned had any objection to this, he would not allow it to occur. Such is the theory, but, in spite of it, I must continue to disapprove the practice. The Egyptians are meticulous in their observance of this point, as indeed they are in everything else which concerns their religion.

There are not a great many wild animals in Egypt, in spite of the fact that it borders on Libya. Such as there are—both wild and tame—are without exception held to be sacred. To explain the reason for this, I should have to enter into a discussion of religious principles, which is a subject I particularly wish to avoid—any slight mention I have already made of such matters having been forced upon me by the needs of my story. But, reasons apart, how they actually behave towards animals I will proceed to describe. The various sorts have guardians appointed for them, sometimes men, sometimes women, who are responsible for feeding them; and the office of guardian is handed down from father to son. Their manner, in the various cities, of performing vows is as follows: praying to the god to whom the particular creature, whichever it may be, is sacred, they shave the heads of their children—sometimes completely, sometimes only a half or a third part—and after weighing the hair in a pair of scales, give an equal weight of silver to the animals' keeper, who then cuts up fish (the animals' usual food) to an equivalent value and gives it to them to eat. Anyone who deliberately kills one of these animals, is punished with death; should one be killed accidentally, the penalty is whatever the priests choose to impose; but for killing an ibis or a hawk, whether deliberately or not, the penalty is inevitably death.

The number, already large, of domestic animals would have been greatly increased, were it not for an odd thing that happens to the cats. The females, when they have kittens, avoid the toms, greatly to the distress of the latter who are thus deprived of their satisfaction. The toms, however, get over the difficulty very ingeniously, for they either openly seize, or secretly steal, the kittens and kill them—but without eating them—and the result is that the females, deprived of their kittens and wanting more (for their maternal instinct is very strong), go off to look for mates again. What happens when a house catches fire is most extraordinary: nobody takes the least trouble to put it out, for it is only the cats that matter; everyone stands in a row, a little distance from his neighbour, trying to protect the cats, who nevertheless slip through the line, or jump over it, and hurl themselves into the flames. This causes the Egyptians deep distress. All the inmates of a house where a cat has died a natural death shave their eyebrows, and when a dog dies they shave the whole body including the head. Cats which have died are taken to Bubastis, where they are embalmed and buried in sacred receptacles; dogs are buried, also in sacred burial-places, in the towns where they belong. Weasels are buried in the same way as dogs; field-mice and hawks are taken to Buto, ibises to Hermopolis. Bears, which are scarce, and wolves (which in Egypt are not much bigger than foxes) are buried wherever they happen to be found lying dead.

The crocodile during the four winter months takes no food. It is a four-footed, amphibious creature, lays and hatches its eggs on land, where it spends the greater part of the day, and stays all night in the river, where the water is warmer than the night-air and the dew. The difference in size between the young and the full-grown crocodile is greater than in any other known creature; for a crocodile's egg is hardly bigger than a goose's, and the young when hatched is small in proportion, yet it grows to a size of some twenty-three feet long or even more. It has eyes like a pig's and great fang-like teeth, and is the only animal to have no tongue and a stationary lower jaw; for when it eats it brings the upper jaw down upon the under. It has powerful claws and a scaly hide, which on its back is impenetrable. It cannot see under water, though on land its sight is remarkably quick. . . .

Of the numerous different ways of catching crocodiles I will describe the one which seems to me the most interesting. They bait a hook with a chine of pork and let it float out into midstream, and at the same time, standing on the bank, beat a live pig to make it squeal. The crocodile makes a rush towards the squealing pig, encounters the bait, gulps it down, and is hauled out of the water. The first thing the huntsman does when he has got the beast on land is to plaster its eyes with mud; this done, it is dispatched easily enough—but without this precaution it will give a lot of trouble.

The hippopotamus is held sacred in the district of Papremis, but not elsewhere. This animal has four legs, cloven hoofs like an ox, a snub nose, a horse's mane and tail, conspicuous tusks, a voice like a horse's neigh, and is about the size of a very large ox. Its hide is so thick and tough that when dried it can be made into spear-shafts. Otters, too, are found in the Nile; they, and the fish called lepidotus, and eels are all considered sacred to the Nile, as is also the bird known as the fox-goose. . . .

The Egyptians who live in the cultivated parts of the country, by their practice of keeping records of the past, have made themselves much the best historians of any nation of which I have had experience. I will describe some of their habits: every month for three successive days they purge themselves, for their health's sake, with emetics and clysters, in the belief that all diseases come from the food a man eats; and it is a fact —even apart from this precaution—that next to the Libyans they are the healthiest people in the world. I should put this down myself to the absence of changes in the climate; for change, and especially change of weather, is the prime cause of disease. They eat loaves made from spelt —*cyllestes* is their word for them—and drink a wine made from barley, as they have no vines in the country. Some kinds of fish they eat raw, either dried in the sun, or salted; quails, too, they eat raw, and ducks and various small birds, after pickling them in brine; other sorts of birds and fish, apart from those which are considered sacred, they either roast or boil. When the rich give a party and the meal is finished, a man carries round amongst the guests a wooden image of a corpse in a coffin, carved and painted to look as much like the real thing as possible, and anything from eighteen inches to three feet long; he shows it to each guest in turn, and says: "Look upon this body as you drink and enjoy yourself; for you will be just like it when you are dead."

The Egyptians keep to their native customs and never adopt any from abroad. Many of these customs are interesting, especially, perhaps, the "Linus" song. This person, under different names, is celebrated in song not only in Egypt but in Phoenicia, Cyprus, and other places, and appears to be the person whom the Greeks celebrate as Linus; if this is so, it is yet one more of the many surprises that Egypt has to offer: for where did the Egyptians get this song from? It is clearly very ancient; the Egyptian name for Linus is Maneros, and their story is that their first king had an only son, who died young, and that this dirge—their first and, at that time, their only melody—was invented to be sung in his honour.

There is another point in which the Egyptians resemble one section of the Greek people—the Lacedaemonians: I mean the custom of young men stepping aside to make room for their seniors when they meet them in the street, and of getting up from their seats when older men come in. But they are unlike any of the Greeks in that they do not greet one another by name in the streets, but make a low bow and drop one hand to the knee. The clothes they wear consist of a linen tunic with a fringe hanging round the legs (called in their language *calasiris*) and a white woollen garment on top of it. It is, however, contrary to religious usage to be buried in a woollen garment, or to wear wool in a temple. They agree in this with those who are known as the followers of Orpheus and Bacchus (actually followers of the Egyptians and of Pythagoras); for anyone initiated into these rites is similarly debarred from burial in a garment of wool. They have a religious doctrine to explain the reason for this.

The Egyptians were also the first to assign each month and each day to a particular deity, and to foretell by the date of a man's birth his character, his fortunes, and the day of his death—a discovery which Greek poets have turned to account. The Egyptians, too, have made more use of omens and prognostics than any other nation; they keep written records of the observed result of any unusual phenomenon, so that they come to expect a similar consequence to follow a similar occurrence in the future. The art of divination is not attributed by them to any man, but only to certain gods: for instance, Heracles, Apollo, Athena, Artemis, Ares, and Zeus all have an oracle in the country, while the oracle of Leto in Buto is held in greater repute than any of them. The method of delivering the responses varies in the different shrines.

The practice of medicine they split up into separate parts, each doctor being responsible for the treatment of only one disease. There are, in consequence, innumerable doctors, some specializing in diseases of the eyes, others of the head, others of the teeth, others of the stomach and so on; while others, again, deal with the sort of troubles which cannot be exactly localized. As regards mourning and funerals, when a distinguished man dies all the women of the household plaster their heads and faces with mud, then, leaving the body indoors, perambulate the town with the dead man's female relatives, their dresses fastened with a girdle, and beat their bared breasts. The men too, for their part, follow the same procedure, wearing a girdle and beating themselves like the women. The ceremony over, they take the body to be embalmed.

(from *The Histories,* Book II)

XENOPHON

IN THE SERVICE OF CYRUS

. . .

From there they marched all the following day through snow, and many of the men fell ill with hunger-faintness. And Xenophon, with the rear-guard, as he came upon the men who were falling by the way, did not know what the trouble was. But as soon as a person who was acquainted with the disease had told him that they manifestly had hunger-faintness, and if they were given something to eat would be able to get up, he went around among the baggage animals, and wherever he saw anything that was edible, he would distribute it among the sick men, or send hither and thither people who had the strength to run along the lines, to give it to them. And when they had eaten something, they would get up and continue the march.

As the army went on, Cheirisophus reached a village about dusk, and found at the spring outside the wall women and girls who had come from the village to fetch water. They asked the Greeks who they were, and the interpreter replied in Persian that they were on their way from the King to the satrap. The women answered that he was not there, but about a parasang away. Then, inasmuch as it was late, the Greeks accompanied the water-carriers within the wall to visit the village chief. So it was that Cheirisophus and all the troops who could muster strength enough to reach the village, went into quarters there, but such of the others as were unable to complete the journey spent the night in the open without food or fire; and in this way some of the soldiers perished.

Meanwhile they were being followed by the enemy, some of whom had banded together and were seizing such of the pack animals as lacked the strength to go on, and fighting over them with one another. Some of the soldiers likewise were falling behind—those whose eyes had been blinded by the snow, or whose toes had rotted off by reason of the cold. It was a protection to the eyes against the snow if a man marched with something black in front of them, and a protection to the feet if one kept moving and never quiet, and if he took off his shoes for the night; but in all cases where men slept with their shoes on, the straps sunk into their flesh and the shoes froze on their feet; for what they were wearing, since their old shoes had given out, were brogues made of freshly flayed ox-hides.

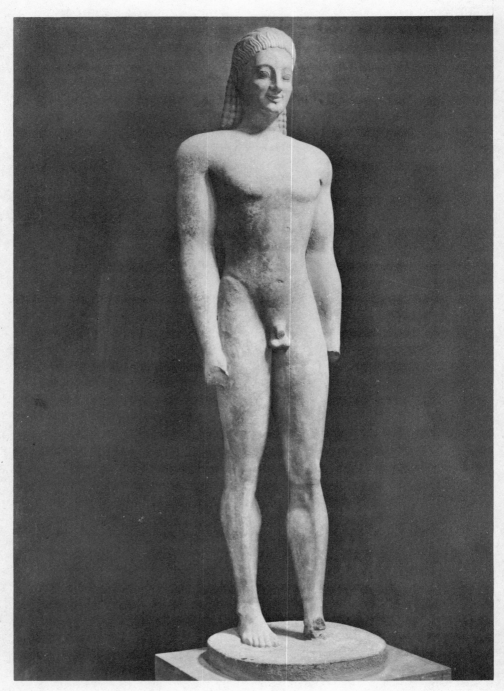

11. Archaic statue of young man.

It was under compulsion of such difficulties that some of the soldiers were falling behind; and espying a spot that was dark because the snow just there had disappeared, they surmised that it had melted; and in fact it had melted, on account of a spring which was near by, steaming in a dell; here they turned aside and sat down, refusing to go any farther. But when Xenophon with some of the rearguard observed them, he begged them by all manner of means not to be left behind, telling them that a large body of the enemy had gathered and were pursuing, and finally he became angry. They told him, however, to kill them, for they could not go on. In this situation it seemed to be best to frighten the pursuing enemy, if they could, in order to prevent their falling upon the sick men. It was dark by this time, and the enemy were coming on with a great uproar, quarrelling over the booty they had. Then the men of the rearguard, since they were sound and well, started up and charged upon the enemy, while the invalids raised as big a shout as they could and clashed their shields against their spears. And the enemy, seized with fear, threw themselves down over the snow into the dell, and not a sound was heard from them afterwards.

Thereupon Xenophon and his men, after telling the invalids that on the next day people would come back after them, continued their march, but before they had gone four stadia they came upon their comrades lying down in the road upon the snow, wrapped up in their cloaks, and without so much as a single guard posted. They tried to get them up, but the men said that the troops in front would not make way for them. Xenophon accordingly passed along and, sending forward the strongest of the peltasts, directed them to see what the hindrance was. They reported back that the whole army was resting in this way. Thereupon Xenophon also and his party bivouacked where they were, without a fire and without dinner, after stationing such guards as they could. When it came toward morning, Xenophon sent the youngest of his troops to the sick men with orders to make them get up and force them to proceed.

.   .   .

From there they journeyed four stages, twenty parasangs, to a large and prosperous inhabited city which was called Gymnias. From this city the ruler of the land sent the Greeks a guide, in order to lead them through territory that was hostile to his own. When the guide came, he said that he would lead them within five days to a place from which they could see the sea; if he failed to do so, he was ready to accept death. Thus taking the lead, as soon as he had brought them into the hostile territory, he kept urging them to spread abroad fire and ruin, thereby making it clear that it was with this end in view that he had come, and not out of good-will toward the Greeks. On the fifth day they did in fact reach the mountain; its name was Theches. Now as soon as the vanguard got to the top of the mountain, a great shout went up. And when Xenophon and the rearguard heard it, they imagined that other enemies were attacking in front; for enemies were following behind them from the district that was in flames, and the rearguard had killed some of them and captured others by setting an ambush, and had also taken about twenty wicker shields covered with raw, shaggy ox-hides. But as the shout kept getting louder and nearer, as the successive ranks that came up all began to run at full speed toward the ranks ahead that were one after another joining in the shout, and as the shout kept growing far louder as the number of men grew steadily greater, it became quite clear to Xenophon that here was something of unusual importance; so he mounted a horse, took with him Lycius and the cavalry, and pushed ahead to lend aid; and in a moment they heard the soldiers shouting, "The Sea! The Sea!" and passing the word along. Then all the troops of the rearguard likewise broke into a run, and the pack animals began racing ahead and the horses. And when all had reached the summit, then indeed they fell to embracing one another, and generals and captains as well, with tears in their eyes. And on a sudden, at the bidding of some one or other, the soldiers began to bring stones and to build a great cairn. Thereon they placed as offerings a quantity of raw ox-hides and walking-sticks and the captured wicker shields; and the guide not only cut these shields to pieces himself, but urged the others to do so. After this the Greeks dismissed the guide with gifts from the common stock— a horse, a silver cup, a Persian dress, and ten darics; but what he particularly asked the men for was their rings, and he got a considerable number of them. Then he showed them a village to encamp in and the road they were to follow to the country of the Macronians, and, as soon as evening came, took his departure.

(from *Anabasis,* Book IV)

Alexander the Great (356-323) is in many respects the epitome of the heroic Greek spirit of adventure. A hero like Achilles, like him young, handsome, physically strong, fearless, Alexander victoriously conquered the greatest part of what was then known of the world. His extraordinary moral nobility, displayed so strikingly in his treatment of prisoners, comes

also to the fore in his salvation of Greek culture; not only did
he refrain from destroying it after conquering the country,
but he was the one who spread it, and thus made possible the
world of Hellenism. This spectacle is indeed unique in history!
The very same hero who put an end to Greek independence,
revived Homeric heroism, was a pupil of Aristotle, and spread
into the world the inexhaustible richness and spirituality of
Greece.

PLUTARCH

ALEXANDER THE GREAT

Once upon a time Philoneicus the Thessalian brought Bucephalas, offering to sell him to Philip for thirteen talents, and they went down into the plain to try the horse, who appeared to be savage and altogether intractable, neither allowing any one to mount him, nor heeding the voice of any of Philip's attendants, but rearing up against all of them. Then Philip was vexed and ordered the horse to be led away, believing him to be altogether wild and unbroken; but Alexander, who was near by, said: "What a horse they are losing, because, for lack of skill and courage, they cannot manage him!" At first, then, Philip held his peace; but as Alexander many times let fall such words and showed great distress, he said: "Dost thou find fault with thine elders in the belief that thou knowest more than they do or art better able to manage a horse?" "This horse, at any rate," said Alexander, "I could manage better than others have." "And if thou shouldst not, what penalty wilt thou undergo for thy rashness?" "Indeed," said Alexander, "I will forfeit the price of the horse." There was laughter at this, and then an agreement between father and son as to the forfeiture, and at once Alexander ran to the horse, took hold of his bridle-rein, and turned him towards the sun; for he had noticed, as it would seem, that the horse was greatly disturbed by the sight of his own shadow falling in front of him and dancing about. And after he had calmed the horse a little in this way, and had stroked him with his hand, when he saw that he was full of spirit and courage, he quietly cast aside his mantle and with a light spring safely bestrode him. Then, with a little pressure of the reins on the bit, and without striking him or tearing his mouth, he held him in hand; but when he saw that the horse was rid of the fear that had beset him, and was impatient for the course, he gave him his head, and at last

12. *Kore in Dorian Peplos.*

urged him on with sterner tone and thrust of foot. Philip and his company were speechless with anxiety at first; but when Alexander made the turn in proper fashion and came back towards them proud and exultant, all the rest broke into loud cries, but his father, as we are told, actually shed tears of joy, and when Alexander had dismounted, kissed him, saying: "My son, seek thee out a kingdom equal to thyself; Macedonia has not room for thee."

And since Philip saw that his son's nature was unyielding and that he resisted compulsion, but was easily led by reasoning into the path of duty, he himself tried to persuade rather than to command him; and because he would not wholly entrust the direction and training of the boy to the ordinary teachers of poetry and the formal studies, feeling that it was a matter of too great importance, and, in the words of Sophocles,

A task for many bits and rudder-sweeps as well,

he sent for the most famous and learned of philosophers, Aristotle, and paid him a noble and appropriate tuition-fee. The city of Stageira, that is, of which Aristotle was a native, and which he had himself destroyed, he peopled again, and restored to it those of its citizens who were in exile or slavery.

Well, then, as a place where master and pupil could labour and study, he assigned them the precinct of the nymphs near Mieza, where to this day the visitor is shown the stone seats and shady walks of Aristotle. It would appear, moreover, that Alexander not only received from his master his ethical and political doctrines, but also participated in those secret and more profound teachings which philosophers designate by the special terms "acroamatic" and "epoptic," and do not impart to many. For after he had already crossed into Asia, and when he learned that certain treatises on these recondite matters had been published in books by Aristotle, he wrote him a letter on behalf of philosophy, and put it in plain language. And this is a copy of the letter. "Alexander, to Aristotle, greeting. Thou hast not done well to publish thy acroamatic doctrines; for in what shall I surpass other men if those doctrines wherein I have been trained are to be all men's common property? But I had rather excel in my acquaintance with the best things than in my power. Farewell." Accordingly, in defending himself, Aristotle encourages this ambition of Alexander by saying that the doctrines of which he spoke were both published and not published; for in truth his treatise on metaphysics is of no use for those who would either teach or learn the science, but is written as a memorandum for those already trained therein.

.   .   .

And now a general assembly of the Greeks was held at the Isthmus, where a vote was passed to make an expedition against Persia with Alexander, and he was proclaimed their leader. Thereupon many statesmen and philosophers came to him with their congratulations, and he expected that Diogenes of Sinope also, who was tarrying in Corinth, would do likewise. But since that philosopher took not the slightest notice of Alexander, and continued to enjoy his leisure in the suburb Craneion, Alexander went in person to see him; and he found him lying in the sun. Diogenes raised himself up a little when he saw so many persons coming towards him, and fixed his eyes upon Alexander. And when that monarch addressed him with greetings, and asked if he wanted anything, "Yes," said Diogenes, "stand a little out of my sun." It is said that Alexander was so struck by this, and admired so much the haughtiness and grandeur of the man who had nothing but scorn for him, that he said to his followers, who were laughing and jesting about the philosopher as they went away, "But verily, if I were not Alexander, I would be Diogenes."

And now, wishing to consult the god concerning the expedition against Asia, he went to Delphi; and since he chanced to come on one of the inauspicious days, when it is not lawful to deliver oracles, in the first place he sent a summons to the prophetess. And when she refused to perform her office and cited the law in her excuse, he went up himself and tried to drag her to the temple, whereupon, as if overcome by his ardour, she said: "Thou art invincible, my son!" On hearing this, Alexander said he desired no further prophecy, but had from her the oracle which he wanted.

.   .   .

As to the number of his forces, those who put it at the smallest figure mention thirty thousand foot and four thousand horse; those who put it at the highest, forty-three thousand foot and five thousand horse. To provision these forces, Aristobulus says he had not more than seventy talents; Duris speaks of maintenance for only thirty days; and Onesicritus says he owed two hundred talents besides. But although he set out with such meagre and narrow resources, he would not set foot upon his ship until he had enquired into the circumstances of his companions and allotted to one a farm, to another a village, and to another the revenue from some hamlet or harbour. And when at last nearly all of the crown property had been expended or allotted, Perdiccas said to him: "But for thyself, O king, what art thou leaving?" And when the king answered, "My hopes," "In these, then," said Perdiccas, "we also will share who make the expedition with thee." Then he declined the possessions which had been allotted to him, and some of the other friends of Alexander did likewise. But upon those who wanted and would accept his favours Alexander bestowed them readily, and most of what he possessed in Macedonia was used up in these distributions. Such was the ardour and such the equipment with which he crossed the Hellespont.

. . .

Meanwhile the generals of Dareius had assembled a large force and set it in array at the crossing of the river Granicus, so that it was practically necessary to fight, as it were at the gates of Asia, for entrance and dominion there. But most of the Macedonian officers were afraid of the depth of the river, and of the roughness and unevenness of the farther banks, up which they would have to climb while fighting. Some, too, thought they ought to observe carefully the customary practice in regard to the month (for in the month of Daesius the kings of Macedonia were not wont to take the field with an army). This objection Alexander removed by bidding them call the month a second Artemisius; and when Parmenio, on the ground that it was too late in the day, objected to their risking the passage, he declared that the Hellespont would blush for shame, if, after having crossed that strait, he should be afraid of the Granicus, and plunged into the stream with thirteen troops of horsemen. And since he was charging against hostile missiles and precipitous positions covered with infantry and cavalry, and through a stream that swept men off their feet and surged about them, he seemed to be acting like a frenzied and foolish commander rather than a wise one. However, he persisted in his attempt to cross, gained the opposite banks with difficulty and much ado, though they were moist and slippery with mud, and was at once compelled to fight pell-mell and engage his assailants man by man, before his troops who were crossing could form into any order. For the enemy pressed upon them with loud shouts, and matching horse with horse, plied their lances, and their swords when their lances were shattered. Many rushed upon Alexander, for he was conspicuous by his buckler and by his helmet's crest, on either side of which was fixed a plume of wonderful size and whiteness. But although a javelin pierced the joint of his breastplate, he was not wounded; and when Rhoesaces and Spithridates, two Persian commanders, made at him together, he avoided the one, and smote Rhoesaces, who wore a breastplate, with his spear; and when this weapon snapped in two with the blow, he took to his sword. Then, while he was thus engaged with Rhoesaces, Spithridates rode up from one side, raised himself up on his horse, and with all his might came down with a barbarian battle-axe upon Alexander's head. Alexander's crest was broken off, together with one of its plumes, and his helmet could barely and with difficulty resist the blow, so that the edge of the battle-axe touched the topmost hair of his head. But while Spithridates was raising his arm again for another stroke, Cleitus, "Black Cleitus," got the start of him and ran him through the body with his spear. At the same time Rhoesaces also fell, smitten by Alexander's sword.

.   .   .

After this, he overpowered such of the Pisidians as had offered him resistance, and subdued Phrygia; and after he had taken the city of Gordium, reputed to have been the home of the ancient Midas, he saw the much-talked-of waggon bound fast to its yoke with bark of the cornel-tree, and heard a story confidently told about it by the Barbarians, to the effect that whosoever loosed the fastening was destined to become king of the whole world. Well, then, most writers say that since the fastenings had their ends concealed, and were intertwined many times in crooked coils, Alexander was at a loss how to proceed, and finally loosened the knot by cutting it through with his sword, and that when it was thus smitten many ends were to be seen. But Aristobulus says that he undid it very easily, by simply taking out the so-called "hestor," or *pin,* of the waggon-pole, by which the yoke-fastening was held together, and then drawing away the yoke.

.   .   .

Dareius was still more encouraged by Alexander's long delay in Cilicia, which he attributed to cowardice. The delay was due, however, to a sickness, which assailed him in consequence of fatigues, according to some, but according to others, because he took a bath in the river Cydnus, whose waters were icy cold. Be that as it may, none of the other physicians had the courage to administer remedies, but thinking that the danger was too great to be overcome by any remedy whatever, they were afraid of the charges which would be made against them by the Macedonians in consequence of their failure; but Philip the Acarnanian, who saw that the king was in an evil plight, put confidence in his friendship, and thinking it a shameful thing not to share his peril by exhausting the resources of art in trying to help him even at great risk, prepared a medicine and persuaded him to drink it boldly, if he was anxious to regain his strength for the war. Meanwhile, however, Parmenio sent a letter to Alexander from the camp, urging him to be on his guard against Philip, for the reason that he had been persuaded by Dareius, with the promise of large gifts and a marriage with his daughter, to kill Alexander. Alexander read the letter and placed it under his pillow, without showing it to any one of his friends. When the time appointed was at hand, and Philip came in with the king's companions, carrying the medicine in a cup, Alexander handed him the letter, while he himself took the medicine from him with readiness and no sign of suspicion. It was an amazing sight, then, and one well worthy of the stage,—the one reading the letter, the other drinking the medicine, and then both together turning their eyes upon one another, but not with the same expression; for Alexander, by his glad and open countenance, showed his good will towards Philip and his trust in him, while Philip was beside himself at the calumny, now lifting up his hands towards heaven and calling upon the gods to witness his innocence, and now falling upon the couch on which Alexander lay and beseeching him to be of good courage and obey his physician. For at first the medicine mastered the patient, and as it were drove back and buried deep his bodily powers, so that his voice failed, he fell into a swoon, and became almost wholly unconscious. However, he was speedily restored to his senses by Philip, and when he had recovered strength he showed himself to the Macedonians, who refused to be comforted until they had seen Alexander.

. . .

While the siege of the city was in progress, he made an expedition against the Arabians who dwelt in the neighbourhood of Mount Antilibanus. On this expedition he risked his life to save his tutor, Lysimachus, who insisted on following him, declaring himself to be neither older nor weaker than Phoenix. But when the force drew near the mountains, they abandoned their horses and proceeded on foot, and most of them got far on in advance. Alexander himself, however, would not consent to abandon the worn and weary Lysimachus, since evening was already coming on and the enemy were near, but sought to encourage him and carry him along. Before he was aware of it, therefore, he was sepa-

13. Archaic sphinx.

rated from his army with a few followers, and had to spend a night of darkness and intense cold in a region that was rough and difficult. In this plight, he saw far off a number of scattered fires which the enemy were burning. So, since he was confident in his own agility, and was ever wont to cheer the Macedonians in their perplexities by sharing their toils, he ran to the nearest camp-fire. Two Barbarians who were sitting at the fire he despatched with his dagger, and snatching up a fire-brand, brought it to his own party. These kindled a great fire and at once frightened some of the enemy into flight, routed others who came up against them, and spent the night without further peril. Such, then, is the account we have from Chares.

The siege of the city had the following issue. While Alexander was giving the greater part of his forces a rest from the many struggles which they had undergone, and was leading up only a few men to attack the walls, in order that the enemy might have no respite, Aristander the seer made a sacrifice, and after taking the omens, declared very confidently to the bystanders that the city would certainly be captured during that month. His words produced laughter and jesting, since it was then the last day of the month, and the king, seeing that he was perplexed, and being always eager to support his prophecies, gave orders to reckon that day, not as the thirtieth of the month, but as the twenty-eighth; and then, after the trumpet had sounded the signal, he attacked the walls with greater vigour than he had at first intended. The assault became fierce, and even those troops which had been left in camp could not restrain themselves, but ran in throngs to help the assailants, and the Tyrians gave up the fight. So Alexander took the city on that day.

·　　·　　·

When Dareius sent to him a letter and friends, begging him to accept ten thousand talents as ransom for the captives, to hold all the territory this side of the Euphrates, to take one of his daughters in marriage, and on these terms to be his ally and friend, Alexander imparted the matter to his companions. "If I were Alexander," said Parmenio, "I would accept these terms." "And so indeed would I," said Alexander, "were I Parmenio." But to Dareius he wrote: "Come to me, and thou shalt receive every courtesy; but otherwise I shall march at once against thee."

·　　·　　·

Now, however, he marched out against Dareius, expecting to fight another battle; but when he heard that Dareius had been seized by Bessus, he sent his Thessalians home, after distributing among them a largess of two thousand talents over and above their pay. In consequence of the pursuit of Dareius, which was long and arduous (for in eleven days he rode thirty-three hundred furlongs), most of his horsemen gave out, and chiefly for lack of water. At this point some Macedonians met him who were carrying water from the river in skins upon their mules. And when they beheld Alexander, it being now midday, in a wretched plight from thirst, they quickly filled a helmet and brought it to him. To his enquiry for whom they were carrying the water, they replied: "For our own sons; but if thou livest, we can get other sons, even if we lose these." On hearing this he took the helmet into his hands, but when he looked around and saw the horsemen about him all stretching out their heads and gazing at the water, he handed it back without drinking any, but with praises for the men who had brought it; "For," said he, "if I should drink of it alone, these horsemen of mine will be out of heart." But when they beheld his self-control and loftiness of spirit, they shouted out to him to lead them forward boldly, and began to goad their horses on, declaring that they would not regard themselves as weary, or thirsty, or as mortals at all, so long as they had such a king.

(from *Lives of Illustrious Men*)

II

The Adventure of the Spirit

The unexamined life is not worth living.

Plato, *Apology*

The spirit of adventure found its most perfect expression in the glorification of courage. *The adventure of the spirit, manifested in the birth of philosophy, the birth of history, and the birth of literature, is deeply linked to the intellectual discovery of* wisdom, *as being the key virtue to which men should aspire.*

The city loads the victor in the games with honors and gifts, and yet he does not deserve them as I do: for this wisdom of ours is better than the strength of men and horses.

Xenophanes

1. The Birth of Philosophy

It is both refreshing and inspiring to go back to the very beginning of philosophical thought, still uninhibited by the burden of hair-splitting distinctions and school disputes. Early Greek philosophy is characterized by the depth of its questions and the classical character of its inner development. If ever the Hegelian process (thesis, antithesis, synthesis) seems to be tailored to history, it is in this history of the pre-Socratics. They seem to base their research on one gigantic intuition: the harmony and order of the cosmos, ruled by definite laws which man's mind can discover and should obey.

THALES

There must be some natural body, one or many, from which all things arise, but which itself remains the same.

But of what sort this first principle is, and how many such there are,

14. *Prium begging Achilles to release Hector's body* (beneath Achilles). Skyphos by Brygos Painter.

this is a point upon which they are not agreed. Thales . . . declares it to be water. (And this is why he said that the earth floats on water.) Possibly he was led to this opinion by observing that the nourishment of all things is moist, and that heat itself is generated and kept alive by moisture. And that from which all things are generated is just what we mean by their first principle.

(from Aristotle, *Metaphysics,* I. 3, 983 B 6)

ANAXIMANDER

Everything either is a first principle or arises from a first principle; but of the boundless there is no first principle, for to find a first principle for it would be to give it bounds. Further, it (the boundless) is unbegotten and indestructible, being a first principle. That which is created perishes, and there is a limit to all destruction. Therefore there is no first principle of the boundless, but it is rather the first principle of other things. And it encompasses all things and rules all things, in the opinion of those who do not assume, in addition to the boundless, some other cause such as "reason," or "love." And this is the divine, for it is deathless and indestructible, as Anaximander holds in agreement with most of the physical philosophers.

(from Aristotle, *Physics,* III. 4, 203 B 6)

XENOPHANES

There is one god, supreme among gods and men; resembling mortals neither in form nor in mind.

Yet if oxen and lions had hands, and could paint with their hands, and fashion images, as men do, they would make the pictures and images of their gods in their own likeness; horses would make them like horses, oxen like oxen.

Homer and Hesiod have ascribed to the gods all deeds that are a shame and a disgrace among men: thieving, adultery, fraud.

There never was, nor ever will be, any man who knows with certainty the things about the gods and about all things which I tell of. For even if he does happen to get most things right, still he himself does not know it. But mere opinions all may have.

Let these opinions of mine pass for semblances of truths.

The gods did not reveal all things to men at the start; but, as time goes on, by searching, they discover more and more.

PARMENIDES

ON TRUTH

Listen, and I will instruct thee—and thou, when thou hearest,
   shalt ponder—
What are the sole two paths of research that are open to
   thinking.
One path is: That Being doth be, and Non-Being is not:
This is the way of Conviction, for Truth follows hard in her
   footsteps.
Th'other path is: That Being is not, and Non-Being must be;
This one, I tell thee in truth, is an all-incredible pathway.
For thou never canst know what is not (for none can conceive
   it),
Nor canst thou give it expression, for one thing are Thinking
   and Being.

One path only: That Being doth be—and on *it* there are
   tokens
Many and many to show that what is is birthless and death-
   less,
Whole and only-begotten and moveless and ever-enduring:
Never it was or shall be; but the ALL simultaneously now is,
One continuous one; for of it what birth shalt thou search for?
How and whence it hath sprung? I shall not permit thee to
   tell me,
Neither to think: "Of what is not," for none can say or imagine
How Not-Is becomes Is; or else what need should have stirred
   it,
After or yet before its beginning, to issue from nothing?
Thus either wholly Being must be or wholly must not be.

HERACLITUS

This Word is everlasting, but men are unable to comprehend it before they have heard it or even after they have heard it for the first time. Although everything happens in accordance with this Word, they behave like inexperienced men whenever they make trial of words and deeds such as I declare as I analyze each thing according to its nature and show what it is. But other men have no idea what they are doing when awake, just as they forget what they do when they are asleep.

One ought to follow the lead of that which is common to all men. But although the Word is common to all, yet most men live as if each had a private wisdom of his own.

If happiness consists in the pleasures of the body, we should call cattle happy when they find grass to eat.

Men seek in vain to purify themselves from blood-guiltiness by defiling themselves with blood; as if, when one has stepped into the mud, he should try to wash himself with mud. And I should deem him mad who should pay heed to any man who does such things. And, forsooth, they offer prayers to these statues here! It is as if one should try to converse with houses. They know nothing of the real nature of gods and heroes.

Most men have no comprehension even of such things as they meet with, nor do they understand what they experience though they themselves think they do.

If you do not expect the unexpected you will never find it, for it is hard to find and inaccessible.

They who seek after gold dig up a lot of earth, and find a little.

Were there no injustice men would never have known the name of justice.

Greater deaths receive greater rewards.

Fools even when they hear the truth are like deaf men. Of them the proverb holds true, "being present they are absent."

Much learning does not teach wisdom, else would it have taught Hesiod and Pythagoras, Xenophanes, too, and Hecataeus.

Wisdom is one thing. It is to know the thought by which all things through all are guided.

15. *A warrior's farewell*. Stamnos by the Kleophon Painter.

Homer ought to be thrown out of the lists and whipped, and Archilochus too.

Let us not make random conjectures about the weightiest matters.

One to me is as good as ten thousand if he be but the best.

It is wise to hearken not to me, but to the Word, and to confess that all things are one.

War is the father of all and the king of all, and some he has made gods and some men, some bond and some free.

The hidden harmony is better than that which is obvious.

We ought to know that war is the common lot, and that justice is strife, and that all things arise through strife and necessity.

The most beautiful ape is ugly as compared with the human race.

The wisest man compared with god is like an ape in wisdom, in beauty, and in everything else.

It is hard to contend against the heart; for it is ready to sell the soul to purchase its desires.

For the most part the knowledge of things divine escapes us because of our unbelief.

One cannot step twice into the same river.

It is best to hide one's folly, but it is hard when relaxed over the wine cups.

To god all things are beautiful and good and right; men deem some things wrong and some right.

No one of all the men whose words I have heard has arrived at the knowledge that wisdom is something apart from all other things.

It were not good for men that all their wishes should be fulfilled.

Wisdom is the foremost virtue, and wisdom consists in speaking the truth, and in lending an ear to nature and acting according to her.

Man's character is his fate.

The Ephesians would do well to hang themselves, every man of them, and to leave the city to beardless boys. For they banished Hermodorus, the best man of them all, declaring: We will have no best man among us; if there be any such let him be so elsewhere and amongst other men.

PYTHAGORAS

THE NUMBER PHILOSOPHY
OF THE PYTHAGOREANS

At this time and even earlier the so-called Pythagoreans applied themselves to mathematics and were the first to advance this branch of knowledge, and spending all their time in these pursuits they came to think that the first principles of mathematics were the first principles of all things that exist. And inasmuch as numbers are what is naturally first in this field, and since they thought they discovered in numbers a great many more similarities with things that exist and that arise in the processes of nature than one could find in fire or earth or water, they thought, for example, that such and such a property of numbers was justice, another the soul and reason, another opportunity, and in the same way of practically everything else; and inasmuch as they saw in numbers the properties and proportions of the different kinds of harmonies, and since all other things so far as their entire nature is concerned were modelled upon numbers, whereas numbers are prior to anything else in nature,—from all this they inferred that the first elements of numbers were the first elements of all things that exist, and that the whole heaven was a harmony and a number. And so all the analogies they could point to between numbers and harmonies on the one hand, and the properties and divisions and the whole arrangement of the heavens on the other hand, these they would collect and piece together, and if any gap appeared anywhere they would greedily seek after something to fill it, in order that their entire system might be coherent. For example, since they thought that the number ten was a perfect thing and included all other numbers they affirmed that the heavenly bodies must also be ten in number, but inasmuch as only nine are visible they invented a tenth, which they called the counter-earth.

These philosophers evidently regarded number as the first principle, both as being the material cause of things that exist and as describing their qualities and states as well. And the elements of number they described as the odd and even, the former being limited and the latter unlimited; and the number one they thought was composed of both of these elements (for it is both even and odd) and from the number one all other numbers spring, and the whole heavens are simply numbers.

(Aristotle, *Metaphysics,* I. 5, 985 B 23)

PYTHAGORAS

Do nothing base with others or alone:
But most of all thyself in reverence hold.

Then practise justice both in deed and word,
Nor let thyself wax thoughtless about aught:
But know that death's the common lot of all.

Be not untimely wasteful of thy wealth,
Like vulgar men, nor yet illiberal.
In all things moderation answers best.

Let never sleep thy drowsy eyelids greet,
Till thou hast pondered each act of the day:
"Wherein have I transgressed? What have I done?
What duty shunned?"—beginning from the first,
Unto the last. Then grieve and fear for what
Was basely done; but in the good rejoice.

EMPEDOCLES

And another thing I shall tell thee: of no one of all the things that perish is there any birth, nor any end in baneful death. There is only a mingling and a separation of what has been mingled. But "birth" is the name men use for this.

Fools! Short is the reach of their thinking who suppose that what before was not comes into being, or that anything perishes and is utterly destroyed.

For it is inconceivable that anything should arise from that which in no way exists, and it is impossible, and a thing unheard of, that what exists should perish, for it will always be wherever one in every case puts it.

We cannot bring God near so as to reach him with our eyes or lay hold of him with our hands—the [two ways] along which the chief highway of persuasion leads into the mind of man.

For he has no human head attached to bodily members, nor do two branching arms dangle from his shoulders; he has neither feet nor swift knees nor any hairy parts. No, he is only mind, sacred and ineffable mind, flashing through the whole universe with swift thoughts.

ANAXAGORAS

All other things contain a portion of everything, but mind is infinite and self-ruled and is mixed with nothing. For if it did not exist by itself, but were mixed with anything else, it would contain a portion of all things . . . For in everything there is a portion of everything, as I have said above. And in that case the things mixed with it would prevent it from having power over anything else such as it now has, being alone and by itself. For it is the thinnest of all things and the purest, and it possesses all knowledge and the greatest power. And whatsoever things are alive, the largest as well as the smallest, over all is mind the ruler. And over the whole revolving universe mind held sway, so that it caused it to revolve in the beginning. . . .

For there is no least of what is small: there is always a still smaller. For it is impossible that that which is should cease to be by being divided. On the other hand there is always a still larger than the large. And (the large) is equal to the small in number (of portions). In itself, however, each thing is both large and small.

We Greeks are wrong in using the expressions "to come into being" and "to be destroyed," for no thing comes into being or is destroyed. Rather, a thing is mixed with or separated from already existing things. And so it would be more accurate to say, instead of origin, commingling; instead of destruction, dissolution.

Because of the weakness of our senses we are unable to discern the truth.

DEMOCRITUS

Of practical wisdom these are the three fruits: to deliberate well, to speak to the point, to do what is right.

He who intends to enjoy life should not be busy about many things, and in what he does should not undertake what exceeds his natural capacity. On the contrary, he should have himself so in hand that even when fortune comes his way, and is apparently ready to lead him on to higher things, he should put her aside and not o'erreach his powers. For a being of moderate size is safer than one that bulks too big.

If one choose the goods of the soul, he chooses the diviner (portion); if the goods of the body, the merely mortal.

'Tis well to restrain the wicked, and in any case not to join him in his wrong-doing.

'Tis not in strength of body nor in gold that men find happiness, but in uprightness and in fulness of understanding.

Not from fear but from a sense of duty refrain from your sins.

Repentance for one's evil deeds is the safeguard of life.

He who does wrong is more unhappy than he who suffers wrong.

Many who have not learned wisdom live wisely, and many who do the basest deeds can make most learned speeches.

One should emulate works and deeds of virtue, not arguments about it.

Strength of body is nobility in beasts of burden, strength of character is nobility in men.

It is better to correct your own faults than those of others.

Good means not [merely] not to do wrong, but rather not to desire to do wrong.

There are many who know many things, yet are lacking in wisdom.

You can tell the man who rings true from the man who rings false, not by his deeds alone, but also by his desires.

My enemy is not the man who wrongs me, but the man who means to wrong me.

The friendship of one wise man is better than the friendship of a host of fools.

No one deserves to live who has not at least one good-man-and-true for a friend.

Seek after the good, and with much toil shall ye find it; the evil turns up of itself without your seeking it.

In the weightiest matters we must go to school to the animals, and learn spinning and weaving from the spider, building from the swallow, singing from the birds,—from the swan and the nightingale, imitating their art.

An evil and foolish and intemperate and irreligious life should not be called a bad life, but rather, dying long drawn out.

Now as of old the gods give men all good things, excepting only those that are baneful and injurious and useless. These, now as of old, are not gifts of the gods: men stumble into them themselves because of their own blindness and folly.

A sensible man takes pleasure in what he has instead of pining for what he has not.

A life without a holiday is like a long journey without an inn to rest at.

Men achieve tranquility through moderation in pleasure and through the symmetry of life. Want and superfluity are apt to upset them and to cause great perturbations in the soul. The souls that are rent by violent conflicts are neither stable nor tranquil. One should therefore set his mind upon the things that are within his power, and be content with his opportunities, nor let his memory dwell very long on the envied and admired of men, nor idly sit and dream of them. Rather, he should contemplate the lives of those who suffer hardship, and vividly bring to mind their sufferings, so that your own present situation may appear to you important and to be envied, and so that it may no longer be your portion to suffer torture in your soul by your longing for more. For he who admires those who have, and whom other men deem blest of fortune, and who spends all his time idly dreaming of them, will be forced to be always contriving some new device because of his (insatiable) desire, until he ends by doing some desperate deed forbidden by the laws. And therefore one ought not to desire other men's blessings, and one ought not to envy those who have more, but rather, comparing his life with that of those who fare worse, and laying to heart their sufferings, deem himself blest of fortune in that he lives and fares so much better than they. Holding fast to this saying you will pass your life in greater tranquility and will avert not a few of the plagues of life—envy and jealousy and bitterness of mind.

2. The Birth of History

Whereas tradition is essentially linked to the formation of every people and of every nation, conscious historical research is typical of the new stage of intellectual alertness reached in Greece. In Herodotus we witness for the first time this passion-

*ate interest in the past, interest which is in no way limited to
the ken of Greece.*

*The greatness of this father of historical research lies in his
capacity of presenting past events with an incredible freshness
and of communicating to the reader not only a colorful world,
but humanity in all its diversity. He deploys before one's eyes
glorious deeds, shameful customs, noble courage and abomin-
able cruelties: the entire gamut of human possibilities. This
wealth of documentation is offered by a writer who succeeds in
transmitting everything in a most lively directness and with
great poetic charm. The* Histories *are presented against the
background of a noble conception of life. Herodotus' work is
not only a thrilling history but also a great work of art.*

HERODOTUS

THE WAR AGAINST PERSIA

Amongst the Athenian commanders opinion was divided: some were
against risking a battle, on the ground that the Athenian force was too
small to stand a chance of success; others—and amongst them Miltiades
—urged it. It seemed for a time as if the more faint-hearted policy would
be adopted—and so it would have been but for the action of Miltiades.
In addition to the ten commanders, there was another person entitled to
a vote, namely the polemarch, or War Archon, an official appointed in
Athens not by vote but by lot. This office (which formerly carried an
equal vote in military decisions with the generals) was held at this time
by Callimachus of Aphidne. To Callimachus, therefore, Miltiades turned.
"It is now in your hands, Callimachus," he said, "either to enslave
Athens, or to make her free and to leave behind you for all future
generations a memory more glorious than ever Harmodius and Aristo-
geiton left. Never in the course of our long history have we Athenians
been in such peril as now. If we submit to the Persian invader, Hippias
will be restored to power in Athens—and there is little doubt what misery
must then ensue; but if we fight and win, then this city of ours may well
grow to pre-eminence amongst all the cities of Greece. If you ask me how
this can be, and how the decision rests with you, I will tell you: we
commanders are ten in number, and we are not agreed upon what action
to take; half of us are for a battle, half against it. If we refuse to fight, I

16. Geometric belly-handled amphora from Dipylon
Cemetery.

have little doubt that the result will be the rise in Athens of bitter political dissension; our purpose will be shaken, and we shall submit to Persia.
But if we fight before the rot can show itself in any of us, then, if God
gives us fair play, we can not only fight but win. Yours is the decision;
all hangs upon you; vote on my side, and our country will be free—yes,
and the mistress of Greece. But if you support those who have voted
against fighting, that happiness will be denied you—you will get the
opposite."

Miltiades' words prevailed. The vote of Callimachus the War Archon
was cast on the right side, and the decision to fight was made.

The generals exercised supreme command in succession, each for a day;
and those of them who had voted with Miltiades, offered, when their
turn for duty came, to surrender it to him. Miltiades accepted the offer,
but would not fight until the day came when he would in any case have

had the supreme command. When it did come, the Athenian army moved into position for the coming struggle. The right wing was commanded by Callimachus—for it was the regular practice at that time in Athens that the War Archon should lead the right wing; then followed the tribes, one after the other, in an unbroken line; and, finally, on the left wing, was the contingent from Plataea. Ever since the battle of Marathon, when the Athenians offer sacrifice at their quadrennial festival, the herald links the names of Athens and Plataea in the prayer for God's blessing.

One result of the disposition of Athenian troops before the battle was the weakening of their centre by the effort to extend the line sufficiently to cover the whole Persian front; the two wings were strong, but the line in the centre was only a few ranks deep. The dispositions made, and the preliminary sacrifice promising success, the word was given to move, and the Athenians advanced at a run towards the enemy, not less than a mile away. The Persians, seeing the attack developing at the double, prepared to meet it confidently enough, for it seemed to them suicidal madness for the Athenians to risk an assault with so small a force—at the double, too, and with no support from either cavalry or archers. Well, that was what they imagined; nevertheless, the Athenians came on, closed with the enemy all along the line, and fought in a way not to be forgotten. They were the first Greeks, so far as I know, to charge at a run, and the first who dared to look without flinching at Persian dress and the men who wore it; for until that day came, no Greek could hear even the word Persian without terror.

The struggle at Marathon was long drawn out. In the centre, held by the Persians themselves and the Sacae, the advantage was with the foreigners, who were so far successful as to break the Greek line and pursue the fugitives inland from the sea; but the Athenians on one wing and the Plataeans on the other were both victorious. Having got the upper hand, they left the defeated Persians to make their escape, and then, drawing the two wings together into a single unit, they turned their attention to the Persians who had broken through in the centre. Here again they were triumphant, chasing the routed enemy, and cutting them down as they ran right to the edge of the sea. Then, plunging into the water, they laid hold of the ships, calling for fire. It was in this phase of the struggle that the War Archon Callimachus was killed, fighting bravely, and also Stesilaus, the son of Thrasylaus, one of the commanders; Cynegirus, too, the son of Euphorion, had his hand cut off with an axe as he was getting hold of a ship's stern, and so lost his life, together with many other well-known Athenians. Nevertheless the Athenians secured in this way seven ships; the rest managed to get off, and the Persians aboard them, after picking up the Eretrian prisoners whom they had left on Aegilia, laid a course round Sunium for Athens, which they hoped to reach in advance of the Athenian army. In Athens the Alcmaeonidae were accused of suggesting this move; they had, it was said, an understanding with the Persians, and raised a shield as a signal to them when they were on board.

While the Persian fleet was on its way round Sunium, the Athenians hurried back with all possible speed to save their city, and succeeded in reaching it before the arrival of the Persians. Just as at Marathon the Athenian camp had been on a plot of ground sacred to Heracles, so now they fixed their camp on another, also sacred to the same god, at Cynosarges. When the Persian fleet appeared, it lay at anchor for a while off Phalerum (at that time the chief harbour of Athens) and then sailed for Asia.

.   .   .

During the night, when the various commanders had returned on board after the break-up of the conference, an Athenian named Mnesiphilus made his way to Themistocles' ship and asked him what plan it had been decided to adopt. On learning that they had resolved to sail to the Isthmus and to fight there in defence of the Peloponnese, "No, no," he exclaimed; "once the fleet leaves Salamis, it will no longer be one country that you'll be fighting for. Everyone will go home, and neither Eurybiades nor anybody else will be able to prevent the total dissolution of our forces. The plan is absurd and will be the ruin of Greece. Now listen to me: try, if you possibly can, to upset the decision of the conference—it may be that you will be able to persuade Eurybiades to change his mind and remain at Salamis."

Themistocles highly approved of this suggestion, and without saying a word he went to the ship of the commander-in-chief and told him that he had something of public importance to discuss. Eurybiades invited him aboard and gave him permission to speak his mind, whereupon Themistocles, taking a seat beside him, repeated Mnesiphilus' arguments as if they were his own, with plenty of new ones added, until he convinced him, by the sheer urgency of his appeal, that the only thing to do was to go ashore and call the officers to another conference. The conference met, and then, before Eurybiades even had time to announce its purpose, Themistocles, unable to restrain his eagerness, broke into a long and passionate speech. At last he was interrupted by Adeimantus, the son of Ocytus, commander of the Corinthian contingent. "Themistocles," he observed, "in the races, the man who starts before the signal is whipped." "Yes," was Themistocles' retort, "but those who start too late win no prizes." It was a mild retort—for the moment. To Eurybiades he used none of his previous arguments about the danger of the force breaking up if they left Salamis; for it would have been unbecoming to accuse any of the confederates actually to their faces. The line he took this time was quite different. "It is now in your power," he said, "to save Greece, if you take my advice and engage the enemy's fleet here in Salamis, instead of withdrawing to the Isthmus as these other people suggest. Let me put the two plans before you, and you can weigh them up and see which is the better. Take the Isthmus first: if you fight there, it will have to be in the open sea, and that will be greatly to our disadvantage, with our smaller numbers and slower ships. Moreover, even if everything else goes well, you will lose Salamis, Megara, and Aegina. Again, if the enemy fleet comes south, the army will follow it; so you will yourself be responsible for drawing it to the Peloponnese, thus putting the whole of Greece in peril.

"Now for my plan: it will bring, if you adopt it, the following advantages: first, we shall be fighting in narrow waters, and that, with our inferior numbers, will ensure our success, provided things go as we may reasonably expect. The open sea is bound to help the enemy, just as fighting in a confined space is bound to help us. Secondly, Salamis, where we have put our women and children, will be preserved; and thirdly— for you the most important point of all—you will be fighting in defence of the Peloponnese by remaining here just as much as by withdrawing to the Isthmus—nor, if you have the sense to follow my advice, will you draw the Persian army to the Peloponnese. If we beat them at sea, as I expect we shall, they will not advance to attack you on the Isthmus, or come any further than Attica; they will retreat in disorder, and we shall gain by the preservation of Megara, Aegina, and Salamis—where an oracle has already foretold our victory. Let a man lay his plans with due regard to common sense, and he will usually succeed; otherwise he will find that God is unlikely to favour human designs."

. . .

This was enough to make Eurybiades change his mind; and no doubt his chief motive was apprehension of losing Athenian support, if he withdrew to the Isthmus; for without the Athenian contingent his strength would not have been adequate to offer battle. So he took the decision to stay where they were and fight it out at Salamis.

The skirmish of words was over; Eurybiades had made up his mind; and at once the ships' commanders began to prepare for action. Day broke; just as the sun rose the shock of an earthquake was felt both on land and at sea, and the Greeks resolved to offer prayers to the gods and to call upon the Sons of Aeacus to fight at their side. As they resolved, so they did: they prayed to all the gods, and called upon Ajax and Telamon there in Salamis, and sent a ship to Aegina for Aeacus himself and his Sons.

.   .   .

Meanwhile the Persian sailors had returned from Trachis to Histiaea after their sight-seeing tour of the battlefield, and three days later the fleet set sail. The ships passed through the Euripus, and in another three days arrived off Phalerum. In my judgement the Persian forces both by land and sea were just as strong at the time of their entry into Attica as they had been at Sepias and Thermopylae; for as an offset to the losses suffered in the storm, at Thermopylae, and at Artemisium, I reckon the reinforcements which had subsequently joined them. These were the Malians, Dorians, Locrians, and Boeotians, who took service under Xerxes with all the troops they had except the Thespians and Plataeans; and in addition to these they were further reinforced by the Carystians, Andrians, Tenians, and all the other island peoples except the five whom I mentioned above. At each forward step into Greece the Persians had received new accessions of men and ships.

All these troops came as far as Attica except the Parians, who had stayed behind in Cythnus to watch the course of the war; and the rest of the fleet arrived, as I have said, at Phalerum.

.   .   .

The command was now given to put to sea, and the ships proceeded towards Salamis, where they took up their respective stations without interference from the enemy. It was late in the evening, with not enough light left to attack at once; so they prepared to go into action on the following day.

The Greeks were in a state of acute alarm, especially those from the

Peloponnese: for there they were, waiting at Salamis to fight for Athenian territory, and certain, in the event of defeat, to be caught and blocked up in an island, while their own country was left without defence, and the Persian army that very night was on the march for the Peloponnese.

Nevertheless everything that ingenuity could contrive had been done to prevent the Persian army from forcing the Isthmus. On the news of the destruction of Leonidas' force at Thermopylae not a moment was lost; and troops from the various towns in the Peloponnese hurried to the Isthmus, where they took up their position under Cleombrotus, the son of Anaxandrides and brother of Leonidas. Their first act was to break up and block the Scironian Way; then, in accordance with a decision taken in council, they began work on a wall across the Isthmus. As there were many thousands there and every man turned to, it was soon finished. Stones, bricks, timbers, sand-baskets—all were used in the building, and the labour went on continuously night and day. The towns which sent men to help in this work were the following: Sparta, all the towns in Arcadia, Elis, Corinth, Sicyon, Epidaurus, Phlius, Troezen, and Hermione: all these, in their overriding fear for the safety of Greece, sent every available man. The other Peloponnesian communities (though the Olympic and Carneian festivals were now over) remained indifferent.

.   .   .

The Greeks at the Isthmus, convinced that all they possessed was now at stake and not expecting any notable success at sea, continued to grapple with their task of fortification. The news of how they were employed nevertheless caused great concern at Salamis; for it brought home to everyone there not so much his own peril as the imminent threat to the Peloponnese. At first there was whispered criticism of the incredible folly of Eurybiades; then the smothered feeling broke out into open resentment, and another meeting was held. All the old ground was gone over again, one side urging that it was useless to stay and fight for a country which was already in enemy hands, and that the fleet should sail and risk an action in defence of the Peloponnese, while the Athenians, Aeginetans, and Megarians still maintained that they should stay and fight at Salamis.

At this point Themistocles, feeling that he would be outvoted by the Peloponnesians, slipped quietly away from the meeting and sent a man over in a boat to the Persian fleet, with instructions upon what to say when he got there. The man—Sicinnus—was one of Themistocles' slaves and used to attend upon his sons; some time afterwards, when the Thespians were admitting outsiders to citizenship, Themistocles established him at Thespia and made him a rich man. Following his instructions, then, Sicinnus made his way to the Persians and said: "I am the bearer of a secret communication from the Athenian commander, who is a well-wisher to your king and hopes for a Persian victory. He has told me to report to you that the Greeks have no confidence in themselves and are planning to save their skins by a hasty withdrawal. Only prevent them from slipping through your fingers, and you have at this moment an opportunity of unparalleled success. They are at daggers drawn with each other, and will offer no opposition—on the contrary, you will see the pro-Persians amongst them fighting the rest."

His message delivered, Sicinnus lost no time in getting away. The Persians believed what he had told them, and proceeded to put ashore a large force on the islet of Psyttaleia, between Salamis and the coast; then, about midnight, they moved one division of the fleet towards the western end of Salamis in order to encircle the enemy, while at the same time the ships off Ceos and Cynosura also advanced and blocked the whole channel as far as Munychia. The object of these movements was to prevent the escape of the Greek fleet from the narrow waters of Salamis, and there to take revenge upon it for the battles at Artemisium. The troops were landed on Psyttaleia because it lay right in the path of the impending action, and once the fighting began, most of the men and damaged vessels would be carried on to it, and could be saved or destroyed according as they were friends or enemies. These tactical moves were carried out in silence, to prevent the enemy from being aware of what was going on; they occupied the whole night, so that none of the men had time for sleep.

.   .   .

The Greek commanders at Salamis were still at loggerheads. They did not yet know that the enemy ships had blocked their escape at both ends of the channel, but supposed them to occupy the same position as they had seen them in during the day. However, while the dispute was still at its height, Aristides came over in a boat from Aegina. This man, an Athenian and the son of Lysimachus, had been banished from Athens by popular vote, but the more I have learned of his character, the more I have come to believe that he was the best and most honourable man that Athens ever produced. Arrived at Salamis, Aristides went to where the conference was being held and, standing outside, called for Themistocles. Themistocles was no friend of his; indeed he was his most determined enemy; but Aristides was willing, in view of the magnitude of the danger which threatened them, to forget old quarrels in his desire to communicate with him. He was already aware of the anxiety of the Peloponnesian commanders to withdraw to the Isthmus; as soon, therefore, as Themistocles came out of the conference in answer to his call, he said: "At this moment, more than ever before, you and I should be rivals; and the object of our rivalry should be to see which of us can do most good to our country. First, let me tell you that the Peloponnesians may talk as much or as little as they please about withdrawing from Salamis—it will make not the least difference. What I tell you, I have seen with my own eyes: they *cannot* now get out of here, however much the Corinthians or Eurybiades himself may wish to do so, because our fleet is surrounded. Go back to the conference, and tell them."

"Good news and good advice," Themistocles answered; "what I most wanted has happened—and you bring me the evidence of your own eyes that it is true. It was I who was responsible for this move of the enemy; for as our men would not fight here of their own free will, it was necessary to make them, whether they wanted to do so or not. But take them the good news yourself; if I tell them, they will think I have invented it and will not believe me. Please, then, go in and make the report yourself. If they believe you, well and good; if they do not, it's no odds; for if we are surrounded, as you say we are, escape is no longer possible."

Aristides accordingly went in and made his report, saying he had come from Aegina and had been hard put to it to slip through the blockading enemy fleet, as the entire Greek force was surrounded. He advised them, therefore, to prepare at once to repel an attack. That said, he left the conference, whereupon another dispute broke out, because most of the Greek commanders refused to believe in the truth of Aristides' report. Nor were their doubts settled until a Tenian warship, commanded by Panaetius, the son of Sosimenes, deserted from the Persian navy and came in with a full account of what had occurred. For this service the name of the Tenians was afterwards inscribed on the tripod at Delphi amongst the other states who helped to defeat the invader. With this ship which came over to them at Salamis, and the Lemnian one which previously joined them at Artemisium, the Greek fleet was brought up to the round number of 380. Up till then it had fallen short of that figure by two.

Forced to accept the Tenians' report, the Greeks now at last prepared for action. At dawn the fighting men were assembled and Themistocles was chosen to address them. The whole burden of what he said was a comparison of the nobler and baser parts of human nature, and an exhortation to the men to follow the former in the coming ordeal. Then, having rounded off his speech, he gave the order for embarkation. The order was obeyed and, just as the men were going aboard, the ship which had been sent to Aegina to fetch the Sons of Aeacus, rejoined the fleet.

The whole fleet now got under way, and in a moment the Persians were on them. The Greeks checked their way and began to back astern; and they were on the point of running aground when Ameinias of Pallene, in command of an Athenian ship, drove ahead and rammed an enemy vessel. Seeing the two ships foul of one another and locked together, the rest of the Greek fleet hurried to Ameinias' assistance, and the general action began. Such is the Athenian account of how the battle started; the Aeginetans claim that the first to go into action was the ship which fetched the Sons of Aeacus from Aegina. There is also a popular belief that the phantom shape of a woman appeared and, in a voice which could be heard by every man in the fleet, contemptuously asked if they proposed to go astern all day, and then cheered them on to the fight.

.   .   .

When the Persian rout began, and they were trying to get back to Phalerum, the Aeginetan squadron, which was waiting to catch them in the narrows, did memorable service. The enemy was in hopeless confusion; such ships as offered resistance or tried to escape were cut to pieces by the Athenians, while the Aeginetans caught and disabled those which attempted to get clear of the strait, so that any ship which escaped the one enemy promptly fell amongst the other. It happened at this stage that Themistocles, chasing an enemy vessel, ran close aboard the ship which was commanded by Polycritus, the son of Crius, the Aeginetan. Polycritus had just rammed a Sidonian, the very ship which captured the Aeginetan guard-vessel off Sciathus—the one, it will be remembered, which had Pytheas on board, the man the Persians kept with them out of admiration for his gallantry in refusing to surrender in spite of his appalling wounds. When the ship was taken with him and the Persian crew on board, he got safe home to Aegina. When Polycritus noticed the Athenian ship, and recognized the admiral's flag, he shouted to Themistocles and asked him in a tone of ironic reproach if he still thought that the people of Aegina were Persia's friends.

Such of the Persian ships as escaped destruction made their way back to Phalerum and brought up there under the protection of the army.

(from *The Histories,* Books VI and VIII)

In the hands of Thucydides, history received a strictly scientific character. In systematic presentation and critical spirit he is superior to Herodotus. Like the latter he embodies a noble moral ethos, particularly evident in his description of the moral decay which led to Athens' ruin. His powerful, masculine style has, however, neither the enchanting colorfulness of Herodotus nor his poetic charm. History in the modern sense of this term was molded in his hands.

THUCYDIDES

THE MELIAN DIALOGUE

The Athenians made an expedition against the island of Melos with thirty ships of their own, six Chian, and two Lesbian, twelve hundred hoplites and three hundred archers and twenty mounted archers of their own, and about fifteen hundred hoplites furnished by their allies in the islands. The Melians are colonists of the Lacedaemonians who would not submit to Athens like the other islanders. At first they were neutral and passive. But when the Athenians tried to coerce them by ravaging their lands, they were driven into open hostilities. The generals, Cleomedes the son of Lycomedes and Tisias the son of Tisimachus, encamped with the Athenian forces on the island. But before they did the country any harm, they sent envoys to negotiate with the Melians. Instead of bringing these envoys before the people, the Melians desired them to explain their errand to the minority who held the magistracies. They spoke as follows:

"Since we are denied a public audience on the ground that the multitude might be deceived by hearing our seductive arguments without refutation if they were set forth in a single uninterrupted oration (for we are perfectly aware that this is what you mean in bringing us before the select few), we ask you who are seated here to proceed with even further caution, to reply on each point, instead of speaking continuously yourselves, and to take up at once any statement of ours of which you do not approve, and so reach your decision. Say first of all how you like our proposal."

The Melian representatives answered: "The quiet interchange of explanations is reasonable, and we do not object to that. But at this very time you are actually engaged in acts of war, which obviously belie your words. We see that you mean to decide the discussion yourselves and that at the end of it, if (as is likely) the justice of our cause prevail and we therefore refuse to yield, we may expect war; if we are convinced by you, slavery."

ATHENIANS. "Of course, if you are going to base your calculations on conjectures of the future or if you meet us with any other purpose than that of looking your circumstances in the face and thinking how to save your city, we might as well have done; but if this is your intention, we will proceed."

MELIANS. "It is natural and excusable that men in our position should resort to many arguments and considerations. But we admit that this conference has met to consider the question of our preservation; and therefore let the argument proceed in the manner which you propose, if you think that best."

ATHENIANS. "Well, then, we Athenians will use no fine words; we will not say at length, without carrying conviction, that we have a right to rule because we overthrew the Persians or that we are attacking you now because we are suffering any injury at your hands. And you should not expect to convince us by arguing that, although a colony of the Lacedaemonians, you have taken no part in their expeditions or that you have never done us any wrong. You must act with realism on the basis of what we both really think, for we both alike know that in human reckoning the question of justice only enters where there is equal power to enforce it and that the powerful exact what they can and the weak grant what they must."

MELIANS. "Well, then, since you thus set aside justice and make expediency the subject of debate, in our judgment it is certainly of advantage that you respect the common good, that to every man in peril fair treatment be accorded, and that any plea which he has urged, even if failing of the point a little, should help his cause. Your interest in this principle is quite as great as ours, since if you fall, you might incur the heaviest vengeance and be an example to mankind."

ATHENIANS. "The end of our empire, even if it should fall, does not dismay us; for ruling states such as Lacedaemon are not cruel to their vanquished enemies. But we are not now contending with the Lacedaemonians; the real danger is from our subjects, who may of their own motion rise up and overcome their masters. But this is a danger which you may leave to us. We will show that we have come in the interests of our empire and that in what we are about to say, we are only seeking the preservation of your city. We wish to subdue you without effort and to preserve you to our mutual advantage."

MELIANS. "It may be your advantage to be our masters, but how can it be ours to be your slaves?"

ATHENIANS. "By submission you would avert the most terrible sufferings, and we should profit from not destroying you."

MELIANS. "But must we be your enemies? Would you not receive us as friends if we are neutral and remain at peace with you?"

ATHENIANS. "No, your enmity does not injure us as much as your friendship; for your enmity is in the eyes of our subjects a demonstration of our power, your friendship of our weakness."

MELIANS. "But do your subjects think it fair not to distinguish between cities in which you have no connection and those which are chiefly your own colonies, and in some cases have revolted and been subdued?"

ATHENIANS. "Why, they believe that neither lack pleas of right, but that by reason of their power some escape us and that we do not attack them out of fear. So that your subjection would give us security, as well as an extension of empire, all the more as you are islanders, and insignificant islanders."

MELIANS. "But do you not think that there is security in our proposal? For, once more, since you drive us from the pleas of justice and urge us to submit to you our interest, we must show you what is for our advantage and try to convince you, if it really coincides with yours: Will you not be making enemies of all who are now neutrals? When they see how you are treating us, they will expect you some day to turn against them; and if so, are you not strengthening the enemies whom you already have and bringing upon you others who, if they could help it, would never dream of being your enemies at all?"

ATHENIANS. "We consider that our really dangerous enemies are not any of the peoples inhabiting the mainland who are secure in their freedom and will defer indefinitely any measures of precaution against us, but islanders who, like you, are under no control, and all who are already irritated by the necessity of submission to our empire; for without calculating, they would be most likely to plunge themselves, as well as us, into a danger for all to foresee."

MELIANS. "Surely then, if you and your subjects will brave all this danger, you to preserve your empire and they to be quit of it, how base and cowardly would it be for us, as we are still free, not to do and suffer anything rather than be your slaves."

ATHENIANS. "Not if you deliberate with sound sense; you are in an unequal contest; not about your good character and avoiding dishonor: you must think of saving yourselves by not resisting far superior forces."

MELIANS. "But we know that the fortune of war is sometimes impartial and not always on the side of numbers. If we yield, hope is at once gone, but if we act, we can still hope to stand unbowed."

ATHENIANS. "Hope comforts men in danger; and when they have ample resources, it may be hurtful, but is not ruinous. But when her spendthrift nature has induced them to stake their all, they see her as she is only in the moment of their ruin; when their eyes are opened, and they would at last take precautions, they are left with nothing. You are weak, and a single turn of the scale may be your ruin: do not desire to be deluded; or to be like the common herd of men; when they still, humanly speaking, have a chance of survival but find themselves, in their extremity, destitute of real grounds for confidence, they resort to illusions, to prophecies and oracles and the like, which ruin men by the hopes which they inspire in them."

MELIANS. "You may be sure that we think it hard to struggle against your power and against fortune if she does not mean to be impartial. But still we trust that we shall not have the worst of the fortune that comes from heaven because we stand as righteous men against your injustice, and we are satisfied that our deficiency in power will be compensated by the alliance of the Lacedaemonians; they are bound to help us, if only because we are their kinsmen and for the sake of their own honor. And therefore our confidence is not so utterly unreasonable."

ATHENIANS. "As for the gods, we expect to have quite as much of their favor as you: for we are not claiming or doing anything which goes beyond what men believe of the gods and desire in human relationships. For we believe of the gods by repute, and of men by clear evidence, that by a necessity of nature, wherever they have the power, they will rule. This law was not made by us, and we are not the first who have acted upon it; we did but inherit it, and shall bequeath it to all time; we obey it in the knowledge that you and all mankind, with our strength would act like us. So much for the gods; we have no reason to fear any lack of their favor. And then as to the Lacedaemonians—when you imagine that out of very shame they will assist you, we congratulate you on your blissful ignorance, but we do not admire your folly. No men do each other more services, by their own local standards, than the Lacedaemonians; but as for their conduct to the rest of the world, much might be said, but it could be most clearly expressed in a few words—of all men whom we know, they are the most conspicuous for identifying pleasure with honor and expediency with justice. But how inconsistent is such a character with your present unreasonable hope of deliverance!"

MELIANS. "That is the very reason why we are now particularly reliant on them; they will look to their interest, and therefore will not be willing to betray the Melians, their own colonists, lest they should be distrusted by their friends in Hellas and play into the hands of their enemies."

ATHENIANS. "Then you do not think that the path of expediency is safe, whereas justice and honor involve action and danger, which none are more generally averse to facing than the Lacedaemonians."

MELIANS. "No, we believe that they would be ready to face dangers for our sake, and will think them safer where we are concerned. If action is required, we are close to the Peloponnese; and they can better trust our loyal feeling because we are their kinsmen."

ATHENIANS. "Yes, but what gives men security in joining in a conflict is clearly not the good will of those who summon help but a decided superiority in real power. To this none look more keenly than the Lacedaemonians; so little confidence have they in their own resources that they only attack their neighbors when they have numerous allies; and therefore they are not likely to find their way by themselves to an island, when we are masters of the sea."

MELIANS. "But they might send others; the Cretan sea is a large place, and the masters of the sea will have more difficulty in seizing vessels than those who would elude detection in making their escape. And if the attempt should fail, they might invade Attica itself and find their way to allies of yours whom Brasidas did not reach; and then you will have to make efforts, not for the conquest of a land which is not yours, but nearer home, for the preservation of your confederacy and of your own territory."

ATHENIANS. "Some of this may happen; we have actually experienced it, and you are not unaware that never once have the Athenians retired

17. *Sea journey of Dionysus*. Interior of an Attic black-figured kylix by Exekias.

from a siege through fear of others. You told us that you would deliberate on the safety of your city; but we remark that, in this long discussion, you have uttered not a word which would justify men in expecting deliverance. Your strongest grounds are hopes deferred; and what power you have, compared with that already arrayed against you, is too little to save you. What you have in mind is most unreasonable, unless you ultimately come to a sounder decision after we have withdrawn. For surely you will not fall back on a sense of honor, which has been the ruin of so many, when danger and dishonor were staring them in the face. Many men with their eyes still open to the consequences have found the word *honor* too much for them and have let a mere name lure them on, until with their own acquiescence it has drawn down upon them real and irretrievable calamities; through their own folly they have incurred a worse dishonor than fortune would have inflicted upon them.

If you are wise, you will not run this risk; you will think it not unfitting to yield to the greatest of cities, which invites you to become her ally on reasonable terms, keeping your own land and merely paying tribute; you will find no honor, when you have a choice between two alternatives, safety and war, in obstinately preferring the worse. To maintain one's rights against equals, to be politic with superiors and to be moderate toward inferiors is generally the right course. Reflect once more when we have withdrawn, and say to yourselves over and over again that you are deliberating about your one and only country, which a single decision will save or destroy."

The Athenians left the conference; the Melians, after consulting among themselves, resolved to persevere in their refusal and gave the following answer: "Men of Athens, our resolution is unchanged; and we will not in a moment surrender that liberty which our city, founded seven hundred years ago, still enjoys; we will trust to the good fortune which, by the favor of the gods, has hitherto preserved us, and for human help, to the Lacedaemonians; and we will endeavor to save ourselves. We are ready, however, to be your friends and the enemies neither of you nor of the Lacedaemonians and we ask you to leave our country when you have made such a peace as appears to be in the interest of both parties."

This was the substance of the Melian answer; the Athenians said as they quitted the conference: "Well, we must say, judging from the decision at which you have arrived, that you are the only men who find things to come plainer than what lies before their eyes: your wishes make you see the secrets of the future as present realities; you put your faith in the Lacedaemonians, in fortune and in your hopes; none have more than you at stake, and none will be more utterly ruined."

(from *The Peloponnesian Wars,* Book V)

3. The Birth of Literature

As Livingstone has pointed out in The Pageant of Greece, *it is characteristic of the Greeks that the different poetic genres develop in turn, and are separated by a clear dividing line that can be drawn down to modern times. First comes the period of gigantic epics in Homer and Hesiod; then the lyrics of Pindar, Sappho, and Anacreon, and finally the blossoming of the drama.*

The Birth of Epos

The amazing feature of Greek literature is that it began with two masterpieces, The Iliad *and* The Odyssey. *These two timeless works are not gropings toward perfection but constitute, each in its own fashion, a height of artistic greatness. In these works, nature is described with a freshness and poetry hard to match in the history of literature; for somehow it is nature itself which speaks, unfettered by conventional approaches or scientific investigations. It is not an easy task for modern man to reconquer this freshness of approach, sober in presentation, vibrant in content. But when he succeeds in doing so, he will have the feeling that scales fall off his eyes; he will be given back an undistorted sense of wonder, a most desirable combination of childlike freshness and spiritual maturity. Homer combines simplicity and grandeur.*

HOMER

THE DEATH OF HECTOR

Then to the city, terrible and strong,
With high and haughty steps he tower'd along.
So the proud courser, victor of the prize,
To the near goal with double ardour flies.
Him, as he blazing shot across the field,
The careful eyes of Priam first beheld.
Not half so dreadful rises to the sight,
Through the thick gloom of some tempestuous night,
Orion's dog (the year when autumn weighs,)
And o'er the feeble stars exerts his rays:
Terrific glory! for his burning breath
Taints the red air with fevers, plagues, and death.
So flamed his fiery mail. Then wept the sage;
He strikes his reverend head now white with age:
He lifts his wither'd arms; obtests the skies;
He calls his much-loved son with feeble cries:
The son resolved Achilles' force to dare,
Full at the Scaean gate expects the war:

While the sad father on the rampart stands,
And thus adjures him with extended hands:
  Ah stay not, stay not! guardless and alone;
Hector! my loved, my dearest, bravest son!
Methinks already I behold thee slain,
And stretch'd beneath that fury of the plain.
Implacable Achilles! might'st thou be
To all the gods no dearer than to me!
The vultures wild should scatter round the shore
And bloody dogs grow fiercer from thy gore.
How many valiant sons I late enjoy'd,
Valiant in vain! by thy cursed arm destroy'd:
Or worse than slaughter'd, sold in distant isles
To shameful bondage and unworthy toils.
Two while I speak my eyes in vain explore,
Two from one mother sprung, my Polydore,
And loved Lycaon: now perhaps no more!
Oh! if in yonder hostile camp they live,
What heaps of gold, what treasures would I give!
(Their grandsire's wealth by right of birth their own,
Consign'd his daughter with Lelegia's throne:)
But if (which Heaven forbid) already lost,
All pale they wander on the Stygian coast,
What sorrows then must their sad mother know
What anguish I! unutterable woe!
Yet less that anguish, less to her, to me,
Less to all Troy, if not deprived of thee.
Yet shun Achilles! enter yet the wall;
And spare thyself, thy father, spare us all!
Save thy dear life; or if a soul so brave
Neglect that thought, thy dearer glory save.
Pity, while yet I live, these silver hairs!
While yet thy father feels the woes he bears,
Yet cursed with sense! a wretch, whom, in his rage
(All trembling on the verge of helpless age)
Great Jove has placed, sad spectacle of pain!
The bitter dregs of Fortune's cup to drain:
To fill with scenes of death his closing eyes,
And number all his days by miseries;
My heroes slain, my bridal bed o'erturn'd,

My daughters ravish'd, and my city burn'd,
My bleeding infants dash'd against the floor;
These I have yet to see, perhaps yet more!
Perhaps e'en I, reserved by angry Fate
The last sad relic of my ruin'd state,
(Dire pomp of sovereign wretchedness!) must fall
And stain the pavement of my regal hall
Where famish'd dogs, late guardians of my door,
Shall lick their man, led master's spatter'd gore.
Yet for my sons I thank ye, gods! 'twas well:
Well have they perish'd, for in fight they fell.
Who dies in youth and vigour dies the best,
Struck through with wounds, all honest on the breast
But when the Fates, in fulness of their rage,
Spurn the hoar head of unresisting age,
In dust the reverend lineaments deform,
And pour to dogs the life blood scarcely warm:
This, this is misery! the last, the worst,
That man can feel; man, fated to be cursed!

He said, and acting what no words could say,
Rent from his head the silver locks away.
With him the mournful mother bears a part;
Yet all their sorrows turn not Hector's heart:
The zone unbraced, her bosom she display'd;
And thus, fast falling the salt tears, she said:

Have mercy on me, O my son! revere
The words of age; attend a parent's prayer!
If ever thee in these fond arms I press'd,
Or still'd thy infant clamours at this breast;
Ah! do not thus our helpless years forego,
But by our walls secured repel the foe.
Against his rage if singly thou proceed,
Shouldst thou (but Heaven avert it!) shouldst thou bleed,
Nor must thy corse lie honour'd on the bier,
Nor spouse nor mother grace thee with a tear;
Far from our pious rites, those dear remains
Must feast the vultures on the naked plains.

So they, while down their cheeks the torrents roll,
But fix'd remains the purpose of his soul:
Resolved he stands, and with a fiery glance

Expects the hero's terrible advance.
So roll'd up in his den, the swelling snake
Beholds the traveller approach the brake;
When fed with noxious herbs his turgid veins
Have gather'd half the poisons of the plains;
He burns, he stiffens with collected ire,
And his red eye-balls glare with living fire.
Beneath a turret, on his shield reclined,
He stood, and question'd thus his mighty mind:
　　Where lies my way? To enter in the wall?
Honour and shame the ungenerous thought recall:
Shall proud Polydamas before the gate
Proclaim his counsels are obey'd too late,
Which timely follow'd but the former night,
What numbers had been saved by Hector's flight?
That wise advice rejected with disdain,
I feel my folly in my people slain.
Methinks my suffering country's voice I hear,
But most her worthless sons insult my ear,
On my rash courage charge the chance of war,
And blame those virtues which they cannot share.
No—If I e'er return, return I must
Glorious, my country's terror laid in dust:
Or if I perish, let her see me fall
In field at least, and fighting for her wall.
And yet suppose these measures I forego,
Approach unarm'd and parley with the foe,
The warrior-shield, the helm, and lance, lay down,
And treat on terms of peace to save the town:
The wife withheld, the treasure ill-detain'd
(Cause of the war, and grievance of the land,)
With honourable justice to restore;
And add half Ilion's yet remaining store,
Which Troy shall sworn produce; that injured Greece
May share our wealth, and leave our walls in peace.
But why this thought? Unarm'd if I should go,
What hope of mercy from this vengeful foe,
But woman-like to fall, and fall without a blow?
We greet not here as man conversing man,
Met at an oak, or journeying o'er a plain;

No season now for calm familiar talk,
Like youths and maidens in an evening walk;
War is our business, but to whom is given
To die or triumph, that determine Heaven!
 Thus pondering, like a god the Greek drew nigh,
His dreadful plumage nodded from on high;
The Pelian javelin in his better hand
Shot trembling rays that glitter'd o'er the land;
And on his breast the beamy splendours shone,
Like Jove's own lightning or the rising sun.
As Hector sees, unusual terrors rise,
Struck by some god, he fears, recedes, and flies;
He leaves the gates, he leaves the walls behind:
Achilles follows like the winged wind.
Thus at the panting dove a falcon flies
(The swiftest racer of the liquid skies;)
Just when he holds or thinks he holds his prey,
Obliquely wheeling through the aerial way,
With open beak and shrilling cries he springs,
And aims his claws and shoots upon his wings;

. . .

Thus three times round the Trojan wall they fly:
The gazing gods lean forward from the sky;

. . .

. . . The silence Hector broke;
His dreadful plumage nodded as he spoke:
 Enough, O son of Peleus! Troy has view'd
Her walls thrice circled, and her chief pursued:
But now some god within me bids me try
Thine, or my fate: I kill thee, or I die.
Yet on the verge of battle let us stay,
And for a moment's space suspend the day;
Let heaven's high power be call'd to arbitrate
The just conditions of this stern debate
(Eternal witnesses of all below,
And faithful guardians of the treasured vow!)

To them I swear; if, victor in the strife,
Jove by these hands shall shed thy noble life
No vile dishonour shall thy corse pursue;
Stripp'd of its arms alone (the conqueror's due)
The rest to Greece uninjured I'll restore:
Now plight thy mutual oath, I ask no more.

　　Talk not of oaths (the dreadful chief replies,
While anger flash'd from his disdainful eyes:)
Detested as thou art, and ought to be,
Nor oath nor pact Achilles plights with thee.
Such pacts as lambs and rabid wolves combine,
Such leagues as men and furious lions join,
To such I call the gods! one constant state
Of lasting rancour and eternal hate:
No thought but rage and never-ceasing strife,
Till death extinguish rage, and thought, and life
Rouse then thy forces this important hour,
Collect thy soul, and call forth all thy power.
No farther subterfuge, no farther chance;
'Tis Pallas, Pallas gives thee to my lance.
Each Grecian ghost by thee deprived of breath
Now hovers round, and calls thee to thy death.

　　He spoke, and launch'd the javelin at the foe:
But Hector shunn'd the meditated blow:
He stoop'd, while o'er his head the flying spear
Sung innocent, and spent its force in air.
Minerva watch'd it falling on the land,
Then drew and gave to great Achilles' hand,
Unseen of Hector, who, elate with joy,
Now shakes his lance, and braves the dread of Troy

　　The life you boasted to that javelin given,
Prince! you have miss'd. My fate depends on Heaven.
To thee presumptuous as thou art, unknown
Or what must prove my fortune or thy own.
Boasting is but an art our fears to blind,
And with false terror sink another's mind.
But know, whatever fate I am to try,
By no dishonest wound shall Hector die;
I shall not fall a fugitive at least,
My soul shall bravely issue from my breast.

But first try thou my arm! and may this dart
End all my country's woes, deep buried in thy heart!
   The weapon flew, its course unerring held;
Unerring, but the heavenly shield repell'd
The mortal dart; resulting with a bound
From off the ringing orb, it struck the ground
Hector beheld his javelin fall in vain,
Nor other lance, nor other hope remain;
He calls Deïphobus, demands a spear,
In vain, for no Deïphobus was there.
All comfortless he stands: then, with a sigh,
'Tis so—Heaven wills it, and my hour is nigh!
I deem'd Deïphobus had heard my call,
But he secure lies guarded in the wall.
A god deceived me: Pallas, 'twas thy deed:
Death and black Fate approach! 'tis I must bleed.
No refuge now, no succour from above,
Great Jove deserts me, and the son of Jove,
Propitious once, and kind! then welcome Fate!
'Tis true I perish, yet I perish great:
Yet in a mighty deed I shall expire,
Let future ages hear it and admire!
   Fierce at the word his weighty sword he drew
And all-collected on Achilles flew
So Jove's bold bird, high balanced in the air,
Stoops from the clouds to truss the quivering hare.
Nor less Achilles his fierce soul prepares;
Before his breast the flaming shield he bears,
Refulgent orb! above his fourfold cone
The gilded horse-hair sparkled in the sun,
Nodding at every step (Vulcanian frame!)
And as he moved his figure seem'd on flame.
As radiant Hesper shines with keener light,
Far beaming o'er the silver host of night,
When all the starry train emblaze the sphere:
So shone the point of great Achilles' spear.
In his right hand he waves the weapon round,
Eyes the whole man, and meditates the wound:
But the rich mail Patroclus lately wore,
Securely ceased the warrior's body o'er!

One place at length he spies to let in Fate,
Where 'twixt the neck and throat the jointed plate
Gave entrance: through that penetrable part
Furious he drove the well-directed dart:
Nor pierced the windpipe yet, nor took the power
Of speech, unhappy! from thy dying hour.
Prone on the field the bleeding warrior lies,
While thus triumphing stern Achilles cries:

    At last is Hector stretch'd upon the plain,
Who fear'd no vengeance for Patroclus slain?
Then, prince, you should have fear'd what now you feel;
Achilles absent was Achilles still.
Yet a short space the great avenger stay'd,
Then low in dust thy strength and glory laid.
Peaceful he sleeps with all our rites adorn'd,
For ever honour'd, and for ever mourn'd:
While cast to all the rage of hostile power,
Thee birds shall mangle and the dogs devour.

    Then Hector, fainting at the approach of death:
By thy own soul! by those who gave thee breath!
By all the sacred prevalence of prayer!
Ah, leave me not for Grecian dogs to tear!
The common rites of sepulture bestow,
To soothe a father's and a mother's woe;
Let their large gifts procure an urn at least,
And Hector's ashes in his country rest.

    No, wretch accursed! relentless he replies
(Flames as he spoke shot flashing from his eyes,)
Not those who gave me breath should bid me spare,
Nor all the sacred prevalence of prayer.
Could I myself the bloody banquet join!
No—to the dogs that carcass I resign.
Should Troy to bribe me bring forth all her store,
And giving thousands, offer thousands more;
Should Dardan Priam, and his weeping dame,
Drain the whole realm to buy one funeral flame:
Their Hector on the pile they should not see,
Nor rob the vultures of one limb of thee.

    Then thus the chief his dying accents drew:
Thy rage implacable too well I knew:

The Furies that relentless breast have steel'd,
And cursed thee with a heart that cannot yield.
Yet think, a day will come, when Fate's decree
And angry gods shall wreak this wrong on thee;
Phoebus and Paris shall avenge my fate,
And stretch thee here before this Scaean gate.
  He ceased. The Fates suppress'd his labouring breath,
And his eyes stiffen'd at the hand of death;
To the dark realm the spirit wings its way
(The manly body left a load of clay,)
And plaintive glides along the dreary coast,
A naked, wandering, melancholy ghost!

      .   .   .

  The mother first beheld with sad survey,
She rent her tresses, venerably gray,
And cast far off the regal veils away.
With piercing shrieks his bitter fate she moans,
While the sad father answers groans with groans
Tears after tears his mournful cheeks o'erflow
And the whole city wears one face of woe:
Not less than if the rage of hostile fires,
From her foundations curling to her spires,
O'er the proud citadel at length should rise,
And the last blaze send Ilion to the skies.
The wretched monarch of the falling state
Distracted presses to the Dardan gate
Scarce the whole people stop his desperate course,
While strong affliction gives the feeble force:
Grief tears his heart, and drives him to and fro,
In all the raging impotence of woe.
At length he roll'd in dust, and thus begun,
Imploring all, and naming one by one:
Ah! let me, let me go where sorrow calls;
I, only I, will issue from your walls
(Guide or companion, friends! I ask you none,)
And bow before the murderer of my son:
My grief perhaps his pity may engage;
Perhaps at least he may respect my age.
He has a father too; a man like me;

THE ADVENTURE OF THE SPIRIT

One not exempt from age and misery:
(Vigorous no more, as when his young embrace
Begot this pest of me and all my race.)
How many valiant sons, in early bloom,
Has that cursed hand sent headlong to the tomb!
Thee, Hector! last: thy loss (divinely brave)
Sinks my sad soul with sorrow to the grave.
Oh had thy gentle spirit pass'd in peace,
The son expiring in the sire's embrace,
While both thy parents wept thy fatal hour,
And bending o'er thee, mix'd the tender shower!
Some comfort that had been, some sad relief,
To melt in full satiety of grief!

Thus wail'd the father, grovelling on the ground,
And all the eyes of Ilion stream'd around.

Amidst her matrons Hecuba appears
(A mourning princess, and a train in tears.)
Ah, why has heaven prolong'd this hated breath,
Patient of horrors, to behold thy death!
O Hector! late thy parents' pride and joy,
The boast of nations! the defence of Troy!
To whom her safety and her fame she owed
Her chief, her hero, and almost her god!
O fatal change! become in one sad day
A senseless corse! inanimated clay!

But not as yet the fatal news had spread
To fair Andromache, of Hector dead;
As yet no messenger had told his fate,
Nor e'en his stay without the Scaean gate.
Far in the close recesses of the dome,
Pensive she plied the melancholy loom;
A growing work employ'd her secret hours,
Confusedly gay with intermingled flowers.
Her fair-hair'd handmaids heat the brazen urn,
The bath preparing for her lord's return:
In vain: alas! her lord returns no more:
Unbathed he lies, and bleeds along the shore!
Now from the walls the clamours reach her ear,
And all her members shake with sudden fear;
Forth from her ivory hand the shuttle falls,

And thus, astonish'd, to her maids she calls:
   Ah! follow me! (she cried) what plaintive noise
Invades my ear? 'Tis sure my mother's voice.
My faltering knees their trembling frame desert,
A pulse unusual flutters at my heart;
Some strange disaster, some reverse of fate
(Ye gods, avert it!) threats the Trojan state.
Far be the omen which my thoughts suggest!
But much I fear my Hector's dauntless breast
Confronts Achilles; chased along the plain,
Shut from our walls! I fear, I fear him slain!
Safe in the crowd he ever scorn'd to wait,
And sought for glory in the jaws of fate:
Perhaps that noble heat has cost his breath,
Now quench'd for ever in the arms of death.
   She spoke; and furious with distracted pace,
Fears in her heart, and anguish in her face,
Flies through the dome (the maids her steps pursue)
And mounts the walls, and sends around her view.
Too soon her eyes the killing object found,
The godlike Hector dragg'd along the ground
A sudden darkness shades her swimming eyes,
She faints, she falls; her breath, her colour flies
Her hair's fair ornaments, the braids that bound
The net that held them, and the wreath that crown'd,
The veil and diadem flew far away
(The gift of Venus on her bridal day,)
Around a train of weeping sisters stands,
To raise her sinking with assisting hands.
Scarce from the verge of death recall'd again
She faints, or but recovers to complain.

(from The Iliad, Book XXII)

HOMER

NAUSICAÄ

   Soon the bright morning came. Nausicaä rose,
Clad royally, as marvelling at her dream

She hastened through the palace to declare
Her purpose to her father and the queen.
She found them both within. Her mother sat
Beside the hearth with her attendant maids,
And turned the distaff loaded with a fleece
Dyed in sea-purple. On the threshold stood
Her father, going forth to meet the chiefs
Of the Phaeacians in a council where
Their noblest asked his presence. Then the maid,
Approaching her beloved father, spake:—
    "I pray, dear father, give command to make
A chariot ready for me, with high sides
And sturdy wheels, to bear to the river-brink,
There to be cleansed, the costly robes that now
Lie soiled. Thee likewise it doth well beseem
At councils to appear in vestments fresh
And stainless. Thou hast also in these halls
Five sons, two wedded, three in boyhood's bloom,
And ever in the dance they need attire
New from the wash. All this must I provide."
    She ended, for she shrank from saying aught
Of her own hopeful marriage. He perceived
Her thought and said: "Mules I deny thee not,
My daughter, nor aught else. Go then; my grooms
Shall make a carriage ready with high sides
And sturdy wheels, and a broad rack above."
    He spake, and gave command. The grooms obeyed,
And, making ready in the outer court
The strong-wheeled chariot, led the harnessed mules
Under the yoke and made them fast; and then
Appeared the maiden, bringing from her bower
The shining garments. In the polished car
She piled them, while with many pleasant meats
And flavoring morsels for the day's repast
Her mother filled a hamper, and poured wine
Into a goatskin. As her daughter climbed
The car, she gave into her hands a cruse
Of gold with smooth anointing oil for her
And her attendant maids. Nausicaä took
The scourge and showy reins, and struck the mules

18. Amphora with Bacchic scenes.

To urge them onward. Onward with loud noise
They went, and with a speed that slackened not,
And bore the robes and her,—yet not alone,
For with her went the maidens of her train.
Now when they reached the river's pleasant brink,
Where lavers had been hollowed out to last
Perpetually, and freely through them flowed
Pure water that might cleanse the foulest stains,
They loosed the mules, and drove them from the wain
To browse the sweet grass by the eddying stream;
And took the garments out, and flung them down
In the dark water, and with hasty feet
Trampled them there in frolic rivalry.
And when the task was done, and all the stains

Were cleansed away, they spread the garments out
Along the beach and where the stream had washed
The gravel cleanest. Then they bathed, and gave
Their limbs the delicate oil, and took their meal
Upon the river's border,—while the robes
Beneath the sun's warm rays were growing dry.
And now, when they were all refreshed by food,
Mistress and maidens laid their veils aside
And played at ball. Nausicaä the white-armed
Began a song. As when the archer-queen
Diana, going forth among the hills,—
The sides of high Taÿgetus or slopes
Of Erymanthus,—chases joyously
Boars and fleet stags, and round her in a throng
Frolic the rural nymphs, Latona's heart
Is glad, for over all the rest are seen
Her daughter's head and brow, and she at once
Is known among them, though they all are fair,
Such was this spotless virgin midst her maids.

  Now when they were about to move for home
With harnessed mules and with the shining robes
Carefully folded, then the blue-eyed maid,
Pallas, bethought herself of this,—to rouse
Ulysses and to bring him to behold
The bright-eyed maiden, that she might direct
The stranger's way to the Phaeacian town.
The royal damsel at a handmaid cast
The ball; it missed, and fell into the stream
Where a deep eddy whirled. All shrieked aloud.
The great Ulysses started from his sleep
And sat upright, discoursing to himself:—

  "Ah me! upon what region am I thrown?
What men are here,—wild, savage, and unjust,
Or hospitable, and who hold the gods
In reverence? There are voices in the air,
Womanly voices, as of nymphs that haunt
The mountain summits, and the river-founts,
And the moist grassy meadows. Or perchance
Am I near men who have the power of speech?
Nay, let me then go forth at once and learn."

Thus having said, the great Ulysses left
The thicket. From the close-grown wood he rent,
With his strong hand, a branch well set with leaves,
And wound it as a covering round his waist.
Then like a mountain lion he went forth,
That walks abroad, confiding in his strength,
In rain and wind; his eyes shoot fire; he falls
On oxen, or on sheep, or forest-deer,
For hunger prompts him even to attack
The flock within its closely guarded fold.
Such seemed Ulysses when about to meet
Those fair-haired maidens, naked as he was,
But forced by strong necessity. To them
His look was frightful, for his limbs were foul
With sea-foam yet. To right and left they fled
Along the jutting river-banks. Alone
The daughter of Alcinoüs kept her place,
For Pallas gave her courage and forbade
Her limbs to tremble. So she waited there.
Ulysses pondered whether to approach
The bright-eyed damsel and embrace her knees
And supplicate, or, keeping yet aloof,
Pray her with soothing words to show the way
Townward and give him garments. Musing thus,
It seemed the best to keep at distance still,
And use soft words, lest, should he clasp her knees,
The maid might be displeased. With gentle words
Skilfully ordered thus Ulysses spake:—

"O queen, I am thy suppliant, whether thou
Be mortal or a goddess. If perchance
Thou art of that immortal race who dwell
In the broad heaven, thou art, I deem, most like
To Dian, daughter of imperial Jove,
In shape, in stature, and in noble air.
If mortal and a dweller of the earth,
Thrice happy are thy father and his queen,
Thrice happy are thy brothers; and their hearts
Must overflow with gladness for thy sake,
Beholding such a scion of their house
Enter the choral dance. But happiest he

Beyond them all, who, bringing princely gifts,
Shall bear thee to his home a bride; for sure
I never looked on one of mortal race,
Woman or man, like thee, and as I gaze
I wonder. Like to thee I saw of late,
In Delos, a young palm-tree growing up
Beside Apollo's altar; for I sailed
To Delos, with much people following me,
On a disastrous voyage. Long I gazed
Upon it wonder-struck, as I am now,—
For never from the earth so fair a tree
Had sprung. So marvel I, and am amazed
At thee, O lady, and in awe forbear
To clasp thy knees. Yet much have I endured.
It was but yestereve that I escaped
From the black sea, upon the twentieth day,
So long the billows and the rushing gales
Farther and farther from Ogygia's isle
Had borne me. Now upon this shore some god
Casts me, perchance to meet new sufferings here;
For yet the end is not, and many things
The gods must first accomplish. But do thou,
O queen, have pity on me, since to thee
I come the first of all. I do not know
A single dweller of the land beside.
Show me, I pray, thy city; and bestow
Some poor old robe to wrap me,—if, indeed,
In coming hither, thou hast brought with thee
Aught poor or coarse. And may the gods vouchsafe
To thee whatever blessing thou canst wish,
Husband and home and wedded harmony.
There is no better, no more blessed state,
Than when the wife and husband in accord
Order their household lovingly. Then those
Repine who hate them, those who wish them well
Rejoice, and they themselves the most of all."
    And then the white-armed maid Nausicaä said:—
"Since then, O stranger, thou are not malign
Of purpose nor weak-minded,—yet, in truth,
Olympian Jupiter bestows the goods

Of fortune on the noble and the base
To each one at his pleasure; and thy griefs
Are doubtless sent by him, and it is fit
That thou submit in patience,—now that thou
Hast reached our lands, and art within our realm,
Thou shalt not lack for garments nor for aught
Due to a suppliant stranger in his need.
The city I will show thee, and will name
Its dwellers,—the Phaeacians,—they possess
The city; all the region lying round
Is theirs, and I am daughter of the prince
Alcinoüs, large of soul, to whom are given
The rule of the Phaeacians and their power."

So spake the damsel, and commanded thus
Her fair-haired maids: "Stay! whither do ye flee,
My handmaids, when a man appears in sight?
Ye think, perhaps, he is some enemy.
Nay, there is no man living now, nor yet
Will live, to enter, bringing war, the land
Of the Phaeacians. Very dear are they
To the great gods. We dwell apart, afar
Within the unmeasured deep, amid its waves
The most remote of men; no other race
Hath commerce with us. This man comes to us
A wanderer and unhappy, and to him
Our cares are due. The stranger and the poor
Are sent by Jove, and slight regards to them
Are grateful. Maidens, give the stranger food
And drink, and take him to the river-side
To bathe where there is shelter from the wind."

So spake the mistress; and they stayed their flight
And bade each other stand, and led the chief
Under a shelter as the royal maid,
Daughter of stout Alcinoüs, gave command,
And laid a cloak and tunic near the spot
To be his raiment, and a golden cruse
Of limpid oil. Then, as they bade him bathe
In the fresh stream, the noble chieftain said:—

"Withdraw, ye maidens, hence, while I prepare
To cleanse my shoulders from the bitter brine,

And to anoint them; long have these my limbs
Been unrefreshed by oil. I will not bathe
Before you. I should be ashamed to stand
Unclothed in presence of these bright-haired maids."

(from *The Odyssey,* Book VI)

HOMER

THE RETURN OF TELEMACHUS

First Eurycleia, who had been his nurse,
Beheld him, as she spread the beautiful thrones
With skins, and ran to him with weeping eyes;
And round him other handmaids of the house
Of resolute Ulysses thronged. They gave
Fond welcome, kissing him upon the brow
And shoulders. Issuing from her chamber next
The chaste Penelope, like Dian's self
In beauty, or like golden Venus, came,
And, weeping, threw her arms about her son,
And kissed him on his forehead and on both
His glorious eyes, and said, amidst her tears:—
    "Light of my eyes! O my Telemachus!
Art thou, then, come? I never thought again
To see thee, when I heard thou hadst embarked
For Pylos,—secretly, and knowing me
Unwilling,—in the hope to gather there
Some tidings of thy father. Tell me now
All that has happened, all that thou hast seen."
    And thus discreet Telemachus replied:
"Nay, mother, waken not my griefs again,
Nor move my heart to rage. I have just now
Escaped a cruel death. But go and bathe,
And put fresh garments on, and when thou com'st
Into thy chamber with thy maidens, make
A vow to all the gods that thou wilt burn
A sacrifice of chosen hecatombs
When Jupiter shall have avenged our wrongs.
Now must I hasten to the market-place

In quest of one who came with me a guest
From Pylos. Him, with all my faithful crew,
I sent before me to this port, and bade
Piraeus lead him to his own abode,
There to be lodged and honored till I came."
   He spake, nor flew his words unheeded by.
The princess bathed, and put fresh garments on,
And vowed to all the gods a sacrifice
Of chosen hecatombs when Jupiter
Should punish the wrong-doers. While she prayed,
Telemachus went forth, his spear in hand.
Two fleet dogs followed him. Minerva shed
A godlike beauty o'er his form and face,
And all the people wondered as he came.
The suitors thronged around him with smooth words,
Yet plotting mischief in their hearts. He turned
From their assembly hastily, and took
His place where Mentor sat with Antiphus,
And Halitherses,—all his father's friends
And his from the beginning. While they asked
Of all that he had seen, Piraeus came,
The famous spearman, bringing through the town
The stranger with him to the market-place.
Nor long Telemachus delayed, but came
To meet his guest, and then Piraeus said:—
   "Telemachus, despatch to where I dwell
Thy serving-women; I would send to thee,
At once, the gifts which Menelaus gave."
   And then discreet Telemachus replied:
"We know not yet, Piraeus, what may be
The event; and if the suitors privily
Should slay me in the palace, and divide
The inheritance among them, I prefer
That thou, instead of them, shouldst have the gifts;
But should they meet the fate which I have planned,
And be cut off, then shalt thou gladly bring
The treasures, which I gladly will receive."
   So spake the prince, and to the palace led
The unhappy man, his guest. When now they reached

The stately pile, they both laid down their cloaks
Upon the benches, and betook themselves
To the well-polished baths. The attendant maids
There ministered and smoothed their limbs with oil,
And each received a tunic at their hands,
And fleecy mantle. Then they left the baths
And took their seats. A damsel came, and poured
Water from a fair ewer wrought of gold
Into a silver basin for their hands,
And spread a polished table near their seats;
And there the matron of the household placed
Bread, and the many dishes which her stores
Supplied. The queen was seated opposite,
Beside a column of the pile, and twirled
A slender spindle, while the son and guest
Put forth their hands and shared the meal prepared.

(from The Odyssey, Book XVII)

The Birth of Lyrics

It is not surprising that Greek lyrics should rank among the highest poetry of all times, if we realize to what extent the spirit of poetry was an integral part of Greek life and Greek culture. Some of the lyrics that follow point to the intimacy reigning between man and nature, whose awesomeness is but one of its aspects; for nature is also man's friend and companion. In Pindar's poems one is struck by the depth of his thought and by his grandiose vision of man and of the world above him.

SAPPHO

THE NIGHTINGALE

The dear good angel of the spring
    The nightingale.

(Translated by Ben Jonson)

EVENING

Thou, Hesper, bringest homeward all
 That radiant dawn sped far and wide,
The sheep to fold, the goat to stall,
 The children to their mother's side.

(Translated by Sir Rennell Rodd)

THE MOON

Bright stars, around the fair Sêlenê peering,
 No more their beauty to the night discover
When she, at full, her silver light ensphering,
 Floods the world over.

(Translated by T. F. Higham)

FLOWERS FOR THE GRACES

Weave garlands, maiden, from the strands
Of dill, and with soft gentle hands
Set the delicious leafage round your head.
The Goddess and the happy Graces
Love to look on flower-crown'd faces,
But turn aside from the ungarlanded.

(Translated by C. M. Bowra)

PINDAR
HUMAN LIFE

Who, in his tenderest years,
Finds some new lovely thing,
His hope is high, and he flies
On the wings of his manhood:
Better than riches are his thoughts.
—But man's pleasure is a short time growing
And it falls to the ground
As quickly, when an unlucky twist of thought
Loosens its roots.

Man's life is a day. What is he?
What is he not? A shadow in a dream
Is man: but when God sheds a brightness,
Shining light is on earth
And life is sweet as honey.
    Aegina, dear mother,
Keep this city in her voyage of freedom:
You, with Zeus and lord Aiakos,
Pêleus, and noble Télamon, and Achilles.

    (Translated by H. T. Wade-Gery, C. M. Bowra)

THE POWER OF MUSIC

O lyre of gold, Apollo's
Treasure, shared with the violet-wreathed Muses,
The light foot hears you, and the brightness begins:
Your notes compel the singer
When to lead out the dance
The prelude is sounded on your trembling strings.
You quench the warrior Thunderbolt's everlasting flame:
On God's sceptre the Eagle sleeps,
Drooping his swift wings on either side,

The King of Birds.
You have poured a cloud on his beak and head,
   and darkened his face:
His eyelids are shut with a sweet seal.
He sleeps, his lithe back heaves:
Your quivering song has conquered him.
Even Arês the violent
Leaving aside his harsh and pointed spears
Comforts his heart in drowsiness.
Your shafts enchant the souls even of the Gods
Through the wisdom of Lâto's son
   and the deep-bosomed Muses.

And things that God loves not
Hear the voice of the maids of Pieria: they shudder
On earth and in the furious sea.
And He is afraid who lies in the horrors of Hell,
God's enemy,

Tȳphôs the hundred-headed,
Nursed once in the famed Cilician Cave.
But now above Kȳmê the foam-fronting heights,
And the land of Sicily, lie
Heavily on his shaggy chest.
The Pillar of Heaven holds him fast,
White *Etna,* which all year round
Suckles its biting snows.

Pure founts of unapproachable fire
Belch from its depths.
In the day-time its rivers
Pour forth a glowing stream of smoke:
But in the darkness red flame rolls
And into the deep level sea
   throws the rocks roaring.
And that huge Worm
Spouts dreadful fountains of flame,—
A marvel and wonder to see it, a marvel even
   to hear from those who are there,
What a monster is held down
Under Etna's dark-leaved peaks, and under the plain.
The bed he lies on
Driving furrows up and down his back
Goads him.

(Translated by H. T. Wade-Gery,
C. M. Bowra)

AN ECLIPSE

When God reveals his plans to men,
Straight is the way to glory then
   And good the end for all;
And God can from the murky night
Create inviolable light
Or hide the stainless day from sight
   Beneath a black cloud's pall.

(Translated by C. M. Bowra)

THE POWER OF CUSTOM

Custom is lord of everything,
Of mortals and immortals king.
High violence it justifies,
With hand uplifted plundering.
For this my testimony lies
In Hêraclês. He sacked the stalls
Of Gêrÿon, and his cattle brought
And stood them by Eurystheus' halls
Cyclopean,—loot unasked, unbought.

(Translated by C. M. Bowra)

THEOCRITUS

AMYCUS

They found
Hard by a slab of rock a bubbling spring
Brimful of purest water. In the depths
Below, like crystal or like silver gleamed
The pebbles: high above it pine and plane
And poplar rose, and cypress tipt with green;
With all rich flowers that throng the mead, when wanes
The Spring, sweet workshops of the furry bee.
There sat and sunned him one of giant bulk
And grisly mien: hard knocks had stov'n his ears:
Broad were his shoulders, vast his orbèd chest:
Like a wrought statue rose his iron frame:
And nigh the shoulder on each brawny arm
Stood out the muscles, huge as rolling stones
Caught by some rain-swoln river and shapen smooth
By its wild eddyings: and o'er nape and spine
Hung, balanced by the claws, a lion's skin.

(Translated by C. S. Calverley)

4. The Birth and Glory of Drama

The Greeks were the first to discover the artistic potentialities that the stage offers. Their dramas were an essential part of Greek life, a lived communal experience. Plays were not read individually, but essentially performed and experienced as the climax of the city life. The Greeks knew a truth we might tend to forget, namely, that great experiences are deepened and enriched by being shared. To listen to a record of Shakespeare—beautiful as it may be—can never afford the soul-resonance that is found in watching a performance on the stage, not only on account of the visual element, but especially because of the mysterious reality of shared vibrations, because of the phenomenon of unison.

Tragedy steps into human life in an amazing variety of forms; there is something in man himself, great and fragile, that predisposes him to suffering; for man seems able to conquer the world and yet is ultimately vanquished by death, death that lies in wait for him, and ironically reminds him that all his human pursuits, glorious as they may be, will end in defeat. Man, whose mind is so rich and so profound, is constantly tempted "not to think human thoughts" (Sophocles, Ajax); *yet he is caught in the nets of "time's insistent, slow erosion" (Aeschylus,* Agamemnon), *time that inexorably pushes men forward, and grants to the fearfully real human concerns an element of unreality, for at the very moment of their climax they cease to be. Man has been granted a sense of justice and knows that justice must be done:*

> For the tongue which hateth, let hate of tongue
> Be rendered! with these words Justice doth
> In a loud voice claim her payment.

Aeschylus, *Choephoroe*

Nevertheless when man takes it upon himself to adjust the scales of justice, the Furies pursue him.

No doubt man cannot, like a dumb animal, remain a passive actor on the stage of human affairs, but when is he to act righteously and when does his act become a sort of hybris for which he will have to pay the price of suffering?

AESCHYLUS

FROM AGAMEMNON

In Aeschylus' trilogy, the so-called Oresteia, *he dramatizes the phenomenon of the ancestral curse upon the House of Atreus. Agamemnon and Menelaus, sons of Atreus, have inherited the curse. Agamemnon, the most powerful king in all Greece, has marshaled an expedition to attack Troy and return Helen to Menelaus. Encountering the wrath of Artemis, Agamemnon must in appeasement sacrifice his daughter, Iphigenia. After ten years, Troy falls and the leaders begin their journeys home.*

The play opens at this point. The scene is before the palace of Agamemnon in Argos. In front of the palace there are statues of the gods and altars prepared for sacrifice. It is night. Word has not yet reached Argos that the Greeks have captured Troy. There is a sense of restless foreboding, of expectation, of hope, as first the Watchman, then the Chorus of Elders search for signs of the returning army. They turn to Clytemnestra, Agamemnon's wife, who has had intimations of the army's success and return. Finally, a Herald enters, an advance messenger from Agamemnon's forces, which have just landed.

HERALD

.   .   .

To us, the remnant of the host of Greece,
Comes weal beyond all counterpoise of woe;
Thus boast we rightfully to yonder sun,
Like him far-fleeted over sea and land.
The Argive host prevailed to conquer Troy,
And in the temples of the gods of Greece
Hung up these spoils, a shining sign to Time.
Let those who learn this legend bless aright
The city and its chieftains, and repay
The meed of gratitude to Zeus who willed
And wrought the deed. So stands the tale fulfilled.

LEADER
Thy words o'erbear my doubt: for news of good,

The ear of age hath ever youth enow:
But those within and Clytemnestra's self
Would fain hear all; glad thou their ears and mine.

(CLYTEMNESTRA *enters*.)

CLYTEMNESTRA

That night, when first the fiery courier came,
In sign that Troy is ta'en and razed to earth,
So wild a cry of joy my lips gave out,
That I was chidden—*Hath the beacon watch*
Made sure unto thy soul the sack of Troy?
A very woman thou, whose heart leaps light
At wandering rumours!—and with words like these
They showed me how I strayed, misled of hope.
Yet on each shrine I set the sacrifice,
And, in the strain they held for feminine,
Went heralds thro' the city, to and fro,
With voice of loud proclaim, announcing joy;
And in each fane they lit and quenched with wine
The spicy perfumes fading in the flame.
All is fulfilled: I spare your longer tale—
The king himself anon shall tell me all.

·   ·   ·

CHORUS (*singing*)

Even now, and in far other tone,
Troy chants her dirge of mighty moan,
  Woe upon Paris, woe and hate!
  Who wooed his country's doom for mate—
This is the burthen of the groan,
  Wherewith she wails disconsolate
The blood, so many of her own
  Have poured in vain, to fend her fate;
Troy! thou hast fed and freed to roam
A lion-cub within thy home!

·   ·   ·

Alone, alone, I deem far otherwise;
  Not bliss nor wealth it is, but impious deed,

From which that after-growth of ill doth rise!
   Woe springs from wrong, the plant is like the seed—
While Right, in honour's house, doth its own likeness breed.

  Some past impiety, some grey old crime
    Breeds the young curse, that wantons in our ill,
  Early or late, when haps th' appointed time—
    And out of light brings power of darkness still,
A master-fiend, a foe, unseen, invincible;

  A pride accursed, that broods upon the race
    And home in which dark Atè holds her sway—
Sin's child and Woe's, that wears its parents' face;
    While Right in smoky cribs shines clear as day,
And decks with weal his life, who walks the righteous way.

  From gilded halls, that hands polluted raise,
    Right turns away with proud averted eyes,
  And of the wealth, men stamp amiss with praise,
    Heedless, to poorer, holier temples hies,
And to Fate's goal guides all, in its appointed wise.

     (AGAMEMNON *enters, followed by* CASSANDRA.)

    Hail to thee, chief of Atreus' race,
    Returning proud from Troy subdued!
    How shall I greet thy conquering face?
    How nor a fulsome praise obtrude,
    Nor stint the meed of gratitude?
    For mortal men who fall to ill
    Take little heed of open truth,
    But seek unto its semblance still:

      .   .   .

    And thou, our leader—when of yore
    Thou badest Greece go forth to war
    For Helen's sake—I dare avow
    That then I held thee not as now;
    That to my vision thou didst seem
    Dyed in the hues of disesteem.
    I held thee for a pilot ill,
    And reckless, of thy proper will,

Endowing others doomed to die
With vain and forced audacity!
Now from my heart, ungrudgingly,
To those that wrought, this word be said—
Well fall the labour ye have sped—
Let time and search, O king, declare
What men within thy city's bound
Were loyal to the kingdom's care,
And who were faithless found.

AGAMEMNON (*still in the chariot*)

First, as is meet, a king's All-hail be said
To Argos, and the gods that guard the land—
Gods who with me availed to speed us home,
With me availed to wring from Priam's town
The due of justice. In the court of heaven
The gods in conclave sat and judged the cause,
Not from a pleader's tongue, and at the close,
Unanimous into the urn of doom
This sentence gave, *On Ilion and her men,*
Death: and where hope drew nigh to pardon's urn
No hand there was to cast a vote therein.
And still the smoke of fallen Ilion
Rises in sight of all men, and the flame
Of Atè's hecatomb is living yet,
And where the towers in dusty ashes sink,
Rise the rich fumes of pomp and wealth consumed
For this must all men pay unto the gods
The meed of mindful hearts and gratitude:
For by our hands the meshes of revenge
Closed on the prey, and for one woman's sake
Troy trodden by the Argive monster lies—
The foal, the shielded band that leapt the wall,
What time with autumn sank the Pleiades.
Yea, o'er the fencing wall a lion sprang
Ravening, and lapped his fill of blood of kings.

Such prelude spoken to the gods in full,
To you I turn, and to the hidden thing
Whereof ye spake but now: and in that thought
I am as you, and what ye say, say I.

For few are they who have such inborn grace,
As to look up with love, and envy not,
When stands another on the height of weal.
Deep in his heart, whom jealousy hath seized,
Her poison lurking doth enhance his load;
For now beneath his proper woes he chafes,
And sighs withal to see another's weal.

I speak not idly, but from knowledge sure—
There be who vaunt an utter loyalty,
That is but as the ghost of friendship dead,
A shadow in a glass, of faith gone by.
One only—he who went reluctant forth
Across the seas with me—Odysseus—he
Was loyal unto me with strength and will,
A trusty trace-horse bound unto my car.
Thus—be he yet beneath the light of day,
Or dead, as well I fear—I speak his praise.

Lastly, whate'er be due to men or gods,
With joint debate, in public council held,
We well decide, and warily contrive
That all which now is well may so abide:
For that which haply needs the healer's art,
That will be medicine, discerning well
If cautery or knife befit the time.

Now, to my palace and the shrines of home,
I will pass in, and greet you first and fair,
Ye gods, who bade me forth, and home again—
And long may Victory tarry in my train!

(CLYTEMNESTRA *enters*.)

CLYTEMNESTRA

Old men of Argos, lieges of our realm,
Shame shall not bid me shrink lest ye should see
The love I bear my lord. Such blushing fear
Dies at the last from hearts of human kind.
From mine own soul and from no alien lips,
I know and will reveal the life I bore,
Reluctant, through the lingering livelong years,
The while my lord beleaguered Ilion's wall.

First, that a wife sat sundered from her lord,
In widowed solitude, was utter woe—
And woe, to hear how rumour's many tongues
All boded evil—woe, when he who came
And he who followed spake of ill on ill,
Keening *Lost, lost, all lost!* thro' hall and bower.
Had this my husband met so many wounds,
As by a thousand channels rumour told,
No network e'er was full of holes as he.
Had he been slain, as oft as tidings came
That he was dead, he well might boast him now
A second Geryon of triple frame,
With triple robe of earth above him laid—
For that below, no matter—triply dead,
Dead by one death for every form he bore.
And thus distraught by news of wrath and woe,
Oft for self-slaughter had I slung the noose,
But others wrenched it from my neck away.
Hence haps it that Orestes, thine and mine,
The pledge and symbol of our wedded troth,
Stands not beside us now, as he should stand.
Nor marvel thou at this: he dwells with one
Who guards him loyally; 'tis Phocis' king,
Strophius, who warned me erst, *Bethink thee, queen,*
What woes of doubtful issue well may fall!
Thy lord in daily jeopardy at Troy,
While here a populace uncurbed may cry,
"Down with the council, down!" bethink thee too,
'Tis the world's way to set a harder heel
On fallen power.

    For thy child's absence then
Such mine excuse, no wily afterthought.
For me, long since the gushing fount of tears
Is wept away; no drop is left to shed.
Dim are the eyes that ever watched till dawn,
Weeping, the bale-fires, piled for thy return,
Night after night unkindled. If I slept,
Each sound—the tiny humming of a gnat,
Roused me again, again, from fitful dreams
Wherein I felt thee smitten, saw thee slain,

Thrice for each moment of mine hour of sleep.

All this I bore, and now, released from woe,
I hail my lord as watch-dog of a fold,
As saving stay-rope of a storm-tossed ship,
As column stout that holds the roof aloft,
As only child unto a sire bereaved,
As land beheld, past hope, by crews forlorn,
As sunshine fair when tempest's wrath is past,
As gushing spring to thirsty wayfarer.
So sweet it is to 'scape the press of pain.
With such salute I bid my husband hail!
Nor heaven be wroth therewith! for long and hard
I bore that ire of old.

                Sweet lord, step forth,
Step from thy car, I pray—nay, not on earth
Plant the proud foot, O king, that trod down Troy!
Women! why tarry ye, whose task it is
To spread your monarch's path with tapestry?
Swift, swift, with purple strew his passage fair,
The justice lead him to a home, at last,
He scarcely looked to see.

                For what remains,
Zeal unsubdued by sleep shall nerve my hand
To work as right and as the gods command.

        ·   ·   ·

(AGAMEMNON *descends from the chariot,
and moves towards the palace.*)

A Sea there is—and who shall stay its springs?
And deep within its breast, a mighty store,
Precious as silver, of the purple dye,
Whereby the dipped robe doth its tint renew.
Enough of such, O king, within thy halls
There lies, a store that cannot fail; but I—
I would have gladly vowed unto the gods
Cost of a thousand garments trodden thus,
(Had once the oracle such gift required)
Contriving ransom for thy life preserved.
For while the stock is firm the foliage climbs,

Spreading a shade, what time the dog-star glows;
And thou, returning to thine hearth and home,
Art as a genial warmth in winter hours,
Or as a coolness, when the lord of heaven
Mellows the juice within the bitter grape.
Such boons and more doth bring into a home
The present footstep of its proper lord.
Zeus, Zeus, Fulfilment's lord! my vows fulfil,
And whatsoe'er it be, work forth thy will!

(*She follows* AGAMEMNON *into the palace.*)

CHORUS

Wherefore for ever on the wings of fear
 Hovers a vision drear
Before my boding heart? a strain,
Unbidden and unwelcome, thrills mine ear,
 Oracular of pain.
Not as of old upon my bosom's throne
 Sits Confidence, to spurn
 Such fears, like dreams we know not to discern.
Old, old and grey long since the time has grown,
 Which saw the linkèd cables moor
The fleet, when erst it came to Ilion's sandy shore;
 And now mine eyes and not another's see
  Their safe return.

Yet none the less in me
The inner spirit sings a boding song,
 Self-prompted, sings the Furies' strain—
  And seeks, and seeks in vain,
  To hope and to be strong!

Ah! to some end of Fate, unseen, unguessed,
 Are these wild throbbings of my heart and breast—
  Yea, of some doom they tell—
  Each pulse, a knell.
 Lief, lief I were, that all
To unfulfilment's hidden realm might fall.

Too far, too far our mortal spirits strive,
 Grasping at utter weal, unsatisfied—
Till the fell curse, that dwelleth hard beside,

146

19. *Achilles and Patroklos.* Detail of cup by Sosia.

Thrust down the sundering wall. Too fair they blow,
 The gales that waft our bark on Fortune's tide!
 Swiftly we sail, the sooner all to drive
 Upon the hidden rock, the reef of woe.
Then if the hand of caution warily
 Sling forth into the sea
Part of the freight, lest all should sink below,
From the deep death it saves the bark: even so,
 Doom-laden though it be, once more may rise
  His household, who is timely wise.

      *   •   •

(CLYTEMNESTRA *comes out of the palace and addresses*
CASSANDRA, *who has remained motionless in her chariot.*)

CLYTEMNESTRA

Get thee within thou too, Cassandra, go!
For Zeus to thee in gracious mercy grants
To share the sprinklings of the lustral bowl,
Beside the altar of his guardianship,
Slave among many slaves. What, haughty still?
Step from the car; Alcmena's son, 'tis said,
Was sold perforce and bore the yoke of old.
Ay, hard it is, but, if such fate befall,
'Tis a fair chance to serve within a home
Of ancient wealth and power. An upstart lord,
To whom wealth's harvest came beyond his hope,
Is as a lion to his slaves, in all
Exceeding fierce, immoderate in sway.
Pass in: thou hearest what our ways will be.

LEADER OF THE CHORUS

Clear unto thee, O maid, is her command,
But thou—within the toils of Fate thou art—
If such thy will, I urge thee to obey;
Yet I misdoubt thou dost nor hear nor heed.

CLYTEMNESTRA

I wot—unless like swallows she doth use
Some strange barbarian tongue from oversea—
My words must speak persuasion to her soul.

LEADER

Obey: there is no gentler way than this.
Step from the car's high seat and follow her.

CLYTEMNESTRA

Truce to this bootless waiting here without!
I will not stay: beside the central shrine
The victims stand, prepared for knife and fire—
Offerings from hearts beyond all hope made glad.
Thou—if thou reckest aught of my command,
'Twere well done soon: but if they sense be shut
From these my words, let thy barbarian hand
Fulfil by gesture the default of speech.

LEADER

No native is she, thus to read thy words
Unaided: like some wild thing of the wood,
New-trapped, behold! she shrinks and glares on thee.

CLYTEMNESTRA

'Tis madness and the rule of mind distraught,
Since she beheld her city sink in fire,
And hither comes, nor brooks the bit, until
In foam and blood her wrath be champed away.
See ye to her; unqueenly 'tis for me,
Unheeded thus to cast away my words.

LEADER

But with me pity sits in anger's place.
Poor maiden, come thou from the car; no way
There is but this—take up thy servitude.

CASSANDRA

Woe, woe, alas! Earth, Mother Earth! and thou
Apollo, Apollo!

LEADER

Peace! shriek not to the bright prophetic god,
Who will not brook the suppliance of woe.

CASSANDRA

Woe, woe, alas! Earth, Mother Earth! and thou
Apollo, Apollo!

LEADER

Hark, with wild curse she calls anew on him,
Who stands far off and loathes the voice of wail.

149

CASSANDRA

Apollo, Apollo!
God of all ways, but only Death's to me,
Once and again, O thou, Destroyer named,
Thou hast destroyed me, thou, my love of old!

LEADER

She grows presageful of her woes to come,
Slave tho' she be, instinct with prophecy.

CASSANDRA

Apollo, Apollo!
God of all ways, but only Death's to me,
O thou Apollo, thou Destroyer named!
What way hast led me, to what evil home?

LEADER

Know'st thou it not? The home of Atreus' race:
Take these my words for sooth and ask no more.

CASSANDRA

Home cursed of God! Bear witness unto me,
  Ye visioned woes within—
The blood-stained hands of them that smite their kin—
The strangling noose, and spattered o'er
With human blood, the reeking door!

LEADER

How like a sleuth-hound questing on the track,
Keen-scented unto blood and death she hies!

CASSANDRA

Ah! can the ghostly guidance fail,
Whereby my prophet-soul is onwards led?
Look! for their flesh the spectre-children wail,
Their sodden limbs on which their father fed!

LEADER

Long since we knew of thy prophetic fame,—
But for those deeds we seek no prophet's tongue.

CASSANDRA

God! 'tis another crime—
Worse than the storied woe of olden time,
Cureless, abhorred, that one is plotting here—
A shaming death, for those that should be dear!

Alas! and far away, in foreign land,
He that should help doth stand!

LEADER

I knew th' old tales, the city rings withal—
But now thy speech is dark, beyond my ken.

CASSANDRA

O wretch, O purpose fell!
Thou for thy wedded lord
The cleansing wave hast poured—
A treacherous welcome!

         How the sequel tell?
Too soon 'twill come, too soon, for now, even now,
  She smites him, blow on blow!

LEADER

Riddles beyond my rede—I peer in vain
Thro' the dim films that screen the prophecy.

CASSANDRA

God! a new sight! a net, a snare of hell,
Set by her hand—herself a snare more fell!
  A wedded wife, she slays her lord,
Helped by another hand!

         Ye powers, whose hate
  Of Atreus' home no blood can satiate,
Raise the wild cry above the sacrifice abhorred!

CHORUS

Why biddest thou some fiend, I know not whom,
Shriek o'er the house? Thine is no cheering word.
  Back to my heart in frozen fear I feel
  My waning life-blood run—
  The blood that round the wounding steel
  Ebbs slow, as sinks life's parting sun—
Swift, swift and sure, some woe comes pressing on!

CASSANDRA

  Away, away—keep him away—
The monarch of the herd, the pasture's pride,
Far from his mate! In treach'rous wrath,
Muffling his swarthy horns, with secret scathe
  She gores his fenceless side!
Hark! in the brimming bath,

The heavy plash—the dying cry—
Hark—in the laver—hark, he falls by treachery!

CHORUS

I read amiss dark sayings such as thine,
Yet something warns me that they tell of ill.
   O dark prophetic speech,
   Ill tidings dost thou teach
   Ever, to mortals here below!
   Ever some tale of awe and woe
   Thro' all thy windings manifold
   Do we unriddle and unfold!

.   .   .

CASSANDRA

'Tis Agamemnon's doom thou shalt behold.

LEADER

Peace, hapless woman, to thy boding words!

CASSANDRA

Far from my speech stands he who sains and saves.

LEADER

Ay—were such doom at hand—which God forbid!

CASSANDRA

Thou prayest idly—these move swift to slay.

LEADER

What man prepares a deed of such despite?

CASSANDRA

Fool! thus to read amiss mine oracles.

LEADER

Deviser and device are dark to me.

CASSANDRA

Dark! all too well I speak the Grecian tongue.

LEADER

Ay—but in thine, as in Apollo's strains,
Familiar is the tongue, but dark the thought.

CASSANDRA

Ah, ah the fire! it waxes, nears me now—

Woe, woe for me, Apollo of the dawn!

Lo, how the woman-thing, the lioness
Couched with the wolf—her noble mate afar—
Will slay me, slave forlorn! Yea, like some witch,
She drugs the cup of wrath, that slays her lord,
With double death—his recompense for me!
Ay, 'tis for me, the prey he bore from Troy,
That she hath sworn his death, and edged the steel!

. . .

Yet shall the gods have heed of me who die,
For by their will shall one requite my doom.
He, to avenge his father's blood outpoured,
Shall smite and slay with matricidal hand.
Ay, he shall come—tho' far away he roam,
A banished wanderer in a stranger's land—
To crown his kindred's edifice of ill,
Called home to vengeance by his father's fall:
Thus have the high gods sworn, and shall fulfil.
And now why mourn I, tarrying on earth,
Since first mine Ilion has found its fate
And I beheld, and those who won the wall
Pass to such issue as the gods ordain?
I too will pass and like them dare to die!
Portal of Hades, thus I bid thee hail!
Grant me one boon—a swift and mortal stroke,
That all unwrung by pain, with ebbing blood
Shed forth in quiet death, I close mine eyes.

LEADER
Maid of mysterious woes, mysterious lore,
Long was thy prophecy: but if aright
Thou readest all thy fate, how, thus unscared,
Dost thou approach the altar of thy doom,
As fronts the knife some victim, heaven-controlled?

CASSANDRA
Friends, there is no avoidance in delay.

. . .

Sun! thou whose beam I shall not see again,
To thee I cry, Let those whom vengeance calls
To slay their kindred's slayers, quit withal
The death of me, the slave, the fenceless prey.

Ah state of mortal man! in time of weal,
A line, a shadow! and if ill fate fall,
One wet sponge-sweep wipes all our trace away—
And this I deem less piteous, of the twain.

(She enters the palace.)

. . .

(A loud cry is heard from within.)

VOICE OF AGAMEMNON
O I am sped—a deep, a mortal blow.

LEADER OF THE CHORUS
Listen, listen! who is screaming as in mortal agony?

VOICE OF AGAMEMNON
O! O! again, another, another blow!

LEADER
The bloody act is over—I have heard the monarch's cry—
Let us swiftly take some counsel, lest we too be doomed to die.

ONE OF THE CHORUS
'Tis best, I judge, aloud for aid to call,
"Ho! loyal Argives! to the palace, all!"

ANOTHER
Better, I deem, ourselves to bear the aid,
And drag the deed to light, while drips the blade.

ANOTHER
Such will is mine, and what thou say'st I say:
Swiftly to act! the time brooks no delay.

ANOTHER
Ay, for 'tis plain, this prelude of their song
Foretells its close in tyranny and wrong.

ANOTHER
Behold, we tarry—but thy name, Delay,
They spurn, and press with sleepless hand to slay.

ANOTHER

I know not what 'twere well to counsel now—
Who wills to act, 'tis his to counsel how.

ANOTHER

Thy doubt is mine: for when a man is slain,
I have no words to bring his life again.

ANOTHER

What? e'en for life's sake, bow us to obey
These house-defilers and their tyrant sway?

ANOTHER

Unmanly doom! 'twere better far to die—
Death is a gentler lord than tyranny.

ANOTHER

Think well—must cry or sign of woe or pain
Fix our conclusion that the chief is slain?

ANOTHER

Such talk befits us when the deed we see—
Conjecture dwells afar from certainty.

LEADER OF THE CHORUS

I read one will from many a diverse word,
To know aright, how stands it with our lord!

(CLYTEMNESTRA *comes forward. She has blood
smeared upon her forehead. The corpse of* CASSANDRA
lies beside the body of AGAMEMNON.)

CLYTEMNESTRA

Ho, ye who heard me speak so long and oft
The glozing word that led me to my will—
Hear how I shrink not to unsay it all!
How else should one who willeth to requite
Evil for evil to an enemy
Disguised as friend, weave the mesh straitly round him,
Not to be overleaped, a net of doom?
This is the sum and issue of old strife,
Of me deep-pondered and at length fulfilled.
All is avowed, and as I smote I stand
With foot set firm upon a finished thing!
I turn not to denial: thus I wrought
So that he could nor flee nor ward his doom.

Even as the trammel hems the scaly shoal,
I trapped him with inextricable toils,
The ill abundance of a baffling robe;
Then smote him, once, again—and at each wound
He cried aloud, then as in death relaxed
Each limb and sank to earth; and as he lay,
Once more I smote him, with the last third blow,
Sacred to Hades, saviour of the dead.
And thus he fell, and as he passed away,
Spirit with body chafed; each dying breath
Flung from his breast swift bubbling jets of gore,
And the dark sprinklings of the rain of blood
Fell upon me; and I was fain to feel
That dew—not sweeter is the rain of heaven
To cornland, when the green sheath teems with grain.
Elders of Argos—since the thing stands so,
I bid you to rejoice, if such your will:
Rejoice or not, I vaunt and praise the deed,
And well I ween, if seemly it could be,
'Twere not ill done to pour libations here,
Justly—ay, more than justly—on his corpse
Who filled his home with curses as with wine,
And thus returned to drain the cup he filled.

LEADER

I marvel at thy tongue's audacity,
To vaunt thus loudly o'er a husband slain.

CLYTEMNESTRA

Ye hold me as a woman, weak of will,
And strive to sway me: but my heart is stout,
Nor fears to speak its uttermost to you,
Albeit ye know its message. Praise or blame,
Even as ye list,—I reck not of your words.
Lo! at my feet lies Agamemnon slain,
My husband once—and him this hand of mine,
A right contriver, fashioned for his death.
Behold the deed!

CHORUS

Woman, what deadly birth,
What venomed essence of the earth

Or dark distilment of the wave,
  To thee such passion gave,
Nerving thine hand
To set upon thy brow this burning crown,
  The curses of thy land?
Our king by thee cut off, hewn down!
   Go forth—they cry—*accursèd and forlorn,*
    To hate and scorn!

CLYTEMNESTRA

O ye just men, who speak my sentence now,
The city's hate, the ban of all my realm!
Ye had no voice of old to launch such doom
On him, my husband, when he held as light
My daughter's life as that of sheep or goat,
One victim from the thronging fleecy fold!
Yea, slew in sacrifice his child and mine,
The well-loved issue of my travail-pangs,
To lull and lay the gales that blew from Thrace.
That deed of his, I say, that stain and shame,
Had rightly been atoned by banishment;
But ye, who then were dumb, are stern to judge
This deed of mine that doth affront your ears.
Storm out your threats, yet knowing this for sooth,
That I am ready, if your hand prevail
As mine now doth, to bow beneath your sway:
If God say nay, it shall be yours to learn
By chastisement a late humility.

CHORUS

  Bold is thy craft, and proud
Thy confidence, thy vaunting loud;
Thy soul, that chose a murd'ress' fate,
  Is all with blood elate—
   Maddened to know
The blood not yet avenged, the damnèd spot
  Crimson upon thy brow.
But Fate prepares for thee thy lot—
Smitten as thou didst smite, without a friend,
   To meet thine end!

CLYTEMNESTRA

Hear then the sanction of the oath I swear—
By the great vengeance for my murdered child,
By Atè, by the Fury unto whom
This man lies sacrificed by hand of mine,
I do not look to tread the hall of Fear,
While in this hearth and home of mine there burns
The light of love—Aegisthus—as of old
Loyal, a stalwart shield of confidence—
As true to me as this slain man was false,
Wronging his wife with paramours at Troy,
Fresh from the kiss of each Chryseis there!
Behold him dead—behold his captive prize,
Seeress and harlot—comfort of his bed,
True prophetess, true paramour—I wot
The sea-bench was not closer to the flesh,
Full oft, of every rower, than was she.
See, ill they did, and ill requites them now.
His death ye know: she as a dying swan
Sang her last dirge, and lies, as erst she lay,
Close to his side, and to my couch has left
A sweet new taste of joys that know no fear.

.　　.　　.

My guilt thou harpest, o'er and o'er!
I bid thee reckon me no more
　　As Agamemnon's spouse.
The old Avenger, stern of mood
For Atreus and his feast of blood,
　　Hath struck the lord of Atreus' house,
And in the semblance of his wife
　　The king hath slain.—
Yea, for the murdered children's life,
　　A chieftain's in requital ta'en.

CHORUS

Thou guiltless of this murder, thou!
　　Who dares such thought avow?
Yet it may be, wroth for the parent's deed,
The fiend hath holpen thee to slay the son.

Dark Ares, god of death, is pressing on
Thro' streams of blood by kindred shed,
Exacting the accompt for children dead,
For clotted blood, for flesh on which their sire did feed.

Yet ah my king, my king no more!
What words to say, what tears to pour
    Can tell my love for thee?
The spider-web of treachery
She wove and wound, thy life around,
    And lo! I see thee lie,
And thro' a coward, impious wound
    Pant forth thy life and die!
A death of shame—ah woe on woe!
A treach'rous hand, a cleaving blow!

CLYTEMNESTRA

I deem not that the death he died
    Had overmuch of shame:
For this was he who did provide
    Foul wrong unto his house and name:
His daughter, blossom of my womb,
He gave unto a deadly doom,
Iphigenia, child of tears!
And as he wrought, even so he fares
Nor be his vaunt too loud in hell;
For by the sword his sin he wrought,
And by the sword himself is brought
    Among the dead to dwell.

.   .   .

Now walks thy word aright, to tell
This ancient truth of oracle;
But I wish vows of sooth will pray
To him, the power that holdeth sway
    O'er all the race of Pleisthenes—
Tho' dark the deed and deep the guilt,
With this last blood, my hands have spilt,
    I pray thee let thine anger cease!
I pray thee pass from us away

To some new race in other lands,
There, if thou wilt, to wrong and slay
  The lives of men by kindred hands.

For me 'tis all sufficient meed,
Tho' little wealth or power were won,
So I can say, *'Tis past and done.*
The bloody lust and murderous,
The inborn frenzy of our house,
  Is ended, by my deed!

AEGISTHUS

Dawn of the day of rightful vengeance, hail!
I dare at length aver that gods above
Have care of men and heed of earthly wrongs.
I, I who stand and thus exult to see
This man lie wound in robes the Furies wove,
Slain in the requital of his father's craft.

·   ·   ·

LEADER OF THE CHORUS

Aegisthus, for this insolence of thine
That vaunts itself in evil, take my scorn.
Of thine own will, thou sayest, thou hast slain
The chieftain, by thine own unaided plot
Devised the piteous death: I rede thee well,
Think not thy head shall 'scape, when right prevails,
The people's ban, the stones of death and doom.

AEGISTHUS

This word from thee, this word from one who rows
Low at the oars beneath, what time we rule,
We of the upper tier? Thou'lt know anon,
'Tis bitter to be taught again in age,
By one so young, submission at the word.
But iron of the chain and hunger's throes
Can minister unto an o'erswoln pride
Marvellous well, ay, even in the old.
Hast eyes, and seest not this? Peace—kick not thus
Against the pricks, unto thy proper pain!

·   ·   ·

LEADER

Thou losel soul, was then thy strength too slight
To deal in murder, while a woman's hand,
Staining and shaming Argos and its gods,
Availed to slay him? Ho, if anywhere
The light of life smite on Orestes' eyes,
Let him, returning by some guardian fate,
Hew down with force her paramour and her!

AEGISTHUS

How thy word and act shall issue, thou shalt shortly understand.

LEADER

Up to action, O my comrades! for the fight is hard at hand.
Swift, your right hands to the sword hilt! bare the weapon as
for strife—

AEGISTHUS

Lo! I too am standing ready, hand on hilt for death or life.

LEADER

'Twas thy word and we accept it: onward to the chance of
war!

CLYTEMNESTRA

Nay, enough, enough, my champion! we will smite and slay
no more.
Already have we reaped enough the harvest-field of guilt:
Enough of wrong and murder, let no other blood be spilt.
Peace, old men! and pass away unto the homes by Fate de-
creed,
Lest ill valour meet our vengeance—'twas a necessary deed.
But enough of toils and troubles—be the end, if ever, now,
Ere thy talon, O Avenger, deal another deadly blow.
'Tis a woman's word of warning, and let who will list thereto.

AEGISTHUS

But that these should loose and lavish reckless blossoms of the
tongue,
And in hazard of their fortune cast upon me words of wrong,
And forget the law of subjects, and revile their ruler's word—

LEADER

Ruler? but 'tis not for Argives, thus to own a dastard lord!

AEGISTHUS

I will follow to chastise thee in my coming days of sway.

LEADER

Not if Fortune guide Orestes safely on his homeward way.

AEGISTHUS

Ah, well I know how exiles feed on hopes of their return.

LEADER

Fare and batten on pollution of the right, while 'tis thy turn.

AEGISTHUS

Thou shalt pay, be well assured, heavy quittance for thy pride.

LEADER

Crow and strut, with her to watch thee, like a cock, his mate beside!

CLYTEMNESTRA

Heed not thou too highly of them—let the cur-pack growl and yell:

I and thou will rule the palace and will order all things well.

SOPHOCLES

FROM OEDIPUS THE KING

OEDIPUS

My children, latest-born to Cadmus who was of old, why are ye set before me thus with wreathed branches of suppliants, while the city reeks with incense, rings with prayers for health and cries of woe? I deemed it unmeet, my children, to hear these things at the mouth of others, and have come hither myself, I, Oedipus renowned of all.

Tell me, then, thou venerable man—since it is thy natural part to speak for these—in what mood are ye placed here, with what dread or what desire? Be sure that I would gladly give all aid; hard of heart were I, did I not pity such suppliants as these.

PRIEST OF ZEUS

Nay, Oedipus, ruler of my land, thou seest of what years we are who beset thy altars,—some, nestlings still too tender for far flights,—some, bowed with age, priests, as I of Zeus,—and these, the chosen youth;

while the rest of the folk sit with wreathed branches in the market-places, and before the two shrines of Pallas, and where Ismenus gives answer by fire.

For the city, as thou thyself seest, is now too sorely vexed, and can no more lift her head from beneath the angry waves of death; a blight is on her in the fruitful blossoms of the land, in the herds among the pastures, in the barren pangs of women; and withal the flaming god, the malign plague, hath swooped on us, and ravages the town; by whom the house of Cadmus is made waste, but dark Hades rich in groans and tears.

.   .   .

And now, Oedipus, king glorious in all eyes, we beseech thee, all we suppliants, to find for us some succour, whether by the whisper of a god thou knowest it, or haply as in the power of man; for I see that, when men have been proved in deeds past, the issues of their counsels, too, most often have effect.

.   .   .

With good omen didst thou give us that past happiness; now also show thyself the same. For if thou art to rule this land, even as thou art now its lord, 'tis better to be lord of men than of a waste: since neither walled town nor ship is anything, if it is void and no men dwell with thee therein.

Oedipus

Oh my piteous children, known, well known to me are the desires wherewith ye have come: well wot I that ye suffer all; yet, sufferers as ye are, there is not one of you whose suffering is as mine. Your pain comes on each one of you for himself alone, and for no other; but my soul mourns at once for the city, and for myself, and for thee.

So that ye rouse me not, truly, as one sunk in sleep: no, be sure that I have wept full many tears, gone many ways in wanderings of thought. And the sole remedy which, well pondering, I could find, this I have put into act. I have sent the son of Menoeceus, Creon, mine own wife's brother, to the Pythian house of Phoebus, to learn by what deed or word I might deliver this town. And already, when the lapse of days is reckoned, it troubles me what he doth; for he tarries strangely, beyond the fitting space. But when he comes, then shall I be no true man if I do not all that the god shows.

PRIEST

Nay, in season hast thou spoken; at this moment these sign to me that Creon draws near.

OEDIPUS

O king Apollo, may he come to us in the brightness of saving fortune, even as his face is bright!

PRIEST

Nay, to all seeming, he brings comfort; else would he not be coming crowned thus thickly with berry-laden bay.

OEDIPUS

We shall know soon: he is at range to hear.—Prince, my kinsman, son of Menoeceus, what news hast thou brought us from the god?

CREON

Good news: I tell thee that even troubles hard to bear,—if haply they find the right issue,—will end in perfect peace.

OEDIPUS

But what is the oracle? So far, thy words make me neither bold nor yet afraid.

CREON

If thou wouldest hear while these are nigh, I am ready to speak; or else to go within.

OEDIPUS

Speak before all: the sorrow which I bear is for these more than for mine own life.

CREON

With thy leave, I will tell what I heard from the god. Phoebus our lord bids us plainly to drive out a defiling thing, which (he saith) hath been harboured in this land, and not to harbour it, so that it cannot be healed.

OEDIPUS

By what rite shall we cleanse us? What is the manner of the misfortune?

CREON

By banishing a man, or by bloodshed in quittance of bloodshed, since it is that blood which brings the tempest on our city.

OEDIPUS

And who is the man whose fate he thus reveals?

CREON

Laius, king, was lord of our land before thou wast pilot of this State.

OEDIPUS

I know it well—by hearsay, for I saw him never.

CREON

He was slain; and the god now bids us plainly to wreak vengeance on his murderers—whosoever they be.

OEDIPUS

And where are they upon the earth? Where shall the dim track of this old crime be found?

CREON

In this land,—said the god. What is sought for can be caught; only that which is not watched escapes.

OEDIPUS

And was it in the house, or in the field, or on strange soil that Laius met this bloody end?

CREON

'Twas on a visit to Delphi, as he said, that he had left our land; and he came home no more, after he had once set forth.

OEDIPUS

And was there none to tell? Was there no comrade of his journey who saw the deed, from whom tidings might have been gained, and used?

CREON

All perished, save one who fled in fear, and could tell for certain but one thing of all that he saw.

OEDIPUS

And what was that? One thing might show the clue to many, could we get but a small beginning for hope.

CREON

He said that robbers met and fell on them, not in one man's might, but with full many hands.

OEDIPUS

How, then, unless there was some trafficking in bribes from here, should the robber have dared thus far?

CREON

Such things were surmised; but, Laius once slain, amid our troubles no avenger arose.

OEDIPUS

But, when royalty had fallen thus, what trouble in your path can have hindered a full search?

CREON

The riddling Sphinx had made us let dark things go, and was inviting us to think of what lay at our doors.

OEDIPUS

Nay, I will start afresh, and once more make dark things plain. Right worthily hath Phoebus, and worthily hast thou, bestowed this care on the cause of the dead; and so, as is meet, ye shall find me too leagued with you in seeking vengeance for this land, and for the god besides. On behalf of no far-off friend, no, but in mine own cause, shall I dispel this taint. For whoever was the slayer of Laius might wish to take vengeance on me also with a hand as fierce. Therefore, in doing right to Laius, I serve myself.

.   .   .

CHORUS

O sweetly-speaking message of Zeus, in what spirit hast thou come from golden Pytho unto glorious Thebes? I am on the rack, terror shakes my soul, O thou Delian healer to whom wild cries rise, in holy fear of thee, what thing thou wilt work for me, perchance unknown before, perchance renewed with the revolving years: tell me, thou immortal Voice, born of Golden Hope!

.   .   .

OEDIPUS

Thou prayest: and in answer to thy prayer,—if thou wilt give a loyal welcome to my words and minister to thine own disease,—thou mayest hope to find succour and relief from woes. These words will I speak publicly, as one who has been a stranger to this report, a stranger to the deed; for I should not be far on the track, if I were tracing it alone, without a clue. But as it is,—since it was only after the time of the deed that I was numbered a Theban among Thebans,—to you, the Cadmeans all, I do thus proclaim.

Whosoever of you knows by whom Laius son of Labdacus was slain, I bid him to declare all to me. And if he is afraid, I tell him to remove the danger of the charge from his path by denouncing himself; for he shall suffer nothing else unlovely, but only leave the land, unhurt. Or if any one knows an alien, from another land, as the assassin, let him not keep silence; for I will pay his guerdon, and my thanks shall rest with him besides.

But if ye keep silence—if any one, through fear, shall seek to screen friend or self from my behest—hear ye what I then shall do. I charge you that no one of this land, whereof I hold the empire and the throne, give shelter or speak word unto that murderer, whosoever he be,—make him partner of his prayer or sacrifice, or serve him with the lustral rite; but that all ban him their homes, knowing that *this* is our defiling thing, as the oracle of the Pythian god hath newly shown me. I then am on this wise the ally of the god and of the slain. And I pray solemnly that the slayer, whoso he be, whether his hidden guilt is lonely or hath partners, evilly, as he is evil, may wear out his unblest life. And for myself I pray that if, with my privity, he should become an inmate of my house, I may suffer the same things which even now I called down upon others. And on you I lay it to make all these words good, for my sake, and for the sake of the god, and for our land's, thus blasted with barrenness by angry heaven.

.   .   .

LEADER OF THE CHORUS

As thou hast put me on my oath, on my oath, O king, I will speak. I am not the slayer, nor can I point to him who slew. As for the question, it was for Phoebus, who sent it, to tell us this thing—who can have wrought the deed.

OEDIPUS

Justly said; but no man on the earth can force the gods to what they will not.

LEADER

I would fain say what seems to me next best after this.

OEDIPUS

If there is yet a third course, spare not to show it.

LEADER

I know that our Lord Teiresias is the seer most like to our lord Phoebus; from whom, O king, a searcher of these things might learn them most clearly.

OEDIPUS

Not even this have I left out of my cares. On the hint of Creon, I have twice sent a man to bring him; and this long while I marvel why he is not here.

.   .   .

LEADER

But there is one to convict him. For here they bring at last the godlike prophet, in whom alone of men doth live the truth.

OEDIPUS

Teiresias, whose soul grasps all things, the lore that may be told and the unspeakable, the secrets of heaven and the low things of earth,—thou feelest, though thou canst not see, what a plague doth haunt our State,—from which, great prophet, we find in thee our protector and only saviour. Now, Phoebus—if indeed thou knowest it not from the messengers—sent answer to our question that the only riddance from this pest which could come was if we should learn aright the slayers of Laius, and slay them, or send them into exile from our land. Do thou, then, grudge neither voice of birds nor any other way of seer-lore that thou hast, but rescue thyself and the State, rescue me, rescue all that is defiled by the dead. For we are in thy hand; and man's noblest task is to help others by his best means and powers.

TEIRESIAS

Alas, how dreadful to have wisdom where it profits not the wise! Aye, I knew this well, but let it slip out of mind; else would I never have come here.

OEDIPUS

What now? How sad thou hast come in!

TEIRESIAS

Let me go home; most easily wilt thou bear thine own burden to the end, and I mine, if thou wilt consent.

OEDIPUS

Thy words are strange, nor kindly to this State which nurtured thee, when thou withholdest this response.

.   .   .

TEIRESIAS

Aye, for ye are all without knowledge; but never will I reveal my griefs—that I say not thine.

OEDIPUS

How sayest thou? Thou knowest the secret, and wilt not tell it, but art minded to betray us and to destroy the State?

TEIRESIAS

I will paint neither myself nor thee. Why vainly ask these things? Thou wilt not learn them from me.

OEDIPUS

What, basest of the base,—for thou wouldest anger a very stone,—wilt thou never speak out? Can nothing touch thee? Wilt thou never make an end?

.   .   .

TEIRESIAS

I will speak no further; rage, then, if thou wilt, with the fiercest wrath thy heart doth know.

OEDIPUS

Aye, verily, I will not spare—so wroth I am—to speak all my thought. Know that thou seemest to me e'en to have helped in plotting the deed, and to have done it, short of slaying with thy hands. Hadst thou eyesight, I would have said that the doing, also, of this thing was thine alone.

TEIRESIAS

In sooth?—I charge thee that thou abide by the decree of thine own mouth, and from this day speak neither to these nor to me: *thou* art the accursed defiler of this land.

OEDIPUS

So brazen with thy blustering taunt? And wherein dost thou trust to escape thy due?

TEIRESIAS

I have escaped: in my truth is my strength.

OEDIPUS

Who taught thee this? It was not, at least, thine art.

TEIRESIAS

Thou: for thou didst spur me into speech against my will.

OEDIPUS

What speech? Speak again that I may learn it better.

TEIRESIAS

Didst thou not take my sense before? Or art thou tempting me in talk?

OEDIPUS

No, I took it not so that I can call it known:—speak again.

TEIRESIAS

I say that thou art the slayer of the man whose slayer thou seekest.

OEDIPUS

Now thou shalt rue that thou hast twice said words so dire.

TEIRESIAS

Wouldst thou have me say more, that thou mayest be more wroth?

OEDIPUS

What thou wilt; it will be said in vain.

TEIRESIAS

I say that thou hast been living in unguessed shame with thy nearest kin, and seest not to what woe thou hast come.

OEDIPUS

Dost thou indeed think that thou shalt always speak thus without smarting?

TEIRESIAS

Yes, if there is any strength in truth.

OEDIPUS

Nay, there is,—for all save thee; for thee that strength is not, since thou art maimed in ear, and in wit, and in eye.

TEIRESIAS

Aye, and thou art a poor wretch to utter taunts which every man here will soon hurl at thee.

OEDIPUS

Night, endless night hath thee in her keeping, so that thou canst never hurt me, or any man who sees the sun.

TEIRESIAS

No, thy doom is not to fall by *me:* Apollo is enough, whose care it is to work that out.

OEDIPUS

Are these Creon's devices, or thine?

TEIRESIAS

Nay, Creon is no plague to thee; thou art thine own.

OEDIPUS

O wealth, and empire, and skill surpassing skill in life's keen rivalries, how great is the envy that cleaves to you, if for the sake, yea, of this power which the city hath put into my hands, a gift unsought, Creon the trusty, Creon mine old friend, hath crept on me by stealth, yearning to thrust me out of it, and hath suborned such a scheming juggler as this, a tricky quack, who hath eyes only for his gains, but in his art is blind!

．　　　．　　　．

LEADER

To our thinking, both this man's words and thine, Oedipus, have been said in anger. Not for such words is our need, but to seek how we shall best discharge the mandates of the god.

TEIRESIAS

King though thou art, the right of reply, at least, must be deemed the same for both; of that I too am lord. Not to thee do I live servant, but to Loxias; and so I shall not stand enrolled under Creon for my patron. And I tell thee—since thou hast taunted me even with blindness—that thou hast sight, yet seest not in what misery thou art, nor where thou dwellest, nor with whom. Dost thou know of what stock thou art? And thou hast been an unwitting foe to thine own kin, in the shades, and on the earth above; and the double lash of thy mother's and thy father's curse shall one day drive thee from this land in dreadful haste, with darkness then on the eyes that now see true.

And what place shall not be harbour to thy shriek, what of all Cithaeron shall not ring with it soon, when thou hast learnt the meaning of the nuptials in which, within that house, thou didst find a fatal haven, after a voyage so fair? And a throng of other ills thou guessest not, which shall make thee level with thy true self and with thine own brood.

Therefore heap thy scorns on Creon and on my message: for no one among men shall ever be crushed more miserably than thou.

OEDIPUS

Are these taunts to be indeed borne from *him?*—Hence, ruin take thee! Hence, this instant! Back!—away!—avaunt thee from these doors!

．　　　．　　　．

TEIRESIAS

This day shall show thy birth and shall bring thy ruin.

OEDIPUS

What riddles, what dark words thou always speakest!

TEIRESIAS

Nay, art not thou most skilled to unravel dark speech?

OEDIPUS

Make that my reproach in which thou shalt find me great.

TEIRESIAS

Yet 'twas just that fortune that undid thee.

OEDIPUS

Nay, if I delivered this town, I care not.

TEIRESIAS

Then I will go: so do thou, boy, take me hence.

OEDIPUS

Aye, let him take thee: while here, thou art a hindrance, thou, a trouble: when thou hast vanished, thou wilt not vex me more.

TEIRESIAS

I will go when I have done mine errand, fearless of thy frown: for thou canst never destroy me. And I tell thee—the man of whom thou hast this long while been in quest, uttering threats, and proclaiming a search into the murder of Laius—that man is here,—in seeming, an alien sojourner, but anon he shall be found a native Theban, and shall not be glad of his fortune. A blind man, he who now hath sight, a beggar, who now is rich, he shall make his way to a strange land, feeling the ground before him with his staff. And he shall be found at once brother and father of the children with whom he consorts; son and husband of the woman who bore him; heir to his father's bed, shedder of his father's blood.

So go thou in and think on that; and if thou find that I have been at fault, say thenceforth that I have no wit in prophecy.

.   .   .

(TEIRESIAS *is led out by the boy.* OEDIPUS
enters the palace. Enter CREON)

CREON

Fellow-citizens, having learned that Oedipus the king lays dire charges against me, I am here, indignant. If, in the present troubles, he thinks that he has suffered from *me,* by word or deed, aught that tends to harm, in truth I crave not my full term of years, when I must bear such blame as this. The wrong of this rumour touches me not in one point alone, but has the largest scope, if I am to be called a traitor in the city, a traitor too by thee and by my friends.

LEADER OF THE CHORUS

Nay, but this taunt came under stress, perchance, of anger, rather than from the purpose of the heart.

CREON

And the saying was uttered, that *my* counsels won the seer to utter his falsehoods?

LEADER

Such things were said—I know not with what meaning.

.   .   .

(Enter OEDIPUS)

OEDIPUS

Sirrah, how camest thou here? Hast thou a front so bold that thou hast come to my house, who art the proved assassin of its master,—the palpable robber of my crown? Come, tell me, in the name of the gods, was it cowardice or folly that thou sawest in me, that thou didst plot to do this thing? Didst thou think that I would not ward it off? Now is not thine attempt foolish,—to seek, without followers or friends, a throne,—a prize which followers and wealth must win?

CREON

Mark me now,—in answer to thy words, hear a fair reply, and then judge for thyself on knowledge.

OEDIPUS

Thou art apt in speech, but I have a poor wit for thy lessons, since I have found thee my malignant foe.

CREON

Now first hear how I will explain this very thing—

OEDIPUS

Explain me not one thing—that thou art not false.

CREON

If thou deemest that stubbornness without sense is a good gift, thou art not wise.

OEDIPUS

If thou deemest that thou canst wrong a kinsman and escape the penalty, thou art not sane.

CREON

Justly said, I grant thee: but tell me what is the wrong that thou sayest thou hast suffered from me.

OEDIPUS

Didst thou advise, or didst thou not, that I should send for that reverend seer?

CREON

And now I am still of the same mind.

OEDIPUS

How long is it, then, since Laius—

CREON

Since Laius . . . ? I take not thy drift . . .

OEDIPUS

—was swept from men's sight by a deadly violence?

CREON

The count of years would run far into the past.

OEDIPUS

Was this seer, then, of the craft in those days?

CREON

Yea, skilled as now, and in equal honour.

OEDIPUS

Made he, then, any mention of me at that time?

CREON

Never, certainly, when I was within hearing.

.　　.　　.

OEDIPUS

And how was it that this sage did not tell his story *then?*

CREON

I know not; where I lack light, 'tis my wont to be silent.

OEDIPUS

Thus much, at least, thou knowest, and couldst declare with light enough.

CREON

What is that? If I know it, I will not deny.

OEDIPUS

That, if he had not conferred with thee, he would never have named *my* slaying of Laius.

CREON

If so he speaks, thou best knowest; but I claim to learn from thee as much as thou hast now from me.

OEDIPUS

Learn thy fill: I shall never be found guilty of the blood.

CREON

Say, then—thou hast married my sister?

OEDIPUS

The question allows not of denial.

CREON

And thou rulest the land as she doth, with like sway?

OEDIPUS

She obtains from me all her desire.

CREON

And rank not I as a third peer of you twain?

OEDIPUS

Aye, 'tis just therein that thou art seen a false friend.

CREON

Not so, if thou wouldst reason with thine own heart as I with mine. And first weigh this,—whether thou thinkest that any one would choose to rule amid terrors rather than in unruffled peace,—granting that he is to have the same powers. . . .

.   .   .

How, then, could royalty be sweeter for me to have than painless rule and influence? Not yet am I so misguided as to desire other honours than those which profit. Now, all wish me joy; now, every man has a greeting for me; now, those who have a suit to thee crave speech with me, since therein is all their hope of success. Then why should I resign these things, and take those? No mind will become false, while it is wise. Nay, I am no lover of such policy, and, if another put it into deed, never could I bear to act with him.

.   .   .

LEADER

Well hath he spoken, O king, for one who giveth heed not to fall: the quick in counsel are not sure.

OEDIPUS

When the stealthy plotter is moving on me in quick sort, I, too, must be quick with my counterplot. If I await him in repose, his ends will have been gained, and mine missed.

CREON

What wouldst thou, then? Cast me out of the land?

OEDIPUS

Not so: I desire thy death—not thy banishment—that thou mayest show forth what manner of thing is envy.

CREON

Thou speakest as resolved not to yield or to believe?

OEDIPUS

No; for thou persuadest me not that thou art worthy of belief.

CREON

No, for I find thee not sane.

.   .   .

LEADER

Cease, princes; and in good time for you I see Jocasta coming yonder from the house, with whose help ye should compose your present feud.

JOCASTA

Misguided men, why have ye raised such foolish strife of tongues? Are ye not ashamed, while the land is thus sick, to stir up troubles of your own? Come, go thou into the house,—and thou, Creon, to thy home,—and forbear to make much of a petty grief.

CREON

Kinswoman, Oedipus thy lord claims to do dread things unto me, even one or other of two ills,—to thrust me from the land of my fathers, or to slay me amain.

OEDIPUS

Yea; for I have caught him, lady, working evil, by ill arts, against my person.

CREON

Now may I see no good, but perish accursed, if I have done aught to thee of that wherewith thou chargest me!

JOCASTA

O, for the gods' love, believe it, Oedipus—first, for the awful sake of this oath unto the gods,—then for my sake and for theirs who stand before thee!

CHORUS

Consent, reflect, hearken, O my king, I pray thee!

OEDIPUS

What grace, then wouldest thou have me grant thee?

CHORUS

Respect him who aforetime was not foolish, and who now is strong in his oath.

OEDIPUS

Now dost thou know what thou cravest?

CHORUS

Yea.

OEDIPUS

Declare, then, what thou meanest.

CHORUS

That thou shouldest never use an unproved rumour to cast a dishonouring charge on the friend who has bound himself with a curse.

.   .   .

OEDIPUS

Then let him go, though I am surely doomed to death, or to be thrust dishonoured from the land. Thy lips, not his, move my compassion by their plaint; but he, where'er he be, shall be hated.

CREON

Sullen in yielding art thou seen, even as vehement in the excesses of thy wrath; but such natures are justly sorest for themselves to bear.

OEDIPUS

Then wilt thou not leave me in peace, and get thee gone?

CREON

I will go my way; I have found thee undiscerning, but in the sight of these I am just.

CHORUS

Lady, why dost thou delay to take yon man into the house?

JOCASTA

I will do so, when I have learned what hath chanced.

CHORUS

Blind suspicion, bred of talk, arose; and, on the other part, injustice wounds.

JOCASTA

It was on both sides?

CHORUS

Aye.

JOCASTA

And what was the story?

CHORUS

Enough, methinks, enough—when our land is already vexed—that the matter should rest where it ceased.

OEDIPUS

Seest thou to what thou hast come, for all thy honest purpose, in seeking to slack and blunt my zeal?

.　　　.　　　.

JOCASTA

In the name of the gods, tell me also, O king, on what account thou hast conceived this steadfast wrath.

OEDIPUS

That will I; for I honour thee, lady, above yonder men:—the cause is Creon, and the plots that he hath laid against me.

JOCASTA

Speak on—if thou canst tell clearly how the feud began.

OEDIPUS

He says that I stand guilty of the blood of Laius.

JOCASTA

As on his own knowledge? Or on hearsay from another?

OEDIPUS

Nay, he hath made a rascal seer his mouthpiece; as for himself, he keeps his lips wholly pure.

JOCASTA

Then absolve thyself of the things whereof thou speakest; hearken to me, and learn for thy comfort that nought of mortal birth is a sharer in the science of the seer. I will give thee pithy proof of that.

An oracle came to Laius once—I will not say from Phoebus himself, but from his ministers—that the doom should overtake him to die by the hand of his child, who should spring from him and me.

Now Laius,—as, at least, the rumour saith,—was murdered one day by foreign robbers at a place where three highways meet. And the child's birth was not three days past, when Laius pinned its ankles together, and had it thrown, by others' hands, on a trackless mountain.

So, in that case, Apollo brought it not to pass that the babe should become the slayer of his sire, or that Laius should die—the dread thing which he feared—by his child's hand. Thus did the messages of seer-craft map out the future. Regard them, thou, not at all. Whatsoever needful things the god seeks, he himself will easily bring to light.

OEDIPUS

What restlessness of soul, lady, what tumult of the mind hath just come upon me since I heard thee speak!

JOCASTA

What anxiety hath startled thee, that thou sayest this?

OEDIPUS

Methought I heard this from thee,—that Laius was slain where three highways meet.

JOCASTA

Yea, that was the story; nor hath it ceased yet.

OEDIPUS

And where is the place where this befell?

JOCASTA

The land is called Phocis; and branching roads lead to the same spot from Delphi and from Daulia.

OEDIPUS

And what is the time that hath passed since these things were?

JOCASTA

The news was published to the town shortly before thou wast first seen in power over this land.

OEDIPUS

O Zeus, what hast thou decreed to do unto me?

JOCASTA

And wherefore, Oedipus, doth this thing weigh upon thy soul?

OEDIPUS

Ask me not yet; but say what was the stature of Laius, and how ripe his manhood.

JOCASTA

He was tall,—the silver just lightly strewn among his hair; and his form was not greatly unlike to thine.

OEDIPUS

Unhappy that I am! Methinks I have been laying myself even now under a dread curse, and knew it not.

JOCASTA

How sayest thou? I tremble when I look on thee, my king.

OEDIPUS

Dread misgivings have I that the seer can see. But thou wilt show better if thou wilt tell me one thing more.

JOCASTA

Indeed—though I tremble—I will answer all thou askest, when I hear it.

OEDIPUS

Went he in small force, or with many armed followers, like a chieftain?

JOCASTA

Five they were in all,—a herald one of them; and there was one carriage, which bore Laius.

OEDIPUS

Alas! 'Tis now clear indeed.—Who was he who gave you these tidings, lady?

JOCASTA

A servant—the sole survivor who came home.

OEDIPUS

Is he haply at hand in the house now?

JOCASTA

No, truly; so soon as he came thence, and found thee reigning in the stead of Laius, he supplicated me, with hand laid on mine, that I would send him to the fields, to the pastures of the flocks, that he might be far from the sight of this town. And I sent him; he was worthy, for a slave, to win e'en a larger boon than that.

OEDIPUS

Would, then, that he could return to us without delay!

JOCASTA

It is easy: but wherefore dost thou enjoin this?

OEDIPUS

I fear, lady, that mine own lips have been unguarded; and therefore am I fain to behold him.

JOCASTA

Nay, he shall come. But I too, methinks, have a claim to learn what lies heavy on thy heart, my king.

OEDIPUS

Yea, and it shall not be kept from thee, now that my forebodings have advanced so far. Who, indeed, is more to me than thou, to whom I should speak in passing through such a fortune as this?

My father was Polybus of Corinth,—my mother, the Dorian Merope; and I was held the first of all the folk in that town, until a chance befell me, worthy, indeed, of wonder, though not worthy of mine own heat concerning it. At a banquet, a man full of wine cast it at me in his cups that I was not the true son of my sire. And I, vexed, restrained myself for that day as best I might; but on the next I went to my mother and father, and questioned them; and they were wroth for the taunt with him who had let that word fly. So on their part I had comfort; yet was this thing ever rankling in my heart; for it still crept abroad with strong rumour. And, unknown to mother or father, I went to Delphi; and Phoebus sent me forth disappointed of that knowledge for which I came, but in his response set forth other things, full of sorrow and terror and woe; even that I was fated to defile my mother's bed; and that I should show unto men a brood which they could not endure to behold; and that I should be the slayer of the sire who begat me.

And I, when I had listened to this, turned to flight from the land of Corinth, thenceforth wotting of its region by the stars alone, to some spot where I should never see fulfilment of the infamies foretold in mine evil doom. And on my way I came to the regions in which thou sayest that this prince perished. Now, lady, I will tell thee the truth. When in my journey I was near to those three roads, there met me a herald, and a man seated in a carriage drawn by colts, as thou hast described; and he who was in front, and the old man himself, were for thrusting me rudely from the path. Then, in anger, I struck him who pushed me aside —the driver; and the old man, seeing it, watched the moment when I was passing, and, from the carriage, brought his goad with two teeth down full upon my head. Yet was he paid with interest; by one swift blow from the staff in this hand he was rolled right out of the carriage, on his back; and I slew every man of them.

But if this stranger had any tie of kinship with Laius, who is now more wretched than the man before thee? What mortal could prove more hated of heaven? Whom no stranger, no citizen, is allowed to receive in his house; whom it is unlawful that any one accost; whom all must repel from their homes! And this—this curse—was laid on me by no mouth but mine own! And I pollute the bed of the slain man with the hands by which he perished. Say, am I vile? Oh, am I not utterly unclean? —seeing that I must be banished, and in banishment see not mine own people, nor set foot in mine own land, or else be joined in wedlock to my mother, and slay my sire, even Polybus, who begat and reared me.

Then would not he speak aright of Oedipus, who judged these things sent by some cruel power above man? Forbid, forbid, ye pure and awful gods, that I should see that day! No, may I be swept from among men, ere I behold myself visited with the brand of such a doom!

LEADER OF THE CHORUS

To us, indeed, these things, O king, are fraught with fear; yet have hope, until at least thou hast gained full knowledge from him who saw the deed.

OEDIPUS

Hope, in truth, rests with me thus far alone; I can await the man summoned from the pastures.

JOCASTA

And when he has appeared—what wouldst thou have of him?

OEDIPUS

I will tell thee. If his story be found to tally with thine, I, at least, shall stand clear of disaster.

JOCASTA

And what of special note didst thou hear from me?

OEDIPUS

Thou wast saying that he spoke of Laius as slain by robbers. If, then, he still speaks, as before, of several, I was not the slayer: a solitary man could not be held the same with that band. But if he names one lonely wayfarer, then beyond doubt this guilt leans to me.

JOCASTA

Nay, be assured that thus, at least, the tale was first told; he cannot revoke that, for the city heard it, not I alone. But even if he should diverge somewhat from his former story, never, king, can he show that the murder of Laius, at least, is truly square to prophecy; of whom Loxias plainly said that he must die by the hand of my child. Howbeit that poor innocent never slew him, but perished first itself. So henceforth, for what touches divination, I would not look to my right hand or my left.

OEDIPUS

Thou judgest well. But nevertheless send some one to fetch the peasant, and neglect not this matter.

JOCASTA

I will send, without delay. But let us come into the house: nothing will I do save at thy good pleasure.

.   .   .

CHORUS

. . . If any man walks haughtily in deed or word, with no fear of Justice, no reverence for the images of gods, may an evil doom seize him for his ill-starred pride, if he will not win his vantage fairly, nor keep him from unholy deeds, but must lay profaning hands on sanctities.

Where such things are, what mortal shall boast any more that he can ward the arrows of the gods from his life? Nay, if such deeds are in honour, wherefore should we join in the sacred dance?

.   .   .

The old prophecies concerning Laius are fading; already men are setting them at nought, and nowhere is Apollo glorified with honours; the worship of the gods is perishing.

.   .   .

JOCASTA

Princes of the land, the thought has come to me to visit the shrines of the gods, with this wreathed branch in my hands, and these gifts of incense. For Oedipus excites his soul overmuch with all manner of alarms, nor, like a man of sense, judges the new things by the old, but is at the will of the speaker, if he speak terrors.

Since, then, by counsel I can do no good, to thee, Lycean Apollo, for thou art nearest, I have come, a suppliant with these symbols of prayer, that thou mayest find us some riddance from uncleanness. For now we are all afraid, seeing *him* affrighted, even as they who see fear in the helmsman of their ship.

(*While* JOCASTA *is offering her prayers to the god, a* MESSENGER, *evidently a stranger, enters and addresses the Elders of the* CHORUS.)

MESSENGER

Might I learn from you, strangers, where is the house of the king Oedipus? Or, better still, tell me where he himself is—if ye know.

LEADER OF THE CHORUS

This is his dwelling, and he himself, stranger, is within; and this lady is the mother of his children.

MESSENGER

Then may she be ever happy in a happy home, since she is his heaven-blest queen.

JOCASTA

Happiness to thee also, stranger! 'tis the due of thy fair greeting.— But say what thou hast come to seek or to tell.

MESSENGER

Good tidings, lady, for thy house and for thy husband.

JOCASTA

What are they? And from whom hast thou come?

MESSENGER

From Corinth: and at the message which I will speak anon thou wilt rejoice—doubtless; yet haply grieve.

JOCASTA

And what is it? How hath it thus a double potency?

MESSENGER

The people will make him king of the Isthmian land, as 'twas said there.

JOCASTA

How then? Is the aged Polybus no more in power?

MESSENGER

No, verily: for death holds him in the tomb.

JOCASTA

How sayest thou? Is Polybus dead, old man?

MESSENGER

If I speak not the truth, I am content to die.

JOCASTA

O handmaid, away with all speed, and tell this to thy master! O ye oracles of the gods, where stand ye now! This is the man whom Oedipus long feared and shunned, lest he should slay him; and now this man hath died in the course of destiny, not by his hand.

OEDIPUS

Jocasta, dearest wife, why hast thou summoned me forth from these doors?

JOCASTA

Hear this man, and judge, as thou listenest, to what the awful oracles of the gods have come.

OEDIPUS

And he—who may he be, and what news hath he for me?

JOCASTA

He is from Corinth, to tell that thy father Polybus lives no longer, but hath perished.

OEDIPUS

How, stranger? Let me have it from thine own mouth.

MESSENGER

If I must first make these tidings plain, know indeed that he is dead and gone.

OEDIPUS

By treachery, or by visit of disease?

MESSENGER

A light thing in the scale brings the aged to their rest.

OEDIPUS

Ah, he died, it seems, of sickness?

MESSENGER

Yea, and of the long years that he had told.

OEDIPUS

Alas, alas! Why, indeed, my wife, should one look to the hearth of the Pythian seer, or to the birds that scream above our heads, on whose showing I was doomed to slay my sire? But he is dead, and hid already beneath the earth; and here am I, who have not put hand to spear. . . .

JOCASTA

Nay, did I not so foretell to thee long since?

OEDIPUS

Thou didst: but I was misled by my fear.

JOCASTA

Now no more lay aught of those things to heart.

OEDIPUS

But surely I must needs fear my mother's bed?

JOCASTA

Nay, what should mortal fear, for whom the decrees of Fortune are supreme, and who hath clear foresight of nothing? 'Tis best to live at random, as one may. But fear not thou touching wedlock with thy mother. Many men ere now have so fared in dreams also: but he to whom these things are as nought bears his life most easily.

OEDIPUS

All these bold words of thine would have been well, were not my mother living; but as it is, since she lives, I must needs fear—though thou sayest well.

JOCASTA

Howbeit thy father's death is a great sign to cheer us.

OEDIPUS

Great, I know; but my fear is of her who lives.

MESSENGER

And who is the woman about whom ye fear?

OEDIPUS

Merope, old man, the consort of Polybus.

MESSENGER

And what is it in her that moves your fear?

OEDIPUS

A heaven-sent oracle of dread import, stranger.

MESSENGER

Lawful, or unlawful, for another to know?

OEDIPUS

Lawful, surely. Loxias once said that I was doomed to espouse mine own mother, and to shed with mine own hands my father's blood. Wherefore my home in Corinth was long kept by me afar; with happy event, indeed,—yet still 'tis sweet to see the face of parents.

MESSENGER

Was it indeed for fear of this that thou wast an exile from that city?

OEDIPUS

And because I wished not, old man, to be the slayer of my sire.

MESSENGER

Then why have I not freed thee, king, from this fear, seeing that I came with friendly purpose?

OEDIPUS

Indeed thou shouldst have guerdon due from me.

MESSENGER

Indeed 'twas chiefly for this that I came—that, on thy return home, I might reap some good.

OEDIPUS

Nay, I will never go near my parents.

MESSENGER

Ah my son, 'tis plain enough that thou knowest not what thou doest.

OEDIPUS

How, old man? For the gods' love, tell me.

MESSENGER

If for these reasons thou shrinkest from going home.

OEDIPUS

Aye, I dread lest Phoebus prove himself true for me.

MESSENGER

Thou dreadest to be stained with guilt through thy parents?

OEDIPUS

Even so, old man—this it is that ever affrights me.

MESSENGER

Dost thou know, then, that thy fears are wholly vain?

OEDIPUS

How so, if I was born of those parents?

MESSENGER

Because Polybus was nothing to thee in blood.

OEDIPUS

What sayest thou? Was Polybus not my sire?

MESSENGER

No more than he who speaks to thee, but just so much.

OEDIPUS

And how can my sire be level with him who is as nought to me?

MESSENGER

Nay, he begat thee not, any more than I.

OEDIPUS

Nay, wherefore, then, called he me his son?

MESSENGER

Know that he had received thee as a gift from my hands of yore.

OEDIPUS

And yet he loved me so dearly, who came from another's hand?

MESSENGER

Yea, his former childlessness won him thereto.

OEDIPUS

And thou—hadst thou bought me or found me by chance, when thou
gavest me to him?

MESSENGER

Found thee in Cithaeron's winding glens.

OEDIPUS

And wherefore wast thou roaming in those regions?

MESSENGER

I was there in charge of mountain flocks.

OEDIPUS

What, thou wast a shepherd—a vagrant hireling?

MESSENGER

But thy preserver, my son, in that hour.

OEDIPUS

And what pain was mine when thou didst take me in thine arms?

MESSENGER

The ankles of thy feet might witness.

OEDIPUS

Ah me, why dost thou speak of that old trouble?

MESSENGER

I freed thee when thou hadst thine ankles pinned together.

OEDIPUS

Aye, 'twas a dread brand of shame that I took from my cradle.

MESSENGER

Such, that from that fortune thou wast called by the name which still
is thine.

OEDIPUS

Oh, for the gods' love—was the deed my mother's or father's? Speak!

MESSENGER

I know not; he who gave thee to me wots better of that than I.

OEDIPUS

What, thou hadst me from another? Thou didst not light on me thyself?

MESSENGER

No: another shepherd gave thee up to me.

OEDIPUS

Who was he? Art thou in case to tell clearly?

MESSENGER

I think he was called one of the household of Laius.

OEDIPUS

The king who ruled this country long ago?

MESSENGER

The same: 'twas in his service that the man was a herd.

OEDIPUS

Is he still alive, that I might see him?

MESSENGER

Nay, ye folk of the country should know best.

OEDIPUS

Is there any of you here present that knows the herd of whom he speaks—that hath seen him in the pastures or the town? Answer! The hour hath come that these things should be finally revealed.

LEADER OF THE CHORUS

Methinks he speaks of no other than the peasant whom thou wast already fain to see; but our lady Jocasta might best tell that.

OEDIPUS

Lady, wottest thou of him whom we lately summoned? Is it of him that this man speaks?

JOCASTA

Why ask of whom he spoke? Regard it not . . . waste not a thought on what he said . . . 'twere idle.

OEDIPUS

It must not be that, with such clues in my grasp, I should fail to bring my birth to light.

JOCASTA

For the gods' sake, if thou hast any care for thine own life, forbear this search! My anguish is enough.

OEDIPUS

Be of good courage; though I be found the son of servile mother,—aye, a slave by three descents,—*thou* wilt not be proved base-born.

JOCASTA

Yet hear me, I implore thee: do not thus.

OEDIPUS

I must not hear of not discovering the whole truth.

JOCASTA

Yet I wish thee well—I counsel thee for the best.

OEDIPUS

These best counsels, then, vex my patience.

JOCASTA

Ill-fated one! Mayst thou never come to know who thou art!

OEDIPUS

Go, some one, fetch me the herdsman hither,—and leave yon woman to glory in her princely stock.

JOCASTA

Alas, alas, miserable!—that word alone can I say unto thee, and no other word henceforth for ever.

LEADER

Why hath the lady gone, Oedipus, in a transport of wild grief? I misdoubt, a storm of sorrow will break forth from this silence.

OEDIPUS

Break forth what will! Be my race never so lowly, I must crave to learn it. Yon woman, perchance,—for she is proud with more than a woman's pride—thinks shame of my base source. But I, who hold myself son of Fortune that gives good, will not be dishonoured. She is the mother from whom I spring; and the months, my kinsmen, have marked me sometimes lowly, sometimes great. Such being my lineage, never more can I prove false to it, or spare to search out the secret of my birth.

.   .   .

(The HERDSMAN is brought in.)

OEDIPUS

I ask thee first, Corinthian stranger, is this he whom thou meanest?

MESSENGER

This man whom thou beholdest.

OEDIPUS

Ho thou, old man—I would have thee look this way, and answer all that I ask thee. Thou wast once in the service of Laius?

HERDSMAN

I was—a slave not bought, but reared in his house.

OEDIPUS

Employed in what labour, or what way of life?

HERDSMAN

For the best part of my life I tended flocks.

OEDIPUS

And what the regions that thou didst chiefly haunt?

HERDSMAN

Sometimes it was Cithaeron, sometimes the neighbouring ground.

OEDIPUS

Then wottest thou of having noted yon man in these parts—

HERDSMAN

Doing what? . . . What man dost thou mean? . . .

OEDIPUS

This man here—or of having ever met him before?

HERDSMAN

Not so that I could speak at once from memory.

MESSENGER

And no wonder, master. But I will bring clear recollection to his ignorance. I am sure that he well wots of the time when we abode in the region of Cithaeron,—he with two flocks, I, his comrade, with one,—three full half-years, from spring to Arcturus; and then for the winter I used to drive my flock to mine own fold, and he took his to the fold of Laius. Did aught of this happen as I tell, or did it not?

HERDSMAN

Thou speakest the truth—though 'tis long ago.

MESSENGER

Come, tell me now—wottest thou of having given me a boy in those days, to be reared as mine own foster-son?

HERDSMAN

What now? Why dost thou ask the question?

MESSENGER

Yonder man, my friend, is he who then was young.

HERDSMAN

Plague seize thee—be silent once for all!

OEDIPUS

Ha! chide him not, old man—thy words need chiding more than his.

HERDSMAN

And wherein, most noble master, do I offend?

OEDIPUS

In not telling of the boy concerning whom he asks.

HERDSMAN

He speaks without knowledge—he is busy to no purpose.

OEDIPUS

Thou wilt not speak with a good grace, but thou shalt on pain.

HERDSMAN

Nay, for the gods' love, misuse not an old man!

OEDIPUS

Ho, some one—pinion him this instant!

HERDSMAN

Alas, wherefore? what more wouldst thou learn?

OEDIPUS

Didst thou give this man the child of whom he asks?

HERDSMAN

I did,—and would I had perished that day!

OEDIPUS

Well, thou wilt come to that, unless thou tell the honest truth.

HERDSMAN

Nay, much more am I lost, if I speak.

OEDIPUS

The fellow is bent, methinks, on more delays . . .

HERDSMAN

No, no!—I said before that I gave it to him.

OEDIPUS

Whence hadst thou got it? In thine own house, or from another?

HERDSMAN

Mine own it was not—I had received it from a man.

OEDIPUS

From whom of the citizens here? from what home?

HERDSMAN

Forbear, for the gods' love, master, forbear to ask more!

OEDIPUS

Thou art lost if I have to question thee again.

HERDSMAN

It was a child, then, of the house of Laius.

OEDIPUS

A slave? or one born of his own race?

HERDSMAN

Ah me—I am on the dreaded brink of speech.

OEDIPUS

And I of hearing; yet must I hear.

HERDSMAN

Thou must know, then, that 'twas said to be his own child—but thy lady within could best say how these things are.

OEDIPUS

How? She gave it to thee?

HERDSMAN

Yea, O king.

OEDIPUS

For what end?

HERDSMAN

That I should make away with it.

OEDIPUS

Her own child, the wretch?

HERDSMAN

Aye, from fear of evil prophecies.

OEDIPUS

What were they?

HERDSMAN

The tale ran that he must slay his sire.

OEDIPUS

Why, then, didst thou give him up to this old man?

HERDSMAN

Through pity, master, as deeming that he would bear him away to another land, whence he himself came; but he saved him for the direst woe. For if thou art what this man saith, know that thou wast born to misery.

OEDIPUS

Oh, oh! All brought to pass—all true! Thou light, may I now look my last on thee—I who have been found accursed in birth, accursed in wedlock, accursed in the shedding of blood!

CHORUS

Alas, ye generations of men, how mere a shadow do I count your life! Where, where is the mortal who wins more of happiness than just the seeming, and, after the semblance, a falling away? Thine is a fate that warns me,—thine, thine, unhappy Oedipus—to call no earthly creature blest.

For he, O Zeus, sped his shaft with peerless skill, and won the prize of an all-prosperous fortune; he slew the maiden with crooked talons who sang darkly; he arose for our land as a tower against death. And from that time, Oedipus, thou hast been called our king, and hast been honoured supremely, bearing sway in great Thebes.

.   .   .

SECOND MESSENGER

Ye who are ever most honoured in this land, what deeds shall ye hear, what deeds behold, what burden of sorrow shall be yours, if, true to your race, ye still care for the house of Labdacus! For I ween that not Ister nor Phasis could wash this house clean, so many are the ills that it shrouds, or will soon bring to light,—ills wrought not unwittingly, but of purpose. And those griefs smart most which are seen to be of our own choice.

LEADER

Indeed those which we knew before fall not short of claiming sore lamentation: besides them, what dost thou announce?

SECOND MESSENGER

This is the shortest tale to tell and to hear: our royal lady Jocasta is dead.

LEADER

Alas, hapless one! From what cause?

SECOND MESSENGER

By her own hand. The worst pain in what hath chanced is not for you, for yours it is not to behold. Nevertheless, so far as mine own memory serves, ye shall learn that unhappy woman's fate.

When, frantic, she had passed within the vestibule, she rushed straight towards her nuptial couch, clutching her hair with the fingers of both hands; once within the chamber, she dashed the doors together at her back; then called on the name of Laius, long since a corpse, mindful of that son, begotten long ago, by whom the sire was slain, leaving the mother to breed accursed offspring with his own.

And she bewailed the wedlock wherein, wretched, she had borne a twofold brood, husband by husband, children by her child. And how thereafter she perished, is more than I know. For with a shriek Oedipus burst in, and suffered us not to watch her woe unto the end; on him, as he rushed around, our eyes were set. To and fro he went, asking us to give him a sword,—asking where he should find the wife who was no wife, but a mother whose womb had borne alike himself and his children. And, in his frenzy, a power above man was his guide; for 'twas none of us mortals who were nigh. And with a dread shriek, as though some one beckoned him on, he sprang at the double doors, and from their sockets forced the bending bolts, and rushed into the room.

There beheld we the woman hanging by the neck in a twisted noose of swinging cords. But he, when he saw her, with a dread, deep cry of misery, loosed the halter whereby she hung. And when the hapless woman was stretched upon the ground, then was the sequel dread to see. For he tore from her raiment the golden brooches wherewith she was decked, and lifted them, and smote full on his own eye-balls, uttering words like these: "No more shall ye behold such horrors as I was suffering and working! long enough have ye looked on those whom ye ought never to have seen, failed in knowledge of those whom I yearned to know—henceforth ye shall be dark!"

To such dire refrain, not once alone but oft struck he his eyes with lifted hand; and at each blow the ensanguined eye-balls bedewed his beard, nor sent forth sluggish drops of gore, but all at once a dark shower of blood came down like hail.

From the deeds of twain such ills have broken forth, not on one alone, but with mingled woe for man and wife. The old happiness of their ancestral fortune was aforetime happiness indeed; but to-day—lamentation, ruin, death, shame, all earthly ills that can be named—all, all are theirs.

LEADER

And hath the sufferer now any respite from pain?

SECOND MESSENGER

He cries for some one to unbar the gates and show to all the Cadmeans his father's slayer, his mother's—the unholy word must not pass my lips, —as purposing to cast himself out of the land, and abide no more, to make the house accursed under his own curse. Howbeit he lacks strength, and one to guide his steps; for the anguish is more than man may bear. And he will show this to thee also; for lo, the bars of the gates are withdrawn, and soon thou shalt behold a sight which even he who abhors it must pity.

CHORUS

O dread fate for men to see, O most dreadful of all that have met mine eyes! Unhappy one, what madness hath come on thee? Who is the unearthly foe that, with a bound of more than mortal range, hath made thine ill-starred life his prey?

Alas, alas, thou hapless one! Nay, I cannot e'en look on thee, though there is much that I would fain ask, fain learn, much that draws my wistful gaze,—with such a shuddering dost thou fill me!

OEDIPUS

Woe is me! Alas, alas, wretched that I am! Whither, whither am I borne in my misery? How is my voice swept abroad on the wings of the air? Oh my Fate, how far hast thou sprung!

CHORUS

To a dread place, dire in men's ears, dire in their sight.

OEDIPUS

O thou horror of darkness that enfoldest me, visitant unspeakable, resistless, sped by a wind too fair!

Ay me! and once again, ay me!

How is my soul pierced by the stab of these goads, and withal by the memory of sorrows!

CHORUS

Yea, amid woes so many a twofold pain may well be thine to mourn and to bear.

OEDIPUS

Ah, friend, thou still art steadfast in thy tendance of me,—thou still hast patience to care for the blind man! Ah me! Thy presence is not hid from me—no, dark though I am, yet know I thy voice full well.

CHORUS

Man of dread deeds, how couldst thou in such wise quench thy vision? What more than human power urged thee?

OEDIPUS

Apollo, friends, Apollo was he that brought these my woes to pass, these my sore, sore woes: but the hand that struck the eyes was none save mine, wretched that I am! Why was I to see, when sight could show me nothing sweet?

CHORUS

These things were even as thou sayest.

OEDIPUS

Say, friends, what can I more behold, what can I love, what greeting can touch mine ear with joy? Haste, lead me from the land, friends, lead me hence, the utterly lost, the thrice accursed, yea, the mortal most abhorred of heaven!

.   .   .

CHORUS

I know not how I can say that thou hast counselled well: for thou wert better dead than living and blind.

OEDIPUS

Show me not at large that these things are not best done thus: give me counsel no more. For, had I sight, I know not with what eyes I could e'en have looked on my father, when I came to the place of the dead, aye, or on my miserable mother, since against both I have sinned such sins as strangling could not punish. But deem ye that the sight of children, born as mine were born, was lovely for me to look upon? No, no, not lovely to mine eyes for ever! No, nor was this town with its towered walls, nor the sacred statues of the gods, since I, thrice wretched that I am,—I, noblest of the sons of Thebes,—have doomed myself to know these no more, by mine own command that all should thrust away the impious one,—even him whom gods have shown to be unholy—and of the race of Laius!

After bearing such a stain upon me, was I to look with steady eyes on this folk? No, verily: no, were there yet a way to choke the fount of hearing, I had not spared to make a fast prison of this wretched frame, that so I should have known nor sight nor sound; for 'tis sweet that our thought should dwell beyond the sphere of griefs.

Alas, Cithaeron, why hadst thou a shelter for me? When I was given to thee, why didst thou not slay me straightway, that so I might never have revealed my source to men? Ah, Polybus,—ah, Corinth, and thou that wast called the ancient house of my fathers, how seeming-fair was I your nurseling, and what ills were festering beneath! For now I am found evil, and of evil birth. O ye three roads, and thou secret glen,—thou coppice, and narrow way where three paths met—ye who drank from my hands that father's blood which was mine own,—remember ye, perchance, what deeds I wrought for you to see,—and then, when I came hither, what fresh deeds I went on to do?

O marriage-rites, ye gave me birth, and when ye had brought me forth, again ye bore children to your child, ye created an incestuous kinship of fathers, brothers, sons,—brides, wives, mothers,—yea, all the foulest shame that is wrought among men! Nay, but 'tis unmeet to name what 'tis unmeet to do:—haste ye, for the gods' love, hide me somewhere beyond the land, or slay me, or cast me into the sea, where ye shall never behold me more! Approach,—deign to lay your hands on a wretched man;—hearken, fear not,—my plague can rest on no mortal beside.

LEADER

Nay, here is Creon, in meet season for thy requests, crave they act or counsel; for he alone is left to guard the land in thy stead.

OEDIPUS

Ah me, how indeed shall I accost him? What claim to credence can be shown on my part? For in the past I have been found wholly false to him.

CREON

I have not come in mockery, Oedipus, nor to reproach thee with any bygone fault. (*To the attendants.*) But ye, if ye respect the children of men no more, revere at least the all-nurturing flame of our lord the Sun,—spare to show thus nakedly a pollution such as this,—one which neither earth can welcome, nor the holy rain, nor the light. Nay, take him into the house as quickly as ye may; for it best accords with piety that kinsfolk alone should see and hear a kinsman's woes.

OEDIPUS

For the gods' love—since thou hast done a gentle violence to my presage, who hast come in a spirit so noble to me, a man most vile—grant me a boon: for thy good I will speak, not for mine own.

CREON

And what wish art thou so fain to have of me?

OEDIPUS

Cast me out of this land with all speed, to a place where no mortal shall be found to greet me more.

CREON

This would I have done, be thou sure, but that I craved first to learn all my duty from the god.

OEDIPUS

Nay, his behest hath been set forth in full,—to let me perish, the parricide, the unholy one, that I am.

CREON

Such was the purport; yet, seeing to what a pass we have come, 'tis better to learn clearly what should be done.

OEDIPUS

Will ye, then, seek a response on behalf of such a wretch as I am?

CREON

Aye, for thou thyself wilt now surely put faith in the god.

OEDIPUS

Yea; and on thee lay I this charge, to thee will I make this entreaty:— give to her who is within such burial as thou thyself wouldest; for thou wilt meetly render the last rites to thine own. But for me—never let this city of my sire be condemned to have me dwelling therein, while I live: no, suffer me to abide on the hills, where yonder is Cithaeron, famed as mine,—which my mother and sire, while they lived, set for my appointed tomb,—that so I may die by their decree who sought to slay me. Howbeit of thus much am I sure,—that neither sickness nor aught else can destroy me; for never had I been snatched from death, but in reserve for some strange doom.

Nay, let *my* fate go whither it will: but as touching my children,—I pray thee, Creon, take no care on thee for my sons; they are men, so that, be they where they may, they can never lack the means to live. But my two girls, poor hapless ones,—who never knew my table spread apart, or lacked their father's presence, but ever in all things shared my daily bread,—I pray thee, care for *them;* and—if thou canst—suffer me to touch them with my hands, and to indulge my grief. Grant it, prince, grant it, thou noble heart! Ah, could I but once touch them with my hands, I should think that they were with me, even as when I had sight.

Ha? O ye gods, can it be my loved ones that I hear sobbing,—can Creon have taken pity on me and sent me my children—my darlings? Am I right?

CREON

Yea: 'tis of my contriving, for I knew thy joy in them of old,—the joy that now is thine.

OEDIPUS

Then blessed be thou, and, for guerdon of this errand, may heaven prove to thee a kinder guardian than it hath to me! My children, where are ye? Come hither,—hither to the hands of him whose mother was your own, the hands whose offices have wrought that your sire's once bright eyes should be such orbs as these,—his, who seeing nought, knowing nought, became your father by her from whom he sprang! For you also do I weep—behold you I cannot—when I think of the bitter life in days to come which men will make you live. To what company of the citizens will ye go, to what festival, from which ye shall not return home in tears, instead of sharing in the holiday? But when ye are now come to years ripe for marriage, who shall he be, who shall be the man, my daughters, that will hazard taking unto him such reproaches as must be baneful alike to my offspring and to yours? For what misery is wanting? Your sire slew his sire, he had seed of her who bare him, and begat you at the sources of his own being! Such are the taunts that will be cast at you; and who then will wed? The man lives not, no, it cannot be, my children, but ye must wither in barren maidenhood.

Ah, son of Menoeceus, hear me—since thou art the only father left to them, for we, their parents, are lost, both of us,—allow them not to wander poor and unwed, who are thy kinswomen, nor abase them to the level of my woes. Nay, pity them, when thou seest them at this tender age so utterly forlorn, save for thee. Signify thy promise, generous man, by the touch of thy hand! To you, my children, I would have given much counsel, were your minds mature; but now I would have this to be your prayer—that ye live where occasion suffers, and that the life which is your portion may be happier than your sire's.

CREON

Thy grief hath had large scope enough: nay, pass into the house.

OEDIPUS

I must obey, though 'tis in no wise sweet.

CREON

Yea: for it is in season that all things are good.

OEDIPUS

Knowest thou, then, on what conditions I will go?

CREON

Thou shalt name them; so shall I know them when I hear.

OEDIPUS

See that thou send me to dwell beyond this land.

CREON

Thou askest me for what the god must give.

OEDIPUS

Nay, to the gods I have become most hateful.

CREON

Then shalt thou have thy wish anon.

OEDIPUS

So thou consentest?

CREON

'Tis not my wont to speak idly what I do not mean.

OEDIPUS

Then 'tis time to lead me hence.

CREON

Come, then,—but let thy children go.

OEDIPUS

Nay, take not these from me!

CREON

Crave not to be master in all things: for the mastery which thou didst win hath not followed thee through life.

CHORUS

Dwellers in our native Thebes, behold, this is Oedipus, who knew the famed riddle, and was a man most mighty; on whose fortunes what citizen did not gaze with envy? Behold into what a stormy sea of dread trouble he hath come!

Therefore, while our eyes wait to see the destined final day, we must call no one happy who is of mortal race, until he hath crossed life's border, free from pain.

EURIPIDES

FROM HIPPOLYTUS

APHRODITE

Wide o'er man my realm extends, and proud the name that I, the goddess Cypris, bear, both in heaven's courts and 'mongst all those who dwell within the limits of the sea and the bounds of Atlas, beholding the sun-god's light; those that respect my power I advance to honour, but bring to ruin all who vaunt themselves at me. For even in the race of gods this feeling finds a home, even pleasure at the honour men pay them. And the truth of this I soon will show; for that son of Theseus, born of the Amazon, Hippolytus, whom holy Pittheus taught, alone of all the dwellers in this land of Troezen, calls me vilest of the deities. Love he scorns, and, as for marriage, will none of it; but Artemis, daughter of Zeus, sister of Phoebus, he doth honour, counting her the chief of goddesses, and ever through the greenwood, attendant on his virgin goddess, he clears the earth of wild beasts with his fleet hounds, enjoying the comradeship of one too high for mortal ken. 'Tis not this I grudge him, no! why should I? But for his sins against me, I will this very day take vengeance on Hippolytus; for long ago I cleared the ground of many obstacles, so it needs but trifling toil. For as he came one day from the home of Pittheus to witness the solemn mystic rites and be initiated therein in Pandion's land, Phaedra, his father's noble wife, caught sight of him, and by my designs she found her heart was seized with wild desire. And ere she came to this Troezenian realm, a temple did she rear to Cypris hard by the rock of Pallas where it o'erlooks this country, for love of the youth in another land; and to win his love in days to come she called after his name the temple she had founded for the goddess. Now, when Theseus left the land of Cecrops, flying the pollution of the blood of Pallas' sons, and with his wife sailed to this shore, content to suffer exile for a year, then began the wretched wife to pine away in silence, moaning 'neath love's cruel scourge, and none of her servants knows what disease afflicts her. But this passion of hers must not fail thus. No, I will discover the matter to Theseus, and all shall be laid bare. Then will the father slay his child, my bitter foe, by curses, for the lord Poseidon granted this boon to Theseus; three wishes of the god to ask, nor ever ask in vain. So Phaedra is to die, an honoured death 'tis true, but still to die; for I will not let her suffering outweigh the payment of such forfeit by my foes as shall satisfy my honour. But lo!

I see the son of Theseus coming hither—Hippolytus, fresh from the labours of the chase. I will get me hence. At his back follows a long train of retainers, in joyous cries of revelry uniting and hymns of praise to Artemis, his goddness; for little he recks that Death hath oped his gates for him, and that this is his last look upon the light.

. . .

(APHRODITE *vanishes.* PHAEDRA, *her* NURSE *and the* CHORUS *enter.*)

PHAEDRA

What is is they mean when they talk of people being in "love"?

NURSE

At once the sweetest and the bitterest thing, my child.

PHAEDRA

I shall only find the latter half.

NURSE

Ha! my child, art thou in love?

PHAEDRA

The Amazon's son, whoever he may be—

NURSE

Mean'st thou Hippolytus?

PHAEDRA

'Twas thou, not I, that spoke his name.

NURSE

O heavens! what is this, my child? Thou hast ruined me. Outrageous! friends; I will not live and bear it; hateful is life, hateful to mine eyes the light. This body I resign, will cast it off, and rid me of existence by my death. Farewell, my life is o'er. Yea, for the chaste have wicked passions, 'gainst their will maybe, but still they have. Cypris, it seems, is not a goddess after all, but something greater far, for she hath been the ruin of my lady and of me and our whole family.

CHORUS

O, too clearly didst thou hear our queen uplift her voice to tell her startling tale of piteous suffering. Come death ere I reach thy state of feeling, loved mistress. O horrible! woe, for these miseries! woe, for the sorrows on which mortals feed! Thou art undone! thou hast disclosed thy sin to heaven's light. What hath each passing day and every hour in store for thee? Some strange event will come to pass in this house. For it is no longer uncertain where the star of thy love is setting, thou hapless daughter of Crete.

PHAEDRA

Women of Troezen, who dwell here upon the frontier edge of Pelops' land, oft ere now in heedless mood through the long hours of night have I wondered why man's life is spoiled; and it seems to me their evil case is not due to any natural fault of judgment, for there be many dowered with sense, but we must view the matter in this light: by teaching and experience we learn the right but neglect it in practice, some from sloth, others from preferring pleasure of some kind or other to duty. Now life has many pleasures, protracted talk, and leisure, that seductive evil; likewise there is shame which is of two kinds, one a noble quality, the other a curse to families; but if for each its proper time were clearly known, these twain could not have had the selfsame letters to denote them. So then since I had made up my mind on these points, 'twas not likely any drug would alter it and make me think the contrary. And I will tell thee too the way my judgment went. When love wounded me, I bethought me how I best might bear the smart. So from that day forth I began to hide in silence what I suffered. For I put no faith in counsellors, who know well to lecture others for presumption, yet themselves have countless troubles of their own. Next I did devise noble endurance of these wanton thoughts, striving by continence for victory. And last when I could not succeed in mastering love hereby, methought it best to die; and none can gainsay my purpose. For fain I would my virtue should to all appear, my shame have few to witness it. I knew my sickly passion now; to yield to it I saw how infamous; and more, I learnt to know so well that I was but a woman, a thing the world detests. Curses, hideous curses on that wife who first did shame her marriage-vow for lovers other than her lord! . . .

LEADER OF THE CHORUS

Now look! how fair is chastity however viewed, whose fruit is good repute amongst men.

NURSE

My queen, 'tis true thy tale of woe, but lately told, did for the moment strike me with wild alarm, but now I do reflect upon my foolishness; second thoughts are often best even with men. Thy fate is no uncommon one nor past one's calculations; thou art stricken by the passion Cypris sends. Thou art in love; what wonder? so are many more. Wilt thou, because thou lov'st, destroy thyself? 'Tis little gain, I trow, for those who love or yet may love their fellows, if death must be their end; for though the Love-Queen's onset in her might is more than man can bear, yet doth she gently visit yielding hearts, and only when she finds a proud unnatural spirit, doth she take and mock it past belief. Her path is in the sky, and mid the ocean's surge she rides; from her all nature springs; she sows the seeds of love, inspires the warm desire to which we sons of earth all owe our being. . . .

LEADER

Although she gives thee at thy present need the wiser counsel, Phaedra, yet do I praise thee. Still my praise may sound more harsh and jar more cruelly on thy ear than her advice.

PHAEDRA

'Tis even this, too plausible a tongue, that overthrows good governments and homes of men. We should not speak to please the ear but point the path that leads to noble fame.

NURSE

What means this solemn speech? Thou needst not rounded phrases,— but a man. Straightway must we move to tell him frankly how it is with thee. Had not thy life to such a crisis come, or wert thou with self-control endowed, ne'er would I to gratify thy passions have urged thee to this course; but now 'tis a struggle fierce to save thy life, and therefore less to blame.

PHAEDRA

Accursed proposal! peace, woman! never utter those shameful words again!

NURSE

Shameful, maybe, yet for thee better than honour's code. Better this deed, if it shall save thy life, than that name thy pride will kill thee to retain.

PHAEDRA

I conjure thee, go no further! for thy words are plausible but infamous; for though as yet love has not undermined my soul, yet, if in specious words thou dress thy foul suggestion, I shall be beguiled into the snare from which I am now escaping.

NURSE

If thou art of this mind, 'twere well thou ne'er hadst sinned; but as it is, hear me; for that is the next best course; I in my house have charms to soothe thy love,—'twas but now I thought of them;—these shall cure

20. Oinochoe (for pouring wine).

thee of thy sickness on no disgraceful terms, thy mind unhurt, if thou wilt be but brave. But from him thou lovest we must get some token, a word or fragment of his robe, and thereby unite in one love's twofold stream.

PHAEDRA

Is thy drug a salve or potion?

NURSE

I cannot tell; be content, my child, to profit by it and ask no questions.

PHAEDRA

I fear me thou wilt prove too wise for me.

NURSE

If thou fear this, confess thyself afraid of all; but why thy terror?

PHAEDRA

Lest thou shouldst breathe a word of this to Theseus' son.

NURSE

Peace, my child! I will do all things well; only be thou, queen Cypris, ocean's child, my partner in the work! And for the rest of my purpose, it will be enough for me to tell it to our friends within the house.

CHORUS

O Love, Love, that from the eyes diffusest soft desire, bringing on the souls of those, whom thou dost camp against, sweet grace, O never in evil mood appear to me, nor out of time and tune approach! Nor fire nor meteor hurl a mightier bolt than Aphrodite's shaft shot by the hands of Love, the child of Zeus.

.　　.　　.

PHAEDRA

Peace, oh women, peace! I am undone.

LEADER OF THE CHORUS

What, Phaedra, is this dread event within thy house?

PHAEDRA

Hush! let me hear what those within are saying.

LEADER

I am silent; this is surely the prelude to evil.

PHAEDRA

Great gods! how awful are my sufferings!

CHORUS

What a cry was there! what loud alarm! say what sudden terror, lady, doth thy soul dismay.

PHAEDRA

I am undone. Stand here at the door and hear the noise arising in the house.

CHORUS

Thou art already by the bolted door; 'tis for thee to note the sounds that issue from within. And tell me, O tell me what evil can be on foot.

PHAEDRA

'Tis the son of the horse-loving Amazon who calls, Hippolytus, uttering foul curses on my servant.

CHORUS

I hear a noise, but cannot clearly tell which way it comes. Ah! 'tis through the door the sound reached thee.

PHAEDRA

Yes, yes, he is calling her plainly enough a go-between in vice, traitress to her master's honour.

CHORUS

Woe, woe is me! thou art betrayed, dear mistress! What counsel shall I give thee? thy secret is out; thou art utterly undone.

PHAEDRA

Ah me! ah me!

CHORUS

Betrayed by friends!

PHAEDRA

She hath ruined me by speaking of my misfortune; 'twas kindly meant, but an ill way to cure my malady.

LEADER OF THE CHORUS

O what wilt thou do now in thy cruel dilemma?

PHAEDRA

I only know one way, one cure for these woes, and that is instant death.

> (HIPPOLYTUS *bursts out of the palace,*
> *followed closely by the* NURSE.)

HIPPOLYTUS

O mother earth! O sun's unclouded orb! What words, unfit for any lips, have reached my ears!

NURSE

Peace, my son, lest some one hear thy outcry.

HIPPOLYTUS

I cannot hear such awful words and hold my peace.

NURSE

I do implore thee by thy fair right hand.

HIPPOLYTUS

Let go my hand, touch not my robe.

NURSE

O by thy knees I pray, destroy me not utterly.

HIPPOLYTUS

Why say this, if, as thou pretendest, thy lips are free from blame?

NURSE

My son, this is no story to be noised abroad.

HIPPOLYTUS

A virtuous tale grows fairer told to many.

NURSE

Never dishonour thy oath, my son.

HIPPOLYTUS

My tongue an oath did take, but not my heart.

NURSE

My son, what wilt thou do? destroy thy friends?

HIPPOLYTUS

Friends indeed! the wicked are no friends of mine.

NURSE

O pardon me; to err is only human, child.

HIPPOLYTUS

Great Zeus, why didst thou, to man's sorrow, put woman, evil counter-feit, to dwell where shines the sun? If thou wert minded that the human race should multiply, it was not from women they should have drawn their stock, but in thy temples they should have paid gold or iron or ponderous bronze and bought a family, each man proportioned to his offering, and so in independence dwelt, from women free. But now as soon as ever we would bring this plague into our home we bring its fortune to the ground. . . . Even thus, vile wretch, thou cam'st to make me partner in an outrage on my father's honour; wherefore I must wash that stain away in running streams, dashing the water into my ears. How could I commit so foul a crime when by the very mention of it I feel myself polluted? Be well assured, woman, 'tis only my religious scruple saves thee. For had not I unawares been caught by an oath, 'fore heaven! I would not have refrained from telling all unto my father. But now I will from the house away, so long as Theseus is abroad, and will maintain a strict silence. But, when my father comes, I will return and see how thou and thy mistress face him, and so shall I learn by experi-ence the extent of thy audacity. Perdition seize you both! I can never satisfy my hate for women, no! not even though some say this is ever my theme, for of a truth they always are evil. So either let some one prove them chaste, or let me still trample on them for ever.

(HIPPOLYTUS *departs angrily*.)

PHAEDRA

. . . I, with all my thought, can but one way discover out of this calamity, that so I may secure my children's honour, and find myself some help as matters stand. For never, never will I bring shame upon my Cretan home, nor will I, to save one poor life, face Theseus after my disgrace.

LEADER

Art thou bent then on some cureless woe?

PHAEDRA

On death; the means thereto must I devise myself.

LEADER

Hush!

PHAEDRA

Do thou at least advise me well. For this very day shall I gladden Cypris, my destroyer, by yielding up my life, and shall own myself vanquished by cruel love. Yet shall my dying be another's curse, that he may learn not to exult at my misfortunes; but when he comes to share the self-same plague with me, he will take a lesson in wisdom.

.   .   .

NURSE

Help! ho! To the recue all who near the palace stand! She hath hung herself, our queen, the wife of Theseus.

LEADER OF THE CHORUS

Woe worth the day! the deed is done; our royal mistress is no more, dead she hangs in the dangling noose.

NURSE

Haste! some one bring a two-edged knife wherewith to cut the knot about her neck.

FIRST SEMI-CHORUS

Friends, what shall we do? think you we should enter the house, and loose the queen from the tight-drawn noose?

SECOND SEMI-CHORUS

Why should *we*? Are there not young servants here? To do too much is not a safe course in life.

NURSE

Lay out the hapless corpse, straighten the limbs. This was a bitter way to sit at home and keep my master's house!

LEADER OF THE CHORUS

She is dead, poor lady; 'tis this I hear. Already are they laying out the corpse.

THE ADVENTURE OF THE SPIRIT

(THESEUS *and his attendants have entered, unnoticed.*)

THESEUS

Women, can ye tell me what the uproar in the palace means? There came the sound of servants weeping bitterly to mine ear. None of my household deign to open wide the gates and give me glad welcome as a traveller from prophetic shrines. Hath aught befallen old Pittheus? No. Though he be well advanced in years, yet should I mourn, were he to quit this house.

LEADER

'Tis not against the old, Theseus, that fate, to strike thee, aims this blow; prepare thy sorrow for a younger corpse.

THESEUS

Woe is me! is it a child's life death robs me of?

LEADER

They live; but, cruellest news of all for thee, their mother is no more.

THESEUS

What! my wife dead? By what cruel stroke of chance?

LEADER

About her neck she tied the hangman's knot.

THESEUS

Had grief so chilled her blood? or what had befallen her?

LEADER

I know but this, for I am myself but now arrived at the house to mourn thy sorrows, O Theseus.

THESEUS

Woe is me! why have I crowned my head with woven garlands, when misfortune greets my embassage? Unbolt the doors, servants, loose their fastenings, that I may see the piteous sight, my wife, whose death is death to me.

CHORUS

Woe! woe is thee for thy piteous lot! thou hast done thyself a hurt deep enough to overthrow this family. Ah! ah! the daring of it! done to death by violence and unnatural means, the desperate effort of thy own poor hand! Who cast the shadow o'er thy life, poor lady?

THESEUS

Ah me, my cruel lot! sorrow hath done her worst on me. O fortune, how heavily hast thou set thy foot on me and on my house, by fiendish hands inflicting an unexpected stain? Nay, 'tis complete effacement of my life, making it not to be lived; for I see, alas! so wide an ocean of grief that I can never swim to shore again, nor breast the tide of this calamity. How shall I speak of thee, my poor wife, what tale of direst suffering tell? Thou art vanished like a bird from the covert of my hand, taking one headlong leap from me to Hades' halls. Alas, and woe! this is a bitter, bitter sight! This must be a judgment sent by God for the sins of an ancestor, which from some far source I am bringing on myself.

LEADER OF THE CHORUS

My prince, 'tis not to thee alone such sorrows come; thou hast lost a noble wife, but so have many others.

．　　．　　．

THESEUS

Ha! what means this letter? clasped in her dear hand it hath some strange tale to tell. Hath she, poor lady, as a last request, written her bidding as to my marriage and her children? Take heart, poor ghost; no wife henceforth shall wed thy Theseus or invade his house. Ah! how yon seal of my dead wife stamped with her golden ring affects my sight! Come, I will unfold the sealed packed and read her letter's message to me.

CHORUS

Woe unto us! Here is yet another evil in the train by heaven sent. Looking to what has happened I should count my lot in life no longer worth one's while to gain. My master's house, alas! is ruined, brought to naught, I say. Spare it, O Heaven, if it may be. Hearken to my prayer, for I see, as with prophetic eye, an omen boding ill.

THESEUS

O horror! woe on woe! and still they come, too deep for words, too heavy to bear. Ah me!

LEADER OF THE CHORUS

What is it? speak, if I may share in it.

THESEUS

This letter loudly tells a hideous tale! where can I escape my load of woe? For I am ruined and undone, so awful are the words I find here written clear as if she cried them to me; woe is me!

LEADER

Alas! thy words declare themselves the harbingers of woe.

THESEUS

I can no longer keep the cursed tale within the portals of my lips, cruel though its utterance be. Ah me! Hippolytus hath dared by brutal force to violate my honour, recking naught of Zeus, whose awful eye is over all. O father Poseidon, once didst thou promise to fulfil three prayers of mine; answer one of these and slay my son, let him not escape this single day, if the prayers thou gavest me were indeed with issue fraught.

LEADER

O king, I do conjure thee, call back that prayer; hereafter thou wilt know thy error. Hear, I pray.

THESEUS

It cannot be! Moreover I will banish him from this land, and by one of two fates shall he be struck down; either Poseidon, out of respect to my prayer, will cast his dead body into the house of Hades; or exiled from this land, a wanderer to some foreign shore, shall he eke out a life of misery.

.   .   .

HIPPOLYTUS

The sentence then, it seems, is passed. Ah, misery! How well I know the truth herein, but know no way to tell it! O daughter of Latona, dearest to me of all deities, partner, comrade in the chase, far from glorious Athens must I fly. Farewell, city and land of Erechtheus; farewell, Troezen, most joyous home wherein to pass the spring of life; 'tis my last sight of thee, farewell! Come, my comrades in this land, young like me, greet me kindly and escort me forth, for never will ye behold a purer soul, for all my father's doubts.

CHORUS

In very deed the thoughts I have about the gods, whenso they come into my mind, do much to soothe its grief, but though I cherish secret hopes of some great guiding will, yet am I at fault when I survey the fate and doings of the sons of men; change succeeds to change, and man's life veers and shifts in endless restlessness.

.   .   .

LEADER OF THE CHORUS

But lo! I see a servant of Hippolytus hasting with troubled looks towards the palace.

MESSENGER

Ladies, where may I find Theseus, king of the country? pray, tell me if ye know; is he within the palace here?

LEADER

Lo! himself approaches from the palace.

MESSENGER

Theseus, I am the bearer of troublous tidings to thee and all citizens who dwell in Athens or the bounds of Troezen.

THESEUS

How now? hath some strange calamity o'ertaken these two neighbouring cities?

MESSENGER

In one brief word, Hippolytus is dead. 'Tis true one slender thread still links him to the light of life.

THESEUS

Who slew him? Did some husband come to blows with him, one whose wife, like mine, had suffered brutal violence?

MESSENGER

He perished through those steeds that drew his chariot, and through the curses thou didst utter, praying to thy sire, the ocean-king, to slay thy son.

THESEUS

Ye gods and king Poseidon, thou hast proved my parentage by hearkening to my prayer! Say how he perished; how fell the uplifted hand of Justice to smite the villain who dishonoured me?

MESSENGER

Hard by the wave-beat shore were we combing out his horses' manes, weeping the while, for one had come to say that Hippolytus was harshly exiled by thee and nevermore would return to set foot in this land. Then came he, telling the same doleful tale to us upon the beach, and with him was a countless throng of friends who followed after. At length he stayed his lamentation and spake: "Why weakly rave on this wise? My father's commands must be obeyed. Ho! servants, harness my horses to the chariot; this is no longer now city of mine." Thereupon each one of us bestirred himself, and, ere a man could say 'twas done, we had the horses standing ready at our master's side. Then he caught up the reins from the chariot-rail, first fitting his feet exactly in the hollows made for them. But first with outspread palms he called upon the gods, "O Zeus, now strike me dead, if I have sinned, and let my father learn how he is wronging me, in death at least, if not in life." Therewith he seized the whip and lashed each horse in turn; while we, close by his chariot, near the reins, kept up with him along the road that leads direct to Argos and Epidaurus. And just as we were coming to a desert spot, a strip of sand beyond the borders of this country, sloping right to the Saronic gulf, there issued thence a deep rumbling sound, as it were an earthquake, a fearsome noise, and the horses reared their heads and pricked their ears, while we were filled with wild alarm to know whence came the sound; when, as we gazed toward the wave-beat shore, a wave tremendous we beheld towering to the skies, so that from our view the cliffs of Sciron vanished, for it hid the isthmus and the rock of Asclepius; then swelling and frothing with a crest of foam, the sea discharged it toward the beach where stood the harnessed car, and in the moment that it broke, that mighty wall of waters, there issued from the wave a monstrous bull, whose bellowing filled the land with fearsome echoes, a sight too awful as it seemed to us who witnessed it. A panic seized the horses there and then, but our master, to horses' ways quite used, gripped in both hands his reins, and tying them to his body pulled them backward as the sailor pulls his oars; but the horses gnashed the forged bits between their teeth and bore him wildly on, regardless of their master's guiding hand or rein or jointed car. And oft as he would take the guiding rein and steer for softer ground, showed that bull in front to turn him back again, maddening his team with terror; but if in their frantic career they ran towards the rocks, he would draw nigh the chariot-rail, keeping up with them, until, suddenly dashing the wheel against a stone, he upset and wrecked the car; then was dire confusion, axle-boxes and linchpins springing into the air. While he, poor youth, entangled in the reins was dragged along, bound by a stubborn knot, his poor head dashed against the rocks, his flesh all torn, the while he cried out piteously, "Stay, stay, my horses whom my own hand hath fed at the manger, destroy me not utterly. O luckless curse of a father! Will no one come and save me for all my virtue?" Now we, though much we longed to help, were left far behind. At last, I know not how, he broke loose from the shapely reins that bound him, a faint breath of life still in him; but the horses disappeared, and that portentous bull, among the rocky ground, I know not where. I am but a slave in thy house, 'tis true, O king, yet will I never believe so monstrous a charge against thy son's character, no! not though the whole race of womankind should hang itself, or one should fill with writing every pine-tree tablet grown on Ida, sure as I am of his uprightness.

LEADER

Alas! new troubles come to plague us, nor is there any escape from fate and necessity.

THESEUS

My hatred for him who hath thus suffered made me glad at thy tidings, yet from regard for the gods and him, because he is my son, I feel neither joy nor sorrow at his sufferings.

MESSENGER

But say, are we to bring the victim hither, or how are we to fulfil thy wishes? Bethink thee; if by me thou wilt be schooled, thou wilt not harshly treat thy son in his sad plight.

THESEUS

Bring him hither, that when I see him face to face, who hath denied having polluted my wife's honour, I may by words and heaven's visitation convict him.

.   .   .

ARTEMIS

Hearken, Theseus; I will put thy wretched case. Yet will it naught avail thee, if I do, but vex thy heart; still with this intent I came, to show thy son's pure heart,—that he may die with honour,—as well the frenzy and, in a sense, the nobleness of thy wife; for she was cruelly stung with a passion for thy son by that goddess whom all we, that joy in virgin purity, detest. And though she strove to conquer love by resolution, yet by no fault of hers she fell, thanks to her nurse's strategy, who did reveal her malady unto thy son under oath. But he would none of her counsels, as indeed was right, nor yet, when thou didst revile him, would he break the oath he swore, from piety. She meantime, fearful of being found out, wrote a lying letter, destroying by guile thy son, but yet persuading thee.

THESEUS

Woe is me!

ARTEMIS

Doth my story wound thee, Theseus? Be still awhile; hear what follows, so wilt thou have more cause to groan. Dost remember those three prayers thy father granted thee, fraught with certain issue? 'Tis one of these thou hast misused, unnatural wretch, against thy son, instead of aiming it at an enemy. Thy sea-god sire, 'tis true, for all his kind intent, hath granted that boon he was compelled, by reason of his promise, to grant. But thou alike in his eyes and in mine hast shewn thy evil heart, in that thou hast forestalled all proof or voice prophetic, hast made no inquiry, nor taken time for consideration, but with undue haste cursed thy son even to the death.

THESEUS

Perdition seize me! Queen revered!

ARTEMIS

An awful deed was thine, but still even for this thou mayest obtain pardon; for it was Cypris that would have it so, sating the fury of her soul. For this is law amongst us gods; none of us will thwart his neighbour's will, but ever we stand aloof. For be well assured, did I not fear Zeus, never would I have incurred the bitter shame of handing over to death a man of all his kind to me most dear. As for thy sin, first thy ignorance absolves thee from its villainy, next thy wife, who is dead, was lavish in her use of convincing arguments to influence thy mind. On thee in chief this storm of woe hath burst, yet is it some grief to me as well; for when the righteous die, there is no joy in heaven, albeit we try to destroy the wicked, house and home.

CHORUS

Lo! where he comes, this hapless youth, his fair young flesh and auburn locks most shamefully handled. Unhappy house! what twofold sorrow doth o'ertake its halls, through heaven's ordinance!

HIPPOLYTUS

Ah! ah! woe is me! foully undone by an impious father's impious imprecation! Undone, undone! woe is me! Through my head dart fearful pains; my brain throbs convulsively. Stop, let me rest my worn-out frame. Oh, oh! Accursed steeds, that mine own hand did feed, ye have been my ruin and my death. O by the gods, good sirs, I beseech ye, softly touch my wounded limbs. Who stands there at my right side? Lift me tenderly; with slow and even step conduct a poor wretch cursed by his mistaken sire. Great Zeus, dost thou see this? Me thy reverent worshipper, me who left all men behind in purity, plunged thus into yawning Hades 'neath the earth, reft of life; in vain the toils I have endured through my piety towards mankind. Ah me! ah me! O the thrill of anguish shooting through me! Set me down, poor wretch I am; come Death to set me free! Kill me, end my sufferings. . . .

ARTEMIS

Poor sufferer! cruel the fate that links thee to it! Thy noble soul hath been thy ruin.

HIPPOLYTUS

Ah! the fragrance from my goddess wafted! Even in my agony I feel thee near and find relief; she is here in this very place, my goddess Artemis.

ARTEMIS

She is, poor sufferer! the goddess thou hast loved the best.

HIPPOLYTUS

Dost see me, mistress mine? dost see my present suffering?

ARTEMIS

I see thee, but mine eyes no tear may weep.

HIPPOLYTUS

Thou hast none now to lead the hunt or tend thy fane.

ARTEMIS

None now; yet e'en in death I love thee still.

HIPPOLYTUS

None to groom thy steeds, or guard thy shrines.

ARTEMIS

'Twas Cypris, mistress of iniquity, devised this evil.

HIPPOLYTUS

Ah me! now know I the goddess who destroyed me.

ARTEMIS

She was jealous of her slighted honour, vexed at thy chaste life.

HIPPOLYTUS

Ah! then I see her single hand hath struck down three of us.

ARTEMIS

Thy sire and thee, and last thy father's wife.

HIPPOLYTUS

My sire's ill-luck as well as mine I mourn.

ARTEMIS

He was deceived by a goddess's design.

HIPPOLYTUS

Woe is thee, my father, in this sad mischance!

THESEUS

My son, I am a ruined man; life has no joys for me.

HIPPOLYTUS

For this mistake I mourn thee rather than myself.

THESEUS

O that I had died for thee, my son!

HIPPOLYTUS

Ah! those fatal gifts thy sire Poseidon gave.

THESEUS

Would God these lips had never uttered that prayer!

HIPPOLYTUS

Why not? thou wouldst in any case have slain me in thy fury then.

THESEUS

Yes; Heaven had perverted my power to think.

HIPPOLYTUS

O that the race of men could bring a curse upon the gods!

ARTEMIS

Enough! for though thou pass to gloom beneath the earth, the wrath of Cypris shall not, at her will, fall on thee unrequited, because thou hadst a noble righteous soul. For I with mine own hand will with these unerring shafts avenge me on another, who is her votary, dearest to her of all the sons of men. And to thee, poor sufferer, for thy anguish now will I grant high honours in the city of Troezen; for thee shall maids unwed before their marriage cut off their hair, thy harvest through the long roll of time of countless bitter tears. Yea, and for ever shall the virgin choir hymn thy sad memory, nor shall Phaedra's love for thee fall into oblivion and pass away unnoticed. But thou, O son of old Aegeus, take thy son in thine arms, draw him close to thee, for unwittingly thou slewest him, and men may well commit an error when gods put it in their way. And thee Hippolytus, I admonish; hate not thy sire, for in this death thou dost but meet thy destined fate. And now farewell! 'tis not for me to gaze upon the dead, or pollute my sight with death-scenes, and e'en now I see thee nigh that evil.

HIPPOLYTUS

Farewell, blest virgin queen! leave me now! Easily thou resignest our long friendship! I am reconciled with my father at thy desire, yea, for ever before I would obey thy bidding. Ah me! the darkness is settling even now upon my eyes. Take me, father, in thy arms, lift me up.

THESEUS

Woe is me, my son! what art thou doing to me thy hapless sire!

HIPPOLYTUS

I am a broken man; yes, I see the gates that close upon the dead.

THESEUS

Canst leave me thus with murder on my soul!

HIPPOLYTUS

No, no; I set thee free from this bloodguiltiness.

THESEUS

What sayest thou? dost absolve me from bloodshed?

HIPPOLYTUS

Artemis, the archer-queen, is my witness that I do.

THESEUS

My own dear child, how generous dost thou show thyself to thy father!

HIPPOLYTUS

Farewell, dear father! a long farewell to thee!

THESEUS

O that holy, noble soul of thine!

HIPPOLYTUS

Pray to have children such as me born in lawful wedlock.

THESEUS

O leave me not, my son; endure awhile.

HIPPOLYTUS

'Tis finished, my endurance; I die, father; quickly veil my face with a mantle.

THESEUS

O glorious Athens, realm of Pallas, what a splendid hero ye have lost! Ah me, ah me! How oft shall I remember thy evil works, O Cypris!

CHORUS

On all our citizens hath come this universal sorrow, unforeseen. Now shall the copious tear gush forth, for sad news about great men takes more than usual hold upon the heart.

ARISTOPHANES

FROM THE BIRDS

Two Greek mortals, Pithetaerus and Euelpides, have come to the land of the birds, seeking a peaceful life. In this political fantasy, they eventually place the supreme cosmic power in the hands of the birds.

.   .   .

EUELPIDES

Are we going to have dinner, or what?

PITHETAERUS

Why no; but by Zeus, I'm warming a speech, a large one,
    luscious and hot,

Which will ravish the hearts of all hearers; [*to the* CHORUS]
    my own so bleeds for you and your fall.

To think that of old you were kings!

LEADER

Us Kings? Why, what were we kings of?

PITHETAERUS

Of all!

Yes, all that there is; of me and of him; of Zeus, that usurper
    so bold.

You are older in birth than Cronos himself, more prime than
    the Titans of old.

And the Earth.

LEADER

And the Earth?

PITHETAERUS

By Apollo, you are.

LEADER

That is something I never had heard.

PITHETAERUS

You are not educated. You never inquire. Of your Aesop you
    don't know a word.

He says in his book that the first thing alive was a lark. All
    lonely she flew,

Before even the Earth, till her father took ill, and died on her
    out of the blue.

And no earth was there, so she sat in despair while for five
    long days he lay dead,

Till at last she thought best to develop a crest and bury him
    there in her head.

EUELPIDES

Is that what the great first Father of larks amounts to, a mere
    dead head?

PITHETAERUS

Then doesn't it follow, since older they are than the gods, yes,
    older than earth

If the laws of primogeniture hold, the Kingdom is theirs by
    birth?

EUELPIDES

Then the first thing for you to devote yourself to is growing
    a beak of your own;

Great Zeus of the Oak won't find it a joke when the Wood-
    pecker sits on his throne.

.   .   .

LEADER

O Humans, ye natures so dimly alive, like leaves that blossom
    and fade,

Ye little-achievers, creations of clay, impermanent tribes of the
    shade,

Ephemeral, wingless, much-suffering mortals, Men! Men that
    are shapes of a dream,

To Us, the immortal, surrender your minds, Us ever alive and
    a-gleam;

Us, dwellers in heaven, eternally young, whose mysteries never
    shall die,

Till ye learn from our teaching the ultimate truths, the secrets
    of stars and of sky,

The Being of Birds, the Becoming of Gods, Streams, Chaos
    and Erebos; so

You can bid the astronomers shut up their shops, for you and
    you only will know.

There was Chaos at first, and Erebos black, and Night, and
    the Void profound,

No earth, no Air, no Heaven; when, lo, in the realm of the
    Dark without bound,

In a vortex of winds the Primordial Egg was engendered by
    black-winged Night;

And out of the Egg; as the seasons revolved, sprang Erôs, the
    world's delight.

His back soft-gleaming with feathers of gold, his heart like a
    whirlwind storm.

And he with Chaos the wingèd and dark, being mixed in the
    Void without form,

Begat the original nestlings of us, and guided them up to the
    sun.

21. Comic scene by Euthymides. Amphora.

The Immortals had never existed at all till Erôs made all
    things one.
For at last, as one kind with another combined, came the
    Earth and the circling Sea,
And the Sky; and the heavenly race of the Gods ever-living;
    but eldest are we,
And foremost of all happy dwellers in heaven; and verily all
    things declare.
We are children of Love; for we fly as He flies, and when true
    lovers meet; we are there.

And pretty young things, at the edge of their bloom, who have
    scorned all love as absurd,
A diligent lover can often beguile through the magic that lives
    in a bird;
The gift of a quail or a coot will not fail, or a goose, or a cock
    in his pride.
Then the things that are most of importance to men are
    precisely the things we provide,
It is birds who make clear the chief dates of the year, of
    autumn and winter and spring;
The croak of the crow gives a signal to sow, when to Libya she
    launches her wing;
It is then that the shipper must hang up his oar: all winter
    his hands he can fold;
It is then that Orestes must weave him a cloak; he'll be
    tempted to steal if he's cold,
Then later the cry of a kite in the sky, when the season begins
    to be fair,
Gives the word for the spring-time shearing of sheep; and the
    swallow darts in to declare
That a man will do well his thick woollens to sell, and buy
    something light. So the powers
Of all the great oracles, Ammon, Apollo, Dôdôna and Delphi
    are ours.
In all undertakings you come for advice to the birds before
    anything's done
Be it getting and giving, or earning your living, or choosing
    a wife for your son.
In the world of the seer any sign that speaks clear is an
    "augury," that is, a bird,

Any opportune sneeze, any sight a man sees on a journey, a
    phrase overheard,
A voice at a critical moment, a donkey, a donkey-boy; doesn't
    it follow
That for you poor mortals on earth We Birds are the real
    prophetic Apollo?

.   .   .

5. The Glory of Philosophy

*The excerpts which follow focus upon one central theme:
the timelessness of Plato's philosophy. As was pointed out in
the introduction there are facets of Platonic philosophy that
are time-bound. The authentic side of his thought, however,
is the one that breaks away from a sociologically determined
set-up and turns to man's essence. The timeliness of Platonic
writings lies in its timelessness, for true timelessness does not
mean unrelated to time, but rather valid at all times.*

Book VI of The Republic *is a magnificent sketch of what a
philosopher should be like in order to be worthy of philosophy. Apart from the inexhaustible metaphysical depth of
the analogy of the cave, Book VII of the same work grants us
a key insight into Platonic epistemology. He who sees nothing
but shadows does not know he is seeing shadows; for it is of
the essence of a shadow that it should be the shadow of something. Analogously, he who is always mistaken necessarily believes he never errs. The fact that men know they make
mistakes is a proof that they do not always err. By that the
possibility of reaching truth and certainty is granted to the
searching mind.*

*Gorgias is centered upon the never-ending conflict existing
between egoistic self-interest and the demands of moral values.
But the amazing contribution of Plato is to show that in spite
of all appearances to the contrary, it is better for man to suffer
injustice than to commit it. Plato advocates that there is no
conflict between moral values and what is good for man, for
on account of the absolute primacy of morality, it is also best*

for man to be morally good. By means of a myth, Plato hints at the possibility of survival after death, a theme fully taken up in Phaedo. *Perhaps the latter is the most sublime of Platonic writings, a work so personally addressed to each man that reading it alone does not suffice. There is an existential call in it, for Plato touches at the very core of human existence, the question of death and immortality.*

In Aristotle, for the first time the different domains of philosophical research are clearly delineated. Whereas in Plato one finds tied in one dialogue a variety of problems belonging to different branches of philosophy, in Aristotle, logic, epistemology, metaphysics, ethics, aesthetics, are clearly separated and every one of these domains is explored in a separate work. In the Posterior Analytics, *which is cited here, Aristotle discusses the nature of first principles.*

PLATO

IMMORTALITY

. . . The truth rather is, that the soul which is pure at departing and draws after her no bodily taint, having never voluntarily during life had connection with the body, which she is ever avoiding, herself gathered into herself;—and making such abstraction her perpetual study—which means that she has been a true disciple of philosophy; and therefore has in fact been always engaged in the practice of dying? For is not philosophy the study of death?—

Certainly—

That soul, I say, herself invisible, departs to the invisible world—to the divine and immortal and rational; thither arriving, she is secure of bliss and is released from the error and folly of men, their fears and wild passions and all other human ills, and for ever dwells, as they say of the initiated, in company with the gods. Is not this true, Cebes?

Yes, said Cebes, beyond a doubt.

But the soul which has been polluted, and is impure at the time of her departure, and is the companion and servant of the body always, and is in love with and fascinated by the body and by the desires and pleasures of the body, until she is led to believe that the truth only exists in a bodily form, which a man may touch and see and taste, and use for the purposes of his lusts,—the soul, I mean, accustomed to hate and fear and avoid the intellectual principle, which to the bodily eye is dark and invisible, and can be attained only by philosophy;—do you suppose that such a soul will depart pure and unalloyed?

Impossible, he replied.

She is held fast by the corporeal, which the continual association and constant care of the body have wrought into her nature.

· · ·

The lovers of knowledge are conscious that the soul was simply fastened and glued to the body—until philosophy received her, she could only view real existence through the bars of a prison, not in and through herself; she was wallowing in the mire of every sort of ignorance, and by reason of lust had become the principal accomplice in her own captivity. This was her original state; and then, as I was saying, and as the lovers of knowledge are well aware, philosophy, seeing how terrible was her confinement, of which she was to herself the cause, received and gently comforted her and sought to release her, pointing out that the eye and the ear and the other senses are full of deception, and persuading her to retire from them, and abstain from all but the necessary use of them, and be gathered up and collected into herself, bidding her trust in herself and her own pure apprehension of pure existence, and to mistrust whatever comes to her through other channels and is subject to variation; for such things are visible and tangible, but what she sees in her own nature is intelligible and invisible. And the soul of the true philosopher thinks that she ought not to resist this deliverance, and therefore abstains from pleasures and desires and pains and fears, as far as she is able; reflecting that when a man has great joys or sorrows or fears or desires, he suffers from them, not merely the sort of evil which might be anticipated—as for example, the loss of his health or property which he has sacrificed to his lusts—but an evil greater far, which is the greatest and worst of all evils, and one of which he never thinks.

What is it, Socrates? said Cebes.

The evil is that when the feeling of pleasure or pain is most intense, every soul of man imagines the objects of this intense feeling to be then plainest and truest: but this is not so, they are really the things of sight.

Very true.

And is not this the state in which the soul is most enthralled by the body?

How so?

Why, because each pleasure and pain is a sort of nail which nails and rivets the soul to the body, until she becomes like the body, and believes that to be true which the body affirms to be true; and from agreeing with the body and having the same delights she is obliged to have the same habits and haunts, and is not likely ever to be pure at her departure to the world below, but is always infected by the body; and so she sinks into another body and there germinates and grows, and has therefore no part in the communion of the divine and pure and simple.

Most true, Socrates, answered Cebes.

And this, Cebes, is the reason why the true lovers of knowledge are temperate and brave; and not for the reason which the world gives.

．　　　．　　　．

PHAEDO. Often, Echecrates, I have wondered at Socrates, but never more than on that occasion. That he should be able to answer was nothing, but what astonished me was, first, the gentle and pleasant and approving manner in which he received the words of the young men, and then his quick sense of the wound which had been inflicted by the argument, and the readiness with which he healed it. He might be compared to a general rallying his defeated and broken army, urging them to accompany him and return to the field of argument.

ECHECRATES. What followed?

PHAEDO. You shall hear, for I was close to him on his right hand, seated on a sort of stool, and he on a couch which was a good deal higher. He stroked my head, and pressed the hair upon my neck—he had a way of playing with my hair; and then he said: To-morrow, Phaedo, I suppose that these fair locks of yours will be severed.

Yes, Socrates, I suppose that they will, I replied.

Not so, if you will take my advice.

What shall I do with them? I said.

To-day, he replied, and not to-morrow, if this argument dies and we cannot bring it to life again, you and I will both shave our locks: and if I were you, and the argument got away from me, and I could not hold my ground against Simmias and Cebes, I would myself take an oath, like the Argives, not to wear hair any more until I had renewed the conflict and defeated them.

Yes, I said; but Heracles himself is said not to be a match for two.

Summon me then, he said, and I will be your Iolaus until the sun goes down.

I summon you rather, I rejoined, not as Hercules summoning Iolaus, but as Iolaus might summon Heracles.

That will do as well, he said. But first let us take care that we avoid a danger.

Of what nature? I said.

Lest we become misologists, he replied: no worse thing can happen to a man than this. For as there are misanthropists or haters of men, there are also misologists or haters of ideas, and both spring from the same cause, which is ignorance of the world. Misanthropy arises out of the too great confidence of inexperience;—you trust a man and think him altogether true and sound and faithful, and then in a little while he turns out to be false and knavish; and then another and another, and when this has happened several times to a man, especially when it happens among those whom he deems to be his own most trusted and familiar friends, and he has often quarrelled with them, he at last hates all men, and believes that no one has any good in him at all. You must have observed this trait of character?

I have.

And is not the feeling discreditable? Is it not obvious that such an one having to deal with other men, was clearly without any experience of human nature; for experience would have taught him the true state of the case, that few are the good and few the evil, and that the great majority are in the interval between them.

What do you mean? I said.

I mean, he replied, as you might say of the very large and very small—that nothing is more uncommon than a very large or very small man; and this applies generally to all extremes, whether of great and small, or swift and slow, or fair and foul, or black and white: and whether the instances you select be men or dogs or anything else, few are the extremes, but many are in the mean between them. Did you never observe this?

Yes, I said, I have.

And do you not imagine, he said, that if there were a competition in evil, the worst would be found to be very few?

Yes, that is very likely, I said.

Yes, that is very likely, he replied; although in this respect arguments are unlike men—there I was led on by you to say more than I had intended; but the point of comparison was, that when a simple man who has no skill in dialectics believes an argument to be true which he afterwards imagines to be false, whether really false or not, and then another and another, he has no longer any faith left, and great disputers, as you know, come to think at last that they have grown to be the wisest of mankind; for they alone perceive the utter unsoundness and instability of all arguments, or indeed, of all things, which, like the currents in the Euripus, are going up and down in never-ceasing ebb and flow.

That is quite true, I said.

Yes, Phaedo, he replied, and how melancholy, if there be such a thing as truth or certainty or possibility of knowledge—that a man should have lighted upon some argument or other which at first seemed true and then turned out to be false, and instead of blaming himself and his own want of wit, because he is annoyed, should at last be too glad to transfer the blame from himself to arguments in general: and for ever afterwards should hate and revile them, and lose truth and the knowledge of realities.

Yes, indeed, I said; that is very melancholy.

Let us then, in the first place, he said, be careful of allowing or of admitting into our souls the notion that there is no health or soundness in any arguments at all. Rather say that we have not yet attained to soundness in ourselves, and that we must struggle manfully and do our best to gain health of mind—you and all other men having regard to the whole of your future life, and I myself in the prospect of death. For at this moment I am sensible that I have not the temper of a philosopher; like the vulgar, I am only a partisan. Now the partisan, when he is engaged in a dispute, cares nothing about the rights of the question, but is anxious only to convince his hearers of his own assertions. And the difference between him and me at the present moment is merely this— that whereas he seeks to convince his hearers that what he says is true, I am rather seeking to convince myself; to convince my hearers is a secondary matter with me. And do but see much I gain by the argument. For if what I say is true, then I do well to be persuaded of the truth; but if there be nothing after death, still, during the short time that remains, I shall not distress my friends with lamentations, and my ignorance will not last, but will die with me, and therefore no harm will be done. This is the state of mind, Simmias and Cebes, in which I approach the argument. And I would ask you to be thinking of the truth and not of Socrates: agree with me, if I seem to you to be speaking the truth; or if not, withstand me might and main, that I may not deceive you as well as myself in my enthusiasm, and like the bee, leave my sting in you before I die.

And now let us proceed, he said. And first of all let me be sure that I have in my mind what you were saying. Simmias, if I remember rightly, has fears and misgivings whether the soul, although a fairer and diviner thing than the body, being as she is in the form of harmony, may not perish first. On the other hand, Cebes appeared to grant that the soul was more lasting than the body, but he said that no one could know whether the soul, after having worn out many bodies, might not perish herself and leave her last body behind her; and that this is death, which is the destruction not of the body but of the soul, for in the body the work of destruction is ever going on. Are not these, Simmias and Cebes, the points which we have to consider?

They both agreed to this statement of them.

He proceeded: And did you deny the force of the whole proceeding argument, or of a part only?

Of a part only, they replied.

And what did you think, he said, of that part of the argument in which we said that knowledge was recollection, and hence inferred that the soul must have previously existed somewhere else before she was enclosed in the body?

Cebes said that he had been wonderfully impressed by that part of the argument, and that his conviction remained absolutely unshaken. Simmias agreed, and added that he himself could hardly imagine the possibility of his ever thinking differently.

But, rejoined Socrates, you will have to think differently, my Theban friend, if you still maintain that harmony is a compound, and that the soul is a harmony which is made out of strings set in the frame of the body; for you will surely never allow yourself to say that a harmony is prior to the elements which compose it.

Never, Socrates.

. . .

I mean to say that a harmony admits of degrees, and is more of a harmony, and more completely a harmony, when more truly and fully harmonized, to any extent which is possible; and less of a harmony, and less completely a harmony, when less truly and fully harmonized.

. . .

. . . For any man, who is not devoid of sense, must fear, if he has no knowledge and can give no account of the soul's immortality. . . .

. . .

But then, O my friends, [Socrates] said, if the soul is really immortal, what care should be taken of her, not only in respect of the portion of time which is called life, but of eternity! and the danger of neglecting her from this point of view does indeed appear to be awful. If death had only been the end of all, the wicked would have had a good bargain in dying, for they would have been happily quit not only of their body, but of their own evil together with their soul. But now, inasmuch as the soul is manifestly immortal, there is no release or salvation from evil except the attainment of the highest virtue and wisdom. For the soul when on her progress to the world below takes nothing with her but nurture and education; and these are said greatly to benefit or greatly to injure the departed, at the very beginning of his journey thither.

.　　.　　.

A man of sense ought not to say, nor will I be very confident, that the description which I have given of the soul and her mansions is exactly true. But I do say that, inasmuch as the soul is shown to be immortal, he may venture to think, not improperly or unworthily, that something of the kind is true. The venture is a glorious one, and he ought to comfort himself with words like these, which is the reason why I lengthen out the tale. Wherefore I say, let a man be of good cheer about his soul, who having cast away the pleasures and ornaments of the body as alien to him and working harm rather than good, has sought after the pleasures of knowledge; and has arrayed the soul, not in some foreign attire, but in her own proper jewels, temperance, and justice, and courage, and nobility, and truth—in these adorned she is ready to go on her journey to the world below, when her hour comes. You, Simmias and Cebes, and all other men, will depart at some time or other. Me already, as a tragic poet would say, the voice of fate calls. Soon I must drink the poison; and I think that I had better repair to the bath first, in order that the women may not have the trouble of washing my body after I am dead.

When he had done speaking, Crito said: And have you any commands for us, Socrates—anything to say about your children, or any other matter in which we can serve you?

Nothing particular, Crito, he replied: only, as I have always told you, take care of yourselves; that is a service which you may be ever rendering to me and mine and to all of us, whether you promise to do so or not. But if you have no thought for yourselves, and care not to walk according to the rule which I have prescribed for you, not now for the first time, however much you may profess or promise at the moment, it will be of no avail.

We will do our best, said Crito: And in what way shall we bury you?

In any way that you like; but you must get hold of me, and take care that I do not run away from you. Then he turned to us, and added with a smile:—I cannot make Crito believe that I am the same Socrates who have been talking and conducting the argument; he fancies that I am the other Socrates whom he will soon see, a dead body—and he asks, How shall he bury me? And though I have spoken many words in the endeavour to show that when I have drunk the poison I shall leave you and go to the joys of the blessed,—these words of mine, with which I was comforting you and myself, have had, as I perceive, no effect upon Crito. And therefore I want you to be surety for me to him now, as at the trial he was surety to the judges for me: but let the promise be of another sort; for he was surety for me to the judges that I would remain, and you must be my surety to him that I shall not remain, but go away and depart; and then he will suffer less at my death, and not be grieved when he sees my body being burned or buried. I would not have him sorrow at my hard lot, or say at the burial, Thus we lay out Socrates, or, Thus we follow him to the grave or bury him; for false words are not only evil in themselves, but they infect the soul with evil. Be of good cheer then, my dear Crito, and say that you are burying my body only, and do with that whatever is usual, and what you think best.

When he had spoken these words, he arose and went into a chamber to bathe; Crito followed him and told us to wait. So we remained behind, talking and thinking of the subject of discourse, and also of the greatness of our sorrow; he was like a father of whom we were being bereaved, and we were about to pass thet rest of our lives as orphans. When he had taken the bath his children were brought to him—(he had two young sons and an elder one); and the women of his family also came, and he talked to them and gave them a few directions in the presence of Crito; then he dismissed them and returned to us.

Now the hour of sunset was near, for a good deal of time had passed while he was within. When he came out, he sat down with us again after his bath, but not much was said. Soon the jailer, who was the servant of the Eleven, entered and stood by him, saying:—To you, Socrates, whom I know to be the noblest and gentlest and best of all who ever came to this place, I will not impute the angry feelings of

other men, who rage and swear at me, when in obedience to the authorities, I bid them drink the poison—indeed, I am sure that you will
not be angry with me; for others, as you are aware, and not I, are to
blame. And so fare you well, and try to bear lightly what must needs
be—you know my errand. Then bursting into tears he turned away and
went out.

Socrates looked at him and said: I return your good wishes, and will
do as you bid. Then turning to us, he said, How charming the man is:
since I have been in prison he has always been coming to see me, and at
times he would talk to me, and was as good to me as could be, and now
see how generously he sorrows on my account. We must do as he says,
Crito; and therefore let the cup he brought, if the poison is prepared:
if not, let the attendant prepare some.

Yet, said Crito, the sun is still upon the hill-tops, and I know that
many a one has taken the draught late, and after the announcement has
been made to him, he has eaten and drunk, and enjoyed the society of
his beloved; do not hurry—there is time enough.

Socrates said: Yes, Crito, and they of whom you speak are right in so
acting, for they think that they will be gainers by the delay; but I am
right in not following their example, for I do not think that I should
gain anything by drinking the poison a little later; I should only be
ridiculous in my own eyes for sparing and saving a life which is already
forfeit. Please then to do as I say, and not to refuse me.

Crito made a sign to the servant, who was standing by; and he went
out, and having been absent for some time, returned with the jailer
carrying the cup of poison. Socrates said: You, my good friends, who are
experienced in these matters, shall give me directions how I am to
proceed. The man answered: You have only to walk about until your
legs are heavy, and then to lie down, and the poison will act. At the
same time he handed the cup to Socrates, who in the easiest and gentlest
manner, without the least fear or change of colour or feature, looking at
the man with all his eyes, Echecrates, as his manner was, took the cup
and said: What do you say about making a libation out of this cup to any
god? May I, or not? The man answered: We only prepare, Socrates, just
so much as we deem enough. I understand, he said: but I may and
must ask the gods to prosper by journey from this to the other world—
even so—and so be it according to my prayer. Then raising the cup to
his lips, quite readily and cheerfully he drank off the poison. And
hitherto most of us had been able to control our sorrow; but now when
we saw him drinking, and saw too that he had finished the draught, we

could no longer forbear, and in spite of myself my own tears were flowing fast; so that I covered my face and wept, not for him, but at the thought of my own calamity in having to part from such a friend. Nor was I the first; for Crito, when he found himself unable to restrain his tears, had got up, and I followed; and at that moment, Apollodorus, who had been weeping all the time, broke out in a loud and passionate cry which made cowards of us all. Socrates alone retained his calmness: what is this strange outcry? he said. I sent away the women mainly in order that they might not misbehave in this way, for I have been told that a man should die in peace. Be quiet then, and have patience. When we heard his words we were ashamed, and refrained our tears; and he walked about until, as he said, his legs began to fail, and then he lay on his back, according to the directions, and the man who gave him the poison now and then looked at his feet and legs; and after a while he pressed his foot hard, and asked him if he could feel; and he said, No; and then his leg, and so upwards and upwards, and showed us that he was cold and stiff. And he felt them himself, and said: When the poison reaches the heart, that will be the end. He was beginning to grow cold about the groin, when he uncovered his face, for he had covered himself up, and said—they were his last words—he said: Crito, I owe a cock to Asclepius; will you remember to pay the debt? The debt shall be paid, said Crito; is there anything else? There was no answer to this question; but in a minute or two a movement was heard, and the attendants uncovered him; his eyes were set, and Crito closed his eyes and mouth.

Such was the end, Echecrates, of our friend; concerning whom I may truly say, that of all the men of his time whom I have known, he was the wisest and justest and best.

(from *Phaedo*)

PLATO

THE TRUE PHILOSOPHER

In the first place, as we began by observing, the nature of the philosopher has to be ascertained. We must come to an understanding about him, and, when we have done so, then, if I am not mistaken, we shall also acknowledge that such an union of qualities is possible, and that those in whom they are united, and those only, should be rulers in the State.

What do you mean?

Let us suppose that philosophical minds always love knowledge of a sort which shows them the eternal nature not varying from generation and corruption.

Agreed.

And further, I said, let us agree that they are lovers of all true being; there is no part whether greater or less, or more or less honourable, which they are willing to renounce; as we said before of the lover and the man of ambition.

True.

And if they are to be what we were describing, is there not another quality which they should also possess?

What quality?

Truthfulness: they will never intentionally receive into their mind falsehood, which is their detestation, and they will love the truth.

Yes, that may be safely affirmed of them.

"May be," my friend, I replied, is not the word; say rather "must be affirmed": for he whose nature is amorous of anything cannot help loving all that belongs or is akin to the object of his affections.

Right, he said.

And is there anything more akin to wisdom than truth?

How can there be?

Can the same nature be a lover of wisdom and a lover of falsehood?

Never.

The true lover of learning then must from his earliest youth, as far as in him lies, desire all truth?

Assuredly.

.   .   .

Here Adeimantus interposed and said: To these statements, Socrates, no one can offer a reply; but when you talk in this way, a strange feeling passes over the minds of your hearers: They fancy that they are led astray a little at each step in the argument, owing to their own want of skill in asking and answering questions; these littles accumulate, and at the end of the discussion they are found to have sustained a mighty overthrow and all their former notions appear to be turned upside down. And as unskilful players of draughts are at last shut up by their more skilful adversaries and have no piece to move, so they too find themselves shut up at last; for they have nothing to say in this new game of which words are the counters; and yet all the time they are in the right. The observation is suggested to me by what is now occurring. For any one of us might say, that although in words he is not able to meet you at each step of the argument, he sees as a fact that the votaries of philosophy, when they carry on the study, not only in youth as a part of education, but as the pursuit of their maturer years, most of them become strange monsters, not to say utter rogues, and that those who may be considered the best of them are made useless to the world by the very study which you extol.

Well, and do you think that those who say so are wrong?

I cannot tell, he replied; but I should like to know what is your opinion.

Hear my answer; I am of opinion that they are quite right.

Then how can you be justified in saying that cities will not cease from evil until philosophers rule in them, when philosophers are acknowledged by us to be of no use to them?

You ask a question, I said, to which a reply can only be given in a parable.

Yes, Socrates; and that is a way of speaking to which you are not at all accustomed, I suppose.

I perceive, I said, that you are vastly amused at having plunged me into such a hopeless discussion; but now hear the parable, and then you will be still more amused at the meagreness of my imagination: for the manner in which the best men are treated in their own States is so grievous that no single thing on earth is comparable to it; and therefore, if I am to plead their cause, I must have recourse to fiction, and put together a figure made up of many things, like the fabulous unions of goats and stags which are found in pictures. Imagine then a fleet or a ship in which there is a captain who is taller and stronger than any of the crew, but he is a little deaf and has a similar infirmity in sight, and his knowledge of navigation is not much better. The sailors are quarrelling with one another about the steering—every one is of opinion that he has a right to steer, though he has never learned the art of navigation and cannot tell who taught him or when he learned, and will further assert that it cannot be taught, and they are ready to cut in pieces any one who says the contrary. They throng about the captain, begging and praying him to commit the helm to them; and if at any time they do not prevail, but others are preferred to them, they kill the others or throw them overboard, and having first chained up the noble captain's senses with drink or some narcotic drug, they mutiny and take possession of the ship and make free with the stores; thus, eating and drinking, they proceed on their voyage in such a manner as might be expected of them. Him who is their partisan and cleverly aids them in their plot for getting the ship out of the captain's hands into their own whether by force or persuasion, they compliment with the name of sailor, pilot, able seaman, and abuse the other sort of man, whom they call a good-for-nothing; but that the true pilot must pay attention to the year and seasons and sky and stars and winds, and whatever else belongs to his art, if he intends to be really qualified for the command of a ship, and that he must and will be the steerer, whether other people like or not— the possibility of this union of authority with the steerer's art has never seriously entered into their thoughts or been made part of their calling. Now in vessels which are in a state of mutiny and by sailors who are mutineers, how will the true pilot be regarded? Will he not be called by them a prater, a star-gazer, a good-for-nothing?

Of course, said Adeimantus.

Then you will hardly need, I said, to hear the interpretation of the figure, which describes the true philosopher in his relation to the State; for you understand already.

Certainly.

Then suppose you now take this parable to the gentleman who is surprised at finding that philosophers have no honour in their cities; explain it to him and try to convince him that their having honour would be far more extraordinary.

I will.

Say to him, that, in deeming the best votaries of philosophy to be useless to the rest of the world, he is right; but also tell him to attribute their uselessness to the fault of those who will not use them, and not to themselves. The pilot should not humbly beg the sailors to be commanded by him—that is not the order of nature; neither are "the wise to go to the doors of the rich"—the ingenious author of this saying told a lie—but the truth is, that, when a man is ill, whether he be rich or poor, to the physician he must go, and he who wants to be governed, to him who is able to govern. The ruler who is good for anything ought not to beg his subjects to be ruled by him; although the present governors of mankind are of a different stamp; they may be justly compared to the mutinous sailors, and the true helmsmen to those who are called by them good-for-nothings and star-gazers.

Precisely so, he said.

For these reasons, and among men like these, philosophy, the noblest pursuit of all, is not likely to be much esteemed by those of the opposite faction; not that the greatest and most lasting injury is done to her by her opponents, but by her own professing followers, the same of whom you suppose the accuser to say, that the greater number of them are arrant rogues, and the best are useless.

.   .   .

And we have next to consider the corruptions of the philosophic nature, why so many are spoiled and so few escape spoiling—I am speaking of those who were said to be useless but not wicked—and, when we have done with them, we will speak of the imitators of philosophy, what manner of men are they who aspire after a profession which is above them and of which they are unworthy, and then, by their manifold inconsistencies, bring upon philosophy, and upon all philosophers, that universal reprobation of which we speak.

What are these corruptions? he said.

I will see if I can explain them to you. Every one will admit that a nature having in perfection all the qualities which we required in a philosopher, is a rare plant which is seldom seen among men.

Rare indeed.

And what numberless and powerful causes tend to destroy these rare natures!

In the first place there are their own virtues, their courage, temperance, and the rest of them, every one of which praiseworthy qualities (and this is a most singular circumstance) destroys and distracts from philosophy the soul which is the possessor of them.

That is very singular, he replied.

Then there are all the ordinary goods of life—beauty, wealth, strength, rank, and great connections in the State—you understand the sort of things—these also have a corrupting and distracting effect.

I understand; but I should like to know more precisely what you mean about them.

Grasp the truth as a whole, I said, and in the right way; you will then have no difficulty in apprehending the preceding remarks, and they will no longer appear strange to you.

And how am I to do so? he asked.

Why, I said, we know that all germs or seeds, whether vegetable or animal, when they fail to meet with proper nutriment or climate or soil, in proportion to their vigour, are all the more sensitive to the want of a suitable environment, for evil is a greater enemy to what is good than what is not.

Very true.

There is reason in supposing that the finest natures, when under alien conditions, receive more injury than the inferior, because the contrast is greater.

Certainly.

And may we not say, Adeimantus, that the most gifted minds, when they are ill-educated, become pre-eminently bad? Do not great crimes and the spirit of pure evil spring out of a fulness of nature ruined by education rather than from any inferiority, whereas weak natures are scarcely capable of any very great good or very great evil?

(from *The Republic,* Book VI)

PLATO

THE MYTH OF THE CAVE

And now, I said, let me show in a figure how far our nature is enlightened or unenlightened:—Behold! human beings living in an underground den, which has a mouth open towards the light and reaching all along the den; here they have been from their childhood, and have their legs and necks chained so that they cannot move, and can only see before them, being prevented by the chains from turning round their heads. Above and behind them a fire is blazing at a distance, and between the fire and the prisoners there is a raised way; and you will see, if you look, a low wall built along the way, like the screen which marionette players have in front of them, over which they show the puppets.

I see.

And do you see, I said, men passing along the wall carrying all sorts of vessels, and statues and figures of animals made of wood and stone and various materials, which appear over the wall? Some of them are talking, others silent.

You have shown me a strange image, and they are strange prisoners.

Like ourselves, I replied; and they see only their own shadows, or the shadows of one another, which the fire throws on the opposite wall of the cave?

True, he said; how could they see anything but the shadows if they were never allowed to move their heads?

And of the objects which are being carried in like manner they would only see the shadows?

Yes, he said.

And if they were able to converse with one another, would they not suppose that they were naming what was actually before them?

Very true.

And suppose further that the prison had an echo which came from the other side, would they not be sure to fancy when one of the passers-by spoke that the voice which they heard came from the passing shadow?

No question, he replied.

To them, I said, the truth would be literally nothing but the shadows of the images.

That is certain.

And now look again, and see what will naturally follow if the prisoners are released and disabused of their error. At first, when any of them is liberated and compelled suddenly to stand up and turn his neck round and walk and look towards the light, he will suffer sharp pains; the glare will distress him, and he will be unable to see the realities of which in his former state he had seen the shadows; and then conceive some one saying to him, that what he saw before was an illusion, but that now, when he is approaching nearer to being and his eye is turned towards more real existence, he has a clearer vision,—what will be his reply? And you may further imagine that his instructor is pointing to the objects as they pass and requiring him to name them,—will he not be perplexed? Will he not fancy that the shadows which he formerly saw are truer than the objects which are now shown to him?

Far truer.

And if he is compelled to look straight at the light, will he not have a pain in his eyes which will make him turn away to take refuge in the objects of vision which he can see, and which he will conceive to be in reality clearer than the things which are now being shown to him?

True, he said.

And suppose once more, that he is reluctantly dragged up a steep and rugged ascent, and held fast until he is forced into the presence of the sun himself, is he not likely to be pained and irritated? When he approaches the light his eyes will be dazzled, and he will not be able to see anything at all of what are now called realities.

Not all in a moment, he said.

He will require to grow accustomed to the sight of the upper world. And first he will see the shadows best, next the objects themselves; then he will gaze upon the light of the moon and the stars and the spangled heaven; and he will see the sky and the stars by night better than the sun or the light of the sun by day?

Certainly.

Last of all he will be able to see the sun, and not mere reflections of him in the water, but he will see him in his own proper place, and not in another; and he will contemplate him as he is.

Certainly.

He will then proceed to argue that this is he who gives the season and the years, and is the guardian of all that is in the visible world, and in a certain way the cause of all things which he and his fellows have been accustomed to behold?

Clearly, he said, he would first see the sun and then reason about him.

And when he remembered his old habitation, and the wisdom of the den and his fellow-prisoners, do you not suppose that he would felicitate himself on the change, and pity them?

Certainly he would.

And if they were in the habit of conferring honours among themselves on those who were quickest to observe the passing shadows and to remark which of them went before, and which followed after, and which were together; and who were therefore best able to draw conclusions as to the future, do you think that he would care for such honours and glories, or envy the possessors of them? Would he not say with Homer.

"Better to be the poor servant of a poor master," and to endure anything, rather than think as they do and live after their manner?

Yes, he said, I think that he would rather suffer anything than entertain these false notions and live in this miserable manner.

Imagine once more, I said, such an one coming suddenly out of the sun to be replaced in his old situation; would he not be certain to have his eyes full of darkness?

To be sure, he said.

And if there were a contest, and he had to compete in measuring the shadows with the prisoners who had never moved out of the den, while his sight was still weak, and before his eyes had become steady (and the time which would be needed to acquire this new habit of sight might be very considerable), would he not be ridiculous? Men would say of him that up he went and down he came without his eyes; and that it was better not even to think of ascending; and if any one tried to loose another and lead him up to the light, let them only catch the offender, and they would put him to death.

(from *The Republic,* Book VII)

PLATO

MORAL VALUE AND THE SUPERMAN

SOCRATES. And I tell you, Polus, that rhetoricians and tyrants have the least possible power in states, as I was just now saying; for they do literally nothing which they will, but only what they think best.

POLUS. And is not that a great power?

SOCRATES. Polus has already said the reverse.

SOCRATES. No, by the great—what do you call him?—not you, for you say that power is a good to him who has the power.

POLUS. I do.

SOCRATES. And would you maintain that if a fool does what he thinks best, this is a good, and would you call this great power?

POLUS. I should not.

SOCRATES. Then you must prove that the rhetorician is not a fool, and that rhetoric is an art and not a flattery—and so you will have refuted me; but if you leave me unrefuted, why, the rhetoricians who do what they think best in states, and the tyrants, will have nothing upon which to congratulate themselves, if as you say, power be indeed a good, admitting at the same time that what is done without sense is an evil.

POLUS. Yes; I admit that.

SOCRATES. How then can the rhetoricians or the tyrants have great power in states, unless Polus can refute Socrates, and prove to him they do as they will?

POLUS. This fellow—

SOCRATES. I say that they do not do as they will;—now refute me.

POLUS. Why, have you not already said that they do as they think best?

SOCRATES. And I say so still.

POLUS. Then surely they do as they will?

SOCRATES. I deny it.

POLUS. But they do what they think best?

SOCRATES. Aye.

POLUS. That, Socrates, is monstrous and absurd.

SOCRATES. Good words, good Polus, as I may say in your own peculiar style; but if you have any questions to ask of me, either prove that I am in error or give the answer yourself.

POLUS. Very well, I am willing to answer that I may know what you mean.

SOCRATES. Do men appear to you to will that which they do, or to will that further end for the sake of which they do a thing? When they take medicine, for example, at the bidding of a physician, do they will the drinking of the medicine which is painful, or the health for the sake of which they drink?

POLUS. Clearly, the health.

SOCRATES. And when men go on a voyage or engage in business, they do not will that which they are doing at the time; for who would desire to take the risk of a voyage or the trouble of business?—But they will, to have the wealth for the sake of which they go on a voyage.

POLUS. Certainly.

SOCRATES. And is not this universally true? If a man does something for the sake of something else, he wills not that which he does, but that for the sake of which he does it.

POLUS. Yes.

SOCRATES. And are not all things either good or evil, or intermediate and indifferent?

POLUS. To be sure, Socrates.

SOCRATES. Wisdom and health and wealth and the like you would call goods, and their opposite evils?

POLUS. I should.

SOCRATES. And the things which are neither good nor evil, and which partake something of the nature of good and at other times of evil, or of neither, are such as sitting, walking, running, sailing; or, again, wood, stones, and the like:—these are the things which you can neither call good nor evil?

POLUS. Exactly so.

SOCRATES. Are these indifferent things done for the sake of the good, or the good for the sake of the indifferent?

POLUS. Clearly, the indifferent for the sake of the good.

SOCRATES. When we walk we walk for the sake of the good, and under the idea that it is better to walk, and when we stand we stand equally for the sake of the good?

POLUS. Yes.

SOCRATES. And when we kill a man we kill him or exile him or despoil him of his goods, because, as we think, it will conduce to our good?

POLUS. Certainly.

SOCRATES. Men who do any of these things do them for the sake of the good?

POLUS. Yes.

SOCRATES. And did we not admit that in doing something for the sake of something else, we do not will those things which we do, but that other thing for the sake of which we do them?

POLUS. Most true.

SOCRATES. Then we do not will simply to kill a man or to exile him or to despoil him of his goods, but we will to do that which conduces to our good, and if the act is not conducive to our good we do not will it; for we will, as you say, that which is our good, but that which is neither good nor evil, or simply evil, we do not will. Why are you silent, Polus? Am I not right?

POLUS. You are right.

SOCRATES. Hence we may infer, that if any one, whether he be a tyrant, or a rhetorician, kills another or exiles another or deprives him of his property, under the idea that the act is for his own interests when really not for his own interests, he may be said to do what seems best to him?

POLUS. Yes.

SOCRATES. But does he do what he wills if he does what is evil? Why do you not answer?

POLUS. Well, I suppose not.

SOCRATES. Then if great power is a good as you allow, will such a one have great power in a state?

POLUS. He will not.

SOCRATES. Then I was right in saying that a man may do what seems good to him in a state, and not have great power, and not do what he wills?

POLUS. As though you, Socrates, would not like to have the power of doing what seemed good to you in the state, rather than not; you would not be jealous when you saw any one killing or despoiling or imprisoning whom he pleased. Oh, no!

245

SOCRATES. Justly or unjustly, do you mean?

POLUS. In either case is he not equally to be envied?

SOCRATES. Forbear, Polus!

POLUS. Why "forbear"?

SOCRATES. Because you ought not to envy wretches who are not to be envied, but only to pity them.

POLUS. And are those of whom I spoke wretches?

SOCRATES. Yes, certainly they are.

POLUS. And so you think that he who slays any one whom he pleases, and justly slays him, is pitiable and wretched?

SOCRATES. No, I do not say that of him: but neither do I think that he is to be envied.

POLUS. Were you not saying just now that he is wretched?

SOCRATES. Yes, my friend, if he killed another unjustly in which case he is also to be pitied; and he is not to be envied if he killed him justly.

POLUS. At any rate you will allow that he who is unjustly put to death is wretched, and to be pitied?

SOCRATES. Not so much, Polus, as he who kills him, and not so much as he who is justly killed.

POLUS. How can that be, Socrates?

SOCRATES. That may very well be, inasmuch as doing injustice is the greatest of evils.

POLUS. But is it the greatest? Is not suffering injustice a greater evil?

SOCRATES. Certainly not.

POLUS. Then would you rather suffer than do injustice?

SOCRATES. I should not like either, but if I must choose between them, I would rather suffer than do.

.   .   .

CALLICLES. By the gods, and I will. Tell me, Socrates, are you in earnest, or only in jest? For if you are in earnest, and what you say is true, is not the whole of human life upside down; and are we not doing, as would appear, in everything the opposite of what we ought to be doing?

SOCRATES. O Callicles, if there were not some community of feelings among mankind, however varying in different persons—I mean to say, if every man's feelings were peculiar to himself and were not shared by the rest of his species—I do not see how we could ever communicate our impressions to one another. I make this remark because I perceive that you and I have a common feeling. For we are lovers both, and both of us have two loves apiece:—I am the lover of Alcibiades, the son of Cleinias, and of philosophy; and you of the Athenian Demus, and of Demus the son of Pyrilampes. Now, I observe that you, with all your cleverness, do not venture to contradict your favourite in any word or opinion of his; but as he changes you change, backwards and forwards. When the Athenian Demus denies anything that you are saying in the assembly, you go over to his opinion; and you do the same with Demus, the fair young son of Pyrilampes. For you have not the power to resist the words and ideas of your loves; and if a person were to express surprise at the strangeness of what you say from time to time when under their influence, you would probably reply to him, if you were honest, that you cannot help saying what your loves say unless they are prevented; and that you can only be silent when they are. Now you must understand that my words are an echo too, and therefore you need not wonder at me; but if you want to silence me, silence philosophy, who is my love, for she is always telling me what I am now telling you, my friend; neither is she capricious like my other love, for the son of Cleinias says one thing to-day and another thing to-morrow, but philosophy is always true. She is the teacher at whose words you are now wondering, and you have heard her yourself. Her you must refute, and either show, as I was saying, that to do injustice and to escape punishment is not the worst of all evils; or, if you leave her word unrefuted, by the dog the god of Egypt, I declare, O Callicles, that Callicles will never be at one with himself, but that his whole life will be a discord. And yet, my friend, I would rather that my lyre should be inharmonious, and that there should be no music in the chorus which I provided; aye, or that the whole world should be at odds with myself, and contradict myself.

CALLICLES. O Socrates, you are a regular declaimer, and seem to be running riot in the argument. And now you are declaiming in this way because Polus has fallen into the same error himself of which he accused Gorgias:—for he said that when Gorgias was asked by you, whether, if some one came to him who wanted to learn rhetoric, and did not know justice, he would teach him justice, Gorgias in his modesty replied that he would, because he thought that mankind in general would be displeased if he answered "No"; and then in consequence of this admission, Gorgias was compelled to contradict himself, that being just the sort of thing in which you delight. Whereupon Polus laughed at you deservedly, as I think; but now he has himself fallen into the same . ˇ ˋ. I cannot say very much for his wit when he conceded to you that to do is more dishonourable than to suffer injustice, for this was the admission which led to his being entangled by you; and because he was too modest to say what he thought, he had his mouth stopped. For the truth is, Socrates, that you, who pretend to be engaged in the pursuit of truth, are appealing now to the popular and vulgar notions of right, which are not natural, but only conventional. Convention and nature are generally at variance with one another: and hence, if a person is too modest to say what he thinks, he is compelled to contradict himself; and you, in your ingenuity perceiving the advantage to be thereby gained, slyly ask of him who is arguing conventionally a question which is to be determined by the rule of nature; and if he is talking of the rule of nature, you slip away to custom: as, for instance, you did in this very discussion about doing and suffering injustice. When Polus was speaking of the conventionally dishonourable, you assailed him from the point of view of nature; for by the rule of nature, to suffer injustice is the greater disgrace because the greater evil; but conventionally, to do evil is the more disgraceful. For the suffering of injustice is not the part of a man, but of a slave, who indeed had better die than live; since when he is wronged and trampled upon, he is unable to help himself, or any other about whom he cares. The reason, as I conceive, is that the makers of laws are the majority who are weak; and they make laws and distribute praises and censures with a view to themselves and to their own interests; and they terrify the stronger sort of men, and those who are able to get the better of them, in order that they may not get the better of them; and they say, that dishonesty is shameful and unjust; meaning, by the word injustice, the desire of a man to have more than his neighbours; for knowing their own inferiority, I suspect that they are too glad of equality. And therefore the endeavour to have more than the many, is conventionally said to be shameful and unjust, and is called injustice, whereas nature herself intimates that it is just for the better to have more than the worse, the more powerful than the weaker; and in many ways she shows, among men as well as among animals, and indeed among whole cities and races, that justice consists in the superior ruling over and having more than the inferior. For on what principle of justice consists in the superior ruling over and having more than the inferior? For on what principle of justice did Xerxes invade Hellas, or his father the Scythians? (not to speak of numberless other examples). Nay, but these are the men who act according to nature; yes, by Heaven, and according to the law of nature: not, perhaps, according to that artificial law, which we invent and impose upon our fellows, of whom we take the best and strongest from their youth upwards, and tame them like young lions, —charming them with the sound of the voice, and saying to them, that with equality they must be content, and the equal is the honourable and the just. But if there were a man who had sufficient force, he would shake off and break through, and escape from all this; he would trample under foot all our formulas and spells and charms, and all our laws which are against nature: the slave would rise in rebellion and be lord over us, and the light of natural justice would shine forth. And this I take to be the sentiment of Pindar, when he says in his poem, that

Law is the king of all, of mortals as well as of immortals.

SOCRATES. And do you mean by the better the same as the superior? for I could not make out what you were saying at the time—whether you meant by the superior the stronger, and that the weaker must obey the stronger, as you seemed to imply when you said that great cities attack small ones in accordance with natural right, because they are superior and stronger, as though the superior and stronger and better were the same; or whether the better may be also the inferior and weaker, and the superior the worse, or whether better is to be defined in the same way as superior: this is the point which I want to have cleared up. Are the superior and better and stronger the same or different?

CALLICLES. I say unequivocally that they are the same.

SOCRATES. Then the many are by nature superior to the one, against whom, as you were saying, they make the laws?

CALLICLES. Certainly.

SOCRATES. Then the laws of the many are the laws of the superior?

CALLICLES. Very true.

SOCRATES. Then they are the laws of the better; for the superior class are far better, as you were saying?

CALLICLES. Yes.

SOCRATES. And since they are superior, the laws which are made by them are by nature good?

CALLICLES. Yes.

SOCRATES. And are not the many of opinion, as you were lately saying, that justice is equality, and that to do is more disgraceful than to suffer injustice?—is that so or not? Answer, Callicles, and let no modesty be found to come in the way; do the many think, or do they not think thus? —I must beg of you to answer, in order that if you agree with me I may fortify myself by the assent of so competent an authority.

CALLICLES. Yes; the opinion of the many is what you say.

SOCRATES. Then not only custom but nature also affirms that to do is more disgraceful than to suffer injustice, and that justice is equality; so that you seem to have been wrong in your former assertion, when accusing me you said that nature and custom are opposed. . . .

.   .   .

CALLICLES. Quite so, Socrates; and they are really fools, for how can a man be happy who is the servant of anything? On the contrary, I plainly assert, that he who would truly live ought to allow his desires to wax to the uttermost, and not to chastise them; but when they have grown to their greatest he should have courage and intelligence to minister to them and to satisfy all his longings. And this I affirm to be natural justice and nobility. To this however the many cannot attain; and they blame the strong man because they are ashamed of their own weakness, which they desire to conceal, and hence they say that intemperance is base. As I have remarked already, they enslave the nobler natures, and being unable to satisfy their pleasures they praise temperance and justice out of their own cowardice. For if a man had been originally the son of a king, or had a nature capable of acquiring an empire or a tyranny or sovereignty, what could be more truly base or evil than temperance—to a man like him, I say, who might freely be enjoying every good, and has no one to stand in his way, and yet has admitted custom and reason and the opinion of other men to be lords over him?—must not he be in a miserable plight whom the reputation of justice and temperance hinders from giving more to his friends than to his enemies, even though he be a ruler in his city? Nay, Socrates, for you profess to be a votary of the truth, and the truth is this:—that luxury and intemperance and licence, if they be provided with means, are virtue and happiness—all the rest is a mere bauble, agreements contrary to nature, foolish talk of men, nothing worth.

SOCRATES. There is a noble freedom, Callicles, in your way of approaching the argument; for what you say is what the rest of the world think, but do not like to say. And I must beg of you to persevere, that the true rule of human life may become manifest. Tell me, then:—you say, do you not, that in the rightly-developed man the passions ought not to be controlled, but that we should let them grow to utmost and somehow or other satisfy them, and that this is virtue?

CALLICLES. Yes; I do.

SOCRATES. Then those who want nothing are not truly said to be happy?

CALLICLES. No indeed, for then stones and dead men would be the happiest of all.

SOCRATES. But surely life according to your view is an awful thing; and indeed I think that Euripides may have been right in saying,

> Who knows if life be not death and death life;

and that we are very likely dead; I have heard a philosopher say that at this moment we are actually dead, and that the body is our tomb, and that the part of the soul which is the seat of the desires is liable to be tossed about by words and blown up and down; and some ingenious person, probably a Sicilian or an Italian, playing with the word, invented a tale in which he called the soul—because of its believing and make-believe nature—a vessel, and the ignorant he called the uninitiated or leaky, and the place in the souls of the uninitiated in which the desires are seated, being the intemperate and incontinent part, he compared to a vessel full of holes, because it can never be satisfied. He is not of your way of thinking, Callicles, for he declares, that of all the souls in Hades, meaning the invisible world, these uninitiated or leaky persons are the most miserable, and that they pour water into a vessel which is full of holes out of a colander which is similarly perforated. The colander, as my informer assures me, is the soul, and the soul which he compares to a colander is the soul of the ignorant, which is likewise full of holes, and therefore incontinent, owing to a bad memory and want of faith. These notions are strange enough, but they show the principle which, if I can, I would fain prove to you; that you should change your mind, and, instead of the intemperate and insatiate life, choose that which is orderly and sufficient and has a due provision for daily needs. Do I make any impression on you, and are you coming over to the opinion that the orderly are happier than the intemperate? Or do I fail to persuade you, and, however many tales I rehearse to you, do you continue of the same opinion still?

CALLICLES. The latter, Socrates, is more like the truth.

SOCRATES. Well, I will tell you another image, which comes out of the same school:—Let me request you to consider how far you would accept this as an account of the two lives of the temperate and intemperate in a figure:—There are two men, both of whom have a number of casks; the one man has his casks sound and full, one of wine, another of honey, and a third of milk, besides others filled with other liquids, and the streams which fill them are few and scanty, and he can only obtain them with a great deal of toil and difficulty; but when his casks are once filled he has no need to feed them any more, and has no further trouble with them or care about them. The other, in like manner, can procure streams, though not without difficulty; but his vessels are leaky and unsound, and night and day he is compelled to be filling them, and if he pauses for a moment, he is in an agony of pain. Such are their respective lives:—And now would you say that the life of the intemperate is happier than that of the temperate? Do I not convince you that the opposite is the truth?

(from *Gorgias*)

ARISTOTLE
FIRST PRINCIPLES

What I now assert is that at all events we do know by demonstration. By demonstration I mean a syllogism productive of scientific knowledge, a syllogism, that is, the grasp of which is *eo ipso* such knowledge. Assuming then that my thesis as to the nature of scientific knowing is correct, the premisses of demonstrated knowledge must be true, primary, immediate, better known than and prior to the conclusion, which is further related to them as effect to cause. Unless these conditions are satisfied, the basic truths will not be "appropriate" to the conclusion. Syllogism there may indeed be without these conditions, but such syllogism, not being productive of scientific knowledge, will not be demonstration. The premisses must be true: for that which is non-existent cannot be known —we cannot know, e.g. that the diagonal of a square is commensurate with its side. The premisses must be primary and indemonstrable; otherwise they will require demonstration in order to be known, since to have knowledge, if it be not accidental knowledge, of things which are demonstrable, means precisely to have a demonstration of them. The premisses must be the causes of the conclusion, better known than it, and prior to it; its causes, since we possess scientific knowledge of a thing only when we know its cause; prior, in order to be causes; antecedently known, this antecedent knowledge being not our mere understanding of the meaning, but knowledge of the fact as well. Now "prior" and "better known" are ambiguous terms, for there is a difference between what is prior and better known in the order of being and what is prior and better known to man. I mean that objects nearer to sense are prior and better known to man; objects without qualification prior and better known are those further from sense. Now the most universal causes are furthest from sense and particular causes are nearest to sense, and they are thus exactly opposed to one another. In saying that the premisses of demonstrated knowledge must be primary, I mean that they must be the "appropriate" basic truths, for I identify primary premiss and basic truth. A "basic truth" in a demonstration is an immediate proposition. An immediate proposition is one which has no other proposition prior to it. A proposition is either part of an enunciation, i.e. it predicates a single attribute of a single subject. If a proposition is dialectical, it assumes either part indifferently; if it is demonstrative, it lays down one part to the definite exclusion of the other because that part is true. The term "enunciation" denotes either part of a contradiction indifferently. A contradiction is an opposition which of its own nature excludes a middle. The part of a contradiction which conjoins a predicate with a subject is an affirmation; the part disjoining them is a negation. I call an immediate basic truth of syllogism a "thesis" when, though it is not susceptible of proof by the teacher, yet ignorance of it does not constitute a total bar to progress on the part of the pupil: one which the pupil must know if he is to learn anything whatever is an axiom. I call it an axiom because there are such truths and we give them the name of axioms *par excellence*. If a thesis assumes one part or the other of an enunciation, i.e. asserts either the existence or the non-existence of a subject, it is a hypothesis; if it does not so assert, it is a definition. Definition is a "thesis" or a "laying something down," since the arithmetician lays it down that to be a unit is to be quantitatively indivisible; but it is not a hypothesis, for to define what a unit is is not the same as to affirm its existence.

Now since the required ground of our knowledge—i.e. of our conviction—of a fact is the possession of such a syllogism as we call demonstration, and the ground of the syllogism is the facts constituting its premisses, we must not only know the primary premisses—some if not all of them—beforehand, but know them better than the conclusion: for the cause of an attribute's inherence in a subject always itself inheres in the subject more firmly than that attribute; e.g. the cause of our loving anything is dearer to us than the object of our love. So since the primary premisses are the cause of our knowledge—i.e. of our conviction—it follows that we know them better—that is, are more convinced of them —than their consequences, precisely because our knowledge of the latter is the effect of our knowledge of the premises. Now a man cannot believe in anything more than in the things he knows, unless he has either actual knowledge of it or something better than actual knowledge. But we are faced with this paradox if a student whose belief rests on demonstration has not prior knowledge; a man must believe in some, if not in all, of the basic truths more than in the conclusion. Moreover, if a man sets out to acquire the scientific knowledge that comes through demonstration, he must not only have a better knowledge of the basic truths and a firmer conviction of them than of the connexion which is being demonstrated: more than this, nothing must be more certain or better known to him than these basic truths in their character as contradicting the fundamental premises which lead to the opposed and erroneous conclusion. For indeed the conviction of pure science must be unshakable.

Some hold that, owing to the necessity of knowing the primary premisses, there is no scientific knowledge. Others think there is, but that all truths are demonstrable. Neither doctrine is either true or a necessary deduction from the premises. The first school, assuming that there is no way of knowing other than by demonstration, maintain that an infinite regress is involved, on the ground that if behind the prior stands no primary, we could not know the posterior through the prior (wherein they are right, for one cannot traverse an infinite series): if on the other hand—they say—the series terminates and there are primary premises, yet these are unknowable because incapable of demonstration, which according to them is the only form of knowledge. And since thus one cannot know the primary premises, knowledge of the conclusions which follow from them is not pure scientific knowledge nor properly knowing at all, but rests on the mere supposition that the premises are true. The other party agree with them as regards knowing, holding that it is only possible by demonstration, but they see no difficulty in holding that all truths are demonstrated, on the ground that demonstration may be circular and reciprocal.

Our own doctrine is that not all knowledge is demonstrative: on the contrary, knowledge of the immediate premises is independent of demonstration. The necessity of this is obvious; for since we must know the prior premises from which the demonstration is drawn, and since the regress must end in immediate truths, those truths must be indemonstrable. Such, then, is our doctrine, and in addition we maintain that besides

254

22. and 23. Paintings around the outside of a cup by Douris. *Top:* youths being instructed in the double flute (aulos) and in writing. *Bottom:* students learning to perform on the lyre and to recite poetry by reading from a scroll held by a master.

scientific knowledge there is its originative source which enables us to recognize the definitions.

Now demonstration must be based on premises prior to and better known than the conclusion; and the same things cannot simultaneously be both prior and posterior to one another: so circular demonstration is clearly not possible in the unqualified sense of "demonstration," but only possible if "demonstration" be extended to include that other method of argument which rests on a distinction between truths prior to us and truths without qualification prior, i.e. the method by which induction produces knowledge. But if we accept this extension of its meaning, our definition of unqualified knowledge will prove faulty; for there seem to be two kinds of it. Perhaps, however, the second form of demonstration, that which proceeds from truths better known to us, is not demonstration in the unqualified sense of the term.

The advocates of circular demonstration are not only faced with the difficulty we have just stated: in addition their theory reduces to the mere statement that if a thing exists, then it does exist—an easy way of proving anything. That this is so can be clearly shown by taking three terms, for to constitute the circle it makes no difference whether many terms or few or even only two are taken. Thus by direct proof, if A is, B must be; if B is, C must be; therefore if A is, C must be. Since then—by the circular proof—if A is, B must be, and if B is, A must be, A may be substituted for C above. Then "if B is, A must be" = "if B is, C must be," which above gave the conclusion "if A is, C must be": but C and A have been identified. Consequently the upholders of circular demonstration are in the position of saying that if A is, A must be—a simple way of proving anything. Moreover, even such circular demonstration is impossible except in the case of attributes that imply one another, viz. "peculiar" properties.

Now, it has been shown that the positing of one thing—be it one term or one premiss—never involves a necessary consequent: two premisses constitute the first and smallest foundation for drawing a conclusion at all and therefore a fortiori for the demonstrative syllogism of science. If, then, A is implied in B and C, and B and C are reciprocally implied in one another and in A, it is possible, as has been shown in my writings on the syllogism, to prove all the assumptions on which the original conclusion rested, by circular demonstration in the first figure. But it has also been shown that in the other figures either no conclusion is possible, or at least none which proves both the original premisses. Propositions the terms of which are not convertible cannot be circularly demonstrated at all, and since convertible terms occur rarely in actual demonstrations, it is clearly frivolous and impossible to say that demonstration is reciprocal and that therefore everything can be demonstrated.

. . .

Demonstrative knowledge must rest on necessary basic truths; for the object of scientific knowledge cannot be other than it is. Now attributes attaching essentially to their subjects attach necessarily to them: for essential attributes are either elements in the essential nature of their subjects or contain their subjects as elements in their own essential nature. (The pairs of opposites which the latter class includes are necessary because one member or the other necessarily inheres.) It follows from this that premisses of the demonstrative syllogism must be connexions essential in the sense explained: for all attributes must inhere essentially or else be accidental, and accidental attributes are not necessary to their subjects.

(from *Posterior Analytics*)

6. The Rise of Theology

From the depth of its philosophical exploration, the Greek spirit reached the height of theological exploration. In his Metaphysics, *Aristotle turns his attention to an analysis of basic problems of being, and elaborates a natural theology characterized by the fact that it has freed itself completely from myth. In Plato, religion and philosophical theology are still deeply interwoven; in Aristotle's proof of God's existence we are confronted with a purely rational analysis of this question.*

PLATO

FROM THE LAWS

. . . May we not conceive each of us living beings to be a puppet of the Gods, either their plaything only, or created with a purpose—which of the two we cannot certainly know?

. . .

. . . The life which is by the Gods deemed to be the happiest is also the best;—we shall affirm this to be a most certain truth; and the minds of our young disciples will be more likely to receive these words of ours than any others which we might address to them.

·   ·   ·

. . . God governs all things, and . . . chance and opportunity cooperate with Him in the government of human affairs.

·   ·   ·

. . . But if states are to be named after their rulers, the true state ought to be called by the name of the God who rules over wise men.

·   ·   ·

In like manner God, in His love of mankind, placed over us the demons, who are a superior race, and they with great ease and pleasure to themselves, and no less to us, taking care of us and giving us peace and reverence and order and justice never failing, made the tribes of men happy and united. And this tradition, which is true, declares that cities of which some mortal man and not God is the ruler have no escape from evils and toils.

·   ·   ·

Now God ought to be to us the measure of all things, and not man, as men commonly say (Protagoras): the words are far more true of Him. And he who would be dear to God must, as far as is possible, be like Him and such as He is. Wherefore the temperate man is the friend of God, for he is like Him; and the intemperate man is unlike Him, and different from Him, and unjust.

·   ·   ·

Of all the things which a man has, next to the Gods, his soul is the most divine and most truly his own.

·   ·   ·

Truth is the beginning of every good thing both to Gods and men; and he who would be blessed and happy, should be from the first a partaker of the truth, that he may live a true man as long as possible, for then he can be trusted; but he is not to be trusted who loves voluntary falsehood, and he who loves involuntary falsehood is a fool.

· · ·

Every man should remember the universal rule, that he who is not a good servant will not be a good master; a man should pride himself more upon serving well than upon commanding well: first upon serving the laws, which is also the service of the Gods; in the second place, upon having served ancient and honourable men in the days of his youth.

· · ·

I say that about serious matters a man should be serious, and about a matter which is not serious he should not be serious; and that God is the natural and worthy object of our most serious and blessed endeavours, for man, as I said before, is made to be the plaything of God, and this, truly considered is the best of him.

· · ·

Men say that we ought not to enquire into the supreme God and the nature of the universe, nor busy ourselves in searching out the causes of things, and that such enquiries are impious; whereas the very opposite is the truth.

· · ·

But when any one has any good and true notion which is for the advantage of the state and in every way acceptable to God, he cannot abstain from expressing it.

· · ·

For we have already said in general terms what shall be the punishment of sacrilege, whether fraudulent or violent, and now we have to determine what is to be the punishment of those who speak or act insolently toward the Gods.

· · ·

But is there any difficulty in proving the existence of the Gods? . . .
In the first place; the earth and the sun, and the stars and the universe,
and the fair order of the seasons, and the division of them into years
and months, furnish proofs of their existence; and also there is the fact
that all Hellenes and barbarians believe in them.

.   .   .

At Athens there are tales preserved in writing which the virtue of your
state, as I am informed, refuses to admit. They speak of the Gods in
prose as well as verse, and the oldest of them tell of the origin of the
heavens and of the world, and not far from the beginning of their story
they proceed to narrate the birth of the Gods, and how after they were
born they behaved to one another: Whether these stories have in other
ways a good or a bad influence, I should not like to be severe upon
them, because they are ancient; but, looking at them with reference to
the duties of children to their parents, I cannot praise them, or think
that they are useful, or at all true. Of the words of the ancients I have
nothing more to say; and I should wish to say of them only what is
pleasing to the Gods. But as to our younger generation and their wisdom,
I cannot let them off when they do mischief. For do but mark the effect
of their words: when you and I argue for the existence of the Gods, and
produce the sun, moon, stars, and earth, claiming for them a divine
being, if we would listen to the aforesaid philosophers we should say
that they are earth and stones only, which can have no care at all of
human affairs, and that all religion is a cooking up of words and a make-
believe.

.   .   .

It is a matter of no small consequence, in some way or other to prove
that there are Gods, and that they are good, and regard justice more than
men do. The demonstration of this would be the best and noblest
prelude of all our laws. And therefore, without impatience and without
hurry, let us unreservedly consider the whole matter, summoning up all
the power of persuasion which we possess.

.   .   .

Who can be calm when he is called upon to prove the existence of the

Gods? Who can avoid hating and abhorring the men who are and have
been the cause of this argument; I speak of those who will not believe
the tales which they have heard as babes and sucklings from their mothers
and nurses; repeated by them both in jest and earnest, like charms, who
have also heard them in the sacrificial prayers, and seen sights accompanying them,—sights and sounds delightful to children,—and their
parents during the sacrifices showing an intense earnestness on behalf of
their children and of themselves, and with eager interest talking to the
Gods, and beseeching them, as though they were firmly convinced of
their existence; who likewise see and hear the prostrations and invoca-
tions which are made by Hellenes and barbarians at the rising and setting
of the sun and moon in all the vicissitudes of life, not as if they thought
that there were no Gods, but as if there could be no doubt of their
existence, and no suspicion of their non-existence; when men, knowing
all these things, despise them on no real grounds, as would be admitted
by all who have any particle of intelligence, and when they force us to
say what we are now saying, how can any one in gentle terms remonstrate
with the like of them, when he has to begin by proving to them the
very existence of the Gods? Yet the attempt must be made; for it would
be unseemly that one half of mankind should go mad in their lust of
pleasure, and the other half in their indignation at such persons. Our
address to these lost and perverted natures should not be spoken in
passion; let us suppose ourselves to select some one of them, and gently
say to him, smothering our anger:—O my son, we will say to him, you
are young, and the advance of time will make you reverse many of the
opinions which you now hold. Wait awhile, and do not attempt to
judge at present of the highest things; and that is the highest of which
you now think nothing—to know the Gods rightly and to live accordingly.
And in the first place let me indicate to you one point which is of great
importance, and about which I cannot be deceived:—You and your
friends are not the first who have held this opinion about the Gods.
There have always been persons more or less numerous who have had
the same disorder. I have known many of them, and can tell you, that no
one who had taken up in youth this opinion, that the Gods do not
exist, ever continued in the same until he was old; the two other notions
certainly do continue in some cases, but not in many; the notion, I
mean, that the Gods exist, but take no heed of human things, and the
other notion that they do take heed of them, but are easily propitiated
with sacrifices and prayers. As to the opinion about the Gods which may
some day become clear to you, I advise you to wait and consider if it be

true or not; ask of others, and above all of the legislator. In the meantime take care that you do not offend against the Gods. For the duty of the legislator is and always will be to teach you the truth of these matters.

.   .   .

Perhaps you have seen impious men growing old and leaving their children's children in high offices, and their prosperity shakes your faith —you have known or heard or been yourself an eyewitness of many monstrous impieties, and have beheld men by such criminal means from small beginnings attaining to sovereignty and the pinnacle of greatness; and considering all these things you do not like to accuse the Gods of them, because they are your relatives; and so from some want of reasoning power, and also from an unwillingness to find fault with them, you have come to believe that they exist indeed, but have no thought or care of human things. Now, that your present evil opinion may not grow to still greater impiety, and that we may if possible use arguments which may conjure away the evil before it arrives, we will add another argument to that originally addressed to him who utterly denied the existence of the Gods.

.   .   .

There will probably be no difficulty in proving to him that the Gods care about the small as well as about the great. For he was present and heard what was said, that they are perfectly good, and that the care of all things is most entirely natural to them.

.   .   .

In the first place, you both acknowledge that the Gods hear and see and know all things, and that nothing can escape them which is a matter of sense and knowledge. . . .

.   .   .

. . . It would not be natural for the Gods who own us, and who are the most careful and the best of owners, to neglect us.

.   .   .

Are we assured that there are two things which lead men to believe in the Gods as we have already stated? . . . One is the argument about the soul, which has been already mentioned—that it is the eldest and most divine of all things, to which motion attaining generation gives perpetual existence; the other was an argument from the order of the motion of the stars, and of all things under the dominion of the mind which ordered the universe. If a man look upon the world not lightly or ignorantly, there was never any one so godless who did not experience an effect opposite to that which the many imagine. For they think that those who handle these matters by the help of astronomy, and the accompanying arts of demonstration, may become godless, because they see, as far as they can see, things happening by necessity, and not by an intelligent will accomplishing good.

But what is the fact?

Just the opposite, as I said, of the opinion which once prevailed among men, that the sun and stars are without soul. Even in those days men wondered about them; and that which is now ascertained was then conjectured by some who had a more exact knowledge of them—that if they had been things without soul, and had no mind, they could never have moved with numerical exactness so wonderful, and even at that time some ventured to hazard the conjecture that mind was the ordered of the universe: But these same persons again mistaking the nature of the soul, which they conceived to be younger and not older than the body, once more overturned the world, or rather, I should say, themselves, for the bodies which they saw moving in heaven all appeared to be full of stones, and earth, and many other lifeless substances, and to these they assigned the causes of all things. Such studies gave rise to much atheism and perplexity, and the poets took occasion to be abusive, —comparing the philosophers to she-dogs uttering vain howlings, and talking other nonsense of the same sort. But now, as I said, the case is reversed.

PLATO

THE ESSENCE OF BEAUTY

. . . For he who would proceed aright in this matter should begin in youth to visit beautiful forms; and first, if he be guided by his instructor aright, to love one such form only—out of that he should create fair thoughts; and soon he will of himself perceive that the beauty of one form is akin to the beauty of another; and then if beauty of form in general is his pursuit, how foolish would he be not to recognize that the beauty in every form is one and the same! And when he perceives this he will abate his violent love of the one, which he will despise and deem a small thing, and will become a lover of all beautiful forms; in the next stage he will consider that the beauty of the mind is more honourable than the beauty of the outward form. So that if a virtuous soul have but a little comeliness, he will be content to love and tend him, and will search out and bring to the birth thoughts which may improve the young, until he is compelled to contemplate and see the beauty of institutions and laws, and to understand that the beauty of them all is of one family, and that personal beauty is a trifle; and after laws and institutions he will go on to the sciences, that he may see their beauty, being not like a servant in love with the beauty of one youth or man or institution, himself a slave mean and narrow-minded, but drawing towards and contemplating the vast sea of beauty, he will create many fair and noble thoughts and notions in boundless love of wisdom; until on that shore he grows and waxes strong, and at last the vision is revealed to him of a single science, which is the science of beauty everywhere. To this I will proceed; please to give me your very best attention.

He who has been instructed thus far in the things of love, and who has learned to see the beautiful in due order and succession, when he comes toward the end will suddenly perceive a nature of wondrous beauty (and this, Socrates, is the final cause of all our former toils)—a nature which in the first place is everlasting, not growing and decaying, or waxing and waning; secondly, not fair in one point of view and foul in another, or at one time or in one relation or at one place fair, at another time or in another relation or at another place foul, as if fair to some and foul to others, or in the likeness of a face or hands or any other part of the bodily frame, or in any form of speech or knowledge, or existing in any other being, as for example, in an animal, or in heaven, or in earth, or in any other place; but beauty absolute, separate, simple, and everlasting, which without diminution and without increase, or any change, is imparted to the ever-growing and perishing beauties of all other things. He who from these ascending under the influence of true love, begins to perceive that beauty, is not far from the end. And the true order of going, or being led by another, to the things of love, is to begin from the beauties of earth and mount upwards for the sake of that other beauty, using these as steps only, and from one going on to two, and from two to all fair forms, and from fair forms to fair practices, and from fair practices to fair notions, until from fair notions he arrives at the notion of absolute beauty, and at last knows what the essence of beauty is.

(from *The Symposium*)

ARISTOTLE

THE PRIME MOVER

Since there were three kinds of substance, two of them physical and one unmovable, regarding the latter we must assert that it is necessary that there should be an eternal unmovable substance. For substances are the first of existing things, and if they are all destructible, all things are destructible. But it is impossible that movement should either have come into being or cease to be (for it must always have existed), or that time should. For there could not be a before and an after if time did not exist. Movement also is continuous, then, in the sense in which time is; for time is either the same thing as movement or an attribute of movement. And there is no continuous movement except movement in place, and of this only that which is circular is continuous.

But if there is something which is capable of moving things or acting on them, but is not actually doing so, there will not necessarily be movement; for that which has a potency need not exercise it. Nothing, then, is gained even if we suppose eternal substances, as the believers in the Forms do, unless there is to be in them some principle which can cause change; nay, even this is not enough, nor is another substance besides the Forms enough; for if it is not to *act*, there will be no movement. Further, even if it acts, this will not be enough, if its essence is potency; for there will not be *eternal* movement, since that which is potentially may possibly not be. There must, then, be such a principle, whose very essence is actuality. Further, then, these substances must be without matter; for they must be eternal, if *anything* is eternal. Therefore they must be actuality.

Yet there is a difficulty; for it is thought that everything that acts is able to act, but that not everything that is able to act acts, so that the potency is prior. But if this is so, nothing that is need be; for it is possible for all things to be capable of existing but not yet to exist.

Yet if we follow the theologians who generate the world from night, or the natural philosophers who say that "all things were together," the same impossible result ensues. For how will there be movement, if there is no actually existing cause? Wood will surely not move itself—the carpenter's art must act on it; nor will the menstrual blood nor the earth set themselves in motion, but the seeds must act on the earth and the semen on the menstrual blood.

This is why some suppose eternal actuality—e.g. Leucippus and Plato; for they say there is always movement. But why and what this movement is they do not say, nor, if the world moves in this way or that, do they tell us the cause of its doing so. Now nothing is moved at random, but there must always be something present to move it; e.g. as a matter of fact a thing moves in one way by nature, and in another by force or through the influence of reason or something else. (Further, what sort of movement is primary? This makes a vast difference.) But again for Plato, at least, it is not permissible to name here that which he sometimes supposes to be the source of movement—that which moves itself; for the soul is later, and coeval with the heavens, according to his account. To suppose potency prior to actuality, then, is in a sense right, and in a sense not; and we have specified these senses. That actuality is prior is testified by Anaxagoras (for his "reason" is actuality) and by Empedocles in his doctrine of love and strife, and by those who say that there is always movement, e.g. Leucippus. Therefore chaos or night did not exist for an infinite time, but the same things have always existed (either passing through a cycle of changes or obeying some other law), since actuality is prior to potency. If, then, there is a constant cycle, something must always remain, acting in the same way. And if there is to be generation and destruction, there must be something else which is always acting in different ways. This must, then, act in one way in virtue of itself, and in another in virtue of something else—either of a third agent, therefore, or of the first. Now it must be in virtue of the first. For otherwise this again causes the motion both of the second agent and of the third. Therefore it is better to say "the first." For it was the cause of eternal uniformity; and something else is the cause of variety, and evidently both together are the cause of eternal variety. This, accordingly, is the character which the motions actually exhibit. What need then is there to seek for other principles?

Since (1) this is a possible account of the matter, and (2) if it were not true, the world would have proceeded out of night and "all things together" and out of non-being, these difficulties may be taken as solved. There is, then, something which is always moved with an unceasing motion, which is motion in a circle; and this is plain not in theory only but in fact. Therefore the first heaven must be eternal. There is therefore also something which moves it. And since that which is moved and moves is intermediate, there is something which moves without being moved, being eternal, substance, and actuality. And the object of desire and the object of thought move in this way; they move without being moved. The primary objects of desire and of thought are the same. For the apparent good is the object of appetite, and the real good is the primary object of rational wish. But desire is consequent on opinion rather than opinion on desire; for the thinking is the starting-point. And thought is moved by the object of thought, and one of the two columns of opposites is in itself the object of thought; and in this, substance is first, and in substance, that which is simple and exists actually. (The one and the simple are not the same; for "one" means a measure, but "simple" means that the thing itself has a certain nature.) But the beautiful, also, and that which is in itself desirable are in the same column; and the first in any class is always best, or analogous to the best.

That a final cause may exist among unchangeable entities is shown by the distinction of its meanings. For the final cause is (*a*) some being for whose good an action is done, and (*b*) something at which the action aims; and of these the latter exists among unchangeable entities though the former does not. The final cause, then, produces motion as being loved, but all other things move by being moved.

Now if something is moved it is capable of being otherwise than as it is. Therefore if its actuality is the primary form of spatial motion, then in so far as it is subject to change, in *this* respect it is capable of being otherwise—in place, even if not in substance. But since there is something which moves while itself unmoved, existing actually, this can in no way be otherwise than as it is. For motion in space is the first of the kinds of change, and motion in a circle the first kind of spatial motion; and this the first mover *produces*. The first mover, then, exists of necessity; and in so far as it exists by necessity, its mode of being is good, and it is in this sense a first principle. For the necessary has all these senses—that which is necessary perforce because it is contrary to the natural impulse, that without which the good is impossible, and that which cannot be otherwise but can exist only in a single way.

On such a principle, then, depend the heavens and the world of nature. And it is a life such as the best which we enjoy, and enjoy for but a short time (for it is ever in this state, which we cannot be), since its actuality is also pleasure. (And for this reason are waking, perception, and thinking most pleasant, and hopes and memories are so on account of these.) And thinking in itself deals with that which is best in itself, and that which is thinking in the fullest sense with that which is best in the fullest sense. And thought thinks on itself because it shares the nature of the object of thought; for it becomes an object of thought in coming into contact with and thinking its objects, so that thought and object of thought are the same. For that which is *capable* of receiving the object of thought, i.e. the essence, is thought. But it is *active* when it *possesses* this object. Therefore the possession rather than the receptivity is the divine element which thought seems to contain, and the act of contemplation is what is most pleasant and best. If, then, God is always in that good state in which we sometimes are, this compels our wonder; and if in a better this compels it yet more. And God *is* in a better state. And life also belongs to God; for the actuality of thought is life, and God is that actuality; and God's self-dependent actuality is life most good and eternal. We say therefore that God is a living being, eternal, most good, so that life and duration continuous and eternal belong to God; for this *is* God.

Those who suppose, as the Pythagoreans and Speusippus do, that supreme beauty and goodness are not present in the beginning, because the beginnings both of plants and of animals are *causes,* but beauty and completeness are in the *effects* of these, are wrong in their opinion. For the seed comes from other individuals which are prior and complete, and the first thing is not seed but the complete being; e.g. we must say that before the seed there is a man—not the man produced from the seed, but another from whom the seed comes.

It is clear then from what has been said that there is a substance which is eternal and unmovable and separate from sensible things. It has been shown also that this substance cannot have any magnitude, but is without part and indivisible (for it produces movement through infinite time, but nothing finite has infinite power; and, while every magnitude is either infinite or finite, it cannot, for the above reason, have finite magnitude, and it cannot have infinite magnitude because there is no infinite magnitude at all). But it has also been shown that it is impassive and unalterable; for all the other changes are posterior to change of place.

(from *Metaphysics,* XII)

III

Fate and Freedom

We are all puppets in the hands of aegis-bearing Zeus.

Homer, *Iliad*

1. Fate, Suffering and Crime

The Greeks were keenly conscious of men's dependence upon higher powers above them. The concern of the gods in human affairs and the pitilessness of fate set the framework of human life and human suffering. Yet, step by step, through a slow process of development, the Greeks achieved an ever sharper awareness of man's freedom of will and his responsibility. The role of fate is predominant in Homer, the elaboration of man's free will is found above all in Aristotle's ethics. The interplay of fate and of man's freedom, the difference between suffering resulting from fate and suffering resulting from crime is the warp and woof of Greek tragedies.

The interplay of fate and freedom as well as the mystery of human suffering remain the very core of Sophocles' dramas: Oedipus *finds himself under the crushing weight of a fate from which escape is unthinkable. But in* Oedipus at Colonus, *Sophocles ushers in a new dimension of moral consciousness. Shortly before his mysterious death, Oedipus exonerates himself from guilt, for he lacked knowledge of whom he was killing and of whom he married. The gods have placed him in a tragedy whose actor he is, but a passive and unwilling actor; he is the puppet of destiny; he is not responsible for his deeds.*

In Sophocles man becomes more keenly conscious of the fundamental difference existing between crime and suffering; for if crime always will carry with it the seed of suffering, the latter can exist in guiltless beings. Condemned by society, Oedipus proclaims his own innocence after having drunk to the very dregs the cup of human sorrow.

In Euripides the complexity of the interplay of fate and freedom gains in drama and assumes at times the character of an

open revolt against the gods and fate (Jaeger, Paideia, *I, p.
348). The inner dynamism of human passions and their psy-
chological laws receive the stage light.*

*Medea typifies a woman who has been slighted and betrayed,
and has a clear consciousness of the situation she is in: Jason,
who was so indebted to her, has abandoned her and her two
children, and is about to contract a new marriage. Medea's
hatred of her former husband is the only thing which, subjec-
tively speaking, remains real, and the series of crimes she per-
petrates is not the result of momentary folly, but rather the
logical, implacable consequence of the hatred.*

HOMER

A FATEFUL WRATH

He [Achilles] said: his finish'd wrath with loud acclaim
The Greeks accept, and shout Pelides' name.
When thus, not rising from his lofty throne,
In state unmoved, the king of men [Agamemnon] begun:
   "Hear me, ye sons of Greece! with silence hear!
And grant your monarch an impartial ear;
Awhile your loud, untimely joy suspend,
And let your rash, injurious clamours end:
Unruly murmurs, or ill-timed applause,
Wrong the best speaker, and the justest cause.
Nor charge on me, ye Greeks, the dire debate:
Know, angry Jove, and all-compelling Fate,
With fell Erinnys, urged my wrath that day
When from Achilles' arms I forced the prey.
What then could I against the will of heaven?
Not by myself, but vengeful Atè driven;
She, Jove's dread daughter, fate to infest
The race of mortals, enter'd in my breast.
Not on the ground that haughty fury treads,
But prints her lofty footsteps on the heads
Of mighty men; inflicting as she goes
Long-festering wounds, inextricable woes!
Of old, she stalk'd amid the bright abodes;
And Jove himself, the sire of men and gods,

The world's great ruler, felt her venom'd dart;
Deceiv'd by Juno's wiles, and female art:
For when Alcmena's nine long months were run,
And Jove expected his immortal son,
To gods and goddesses the unruly joy
He show'd, and vaunted of his matchless boy:
'From us (he said) this day an infant springs,
Fated to rule, and born a king of kings.'
Saturnia ask'd an oath, to vouch the truth,
And fix dominion on the favour'd youth.
The Thunderer, unsuspicious of the fraud,
Pronounced those solemn words that bind a god.
The joyful goddess, from Olympus' height,
Swift to Achaian Argos bent her flight:
Scarce seven moons gone, lay Sthenelus' wife;
She push'd her lingering infant into life:
Her charms Alcmena's coming labours stay,
And stop the babe, just issuing to the day.
Then bids Saturnius bear his oath in mind;
'A youth (said she) of Jove's immortal kind
Is this day born: from Sthenelus he springs,
And claims thy promise to be king of kings.'
Grief seized the Thunderer, by his oath engaged;
Stung to the soul, he sorrow'd, and he raged.
From his ambrosial head, where perch'd she sate,
He snatch'd the fury-goddess of debate,
The dread, the irrevocable oath he swore,
The immortal seats should ne'er behold her more;
And whirl'd her headlong down, for ever driven
From bright Olympus and the starry heaven:
Thence on the nether world the fury fell;
Ordain'd with man's contentious race to dwell.
Full oft the god his son's hard toils bemoan'd,
Cursed the dire fury, and in secret groan'd.
Even thus, like Jove himself, was I misled,
While raging Hector heap'd our camps with dead.
What can the errors of my rage atone?
My martial troops, my treasures are thy own:
This instant from the navy shall be sent
Whate'er Ulysses promised at thy tent:

But thou! appeased, propitious to our prayer,
Resume thy arms, and shine again in war."

(from The Iliad, Book XIX)

SOPHOCLES

from OEDIPUS AT COLONUS

The Chorus of Elders of Colonus *encounters the blind* Oedipus *and his daughter,* Antigone. *The two wanderers are poorly dressed and have clearly undergone great hardships.*

CHORUS
What is thy lineage, stranger,—speak!—and who thy sire?

OEDIPUS
Woe is me!—What will become of me, my child?

ANTIGONE
Speak,—for thou art driven to the verge.

OEDIPUS
Then speak I will—I have no way to hide it.

CHORUS
Ye twain make a long delay—come, haste thee!

OEDIPUS
Know ye a son of Laius . . . O! . . . and the race of the Labdacidae?

CHORUS
O Zeus!

OEDIPUS
The hapless Oedipus?

CHORUS
Thou art he?

OEDIPUS
Have no fear of any words that I speak—

(The Chorus *drowns his voice with a shout of execration.)*

OEDIPUS
Unhappy that I am! Daughter, what is about to befall?

CHORUS
Out with you! forth from the land!

24. Caryatids of south porch, Erechtheum. Athens, Acropolis.

OEDIPUS

And thy promise—to what fulfilment wilt thou bring it?

CHORUS

No man is visited by fate if he requites deeds which were first done to himself; deceit on the one part matches deceits on the other, and gives pain, instead of benefit, for reward. And thou—back with thee! out from these seats! avaunt! away from my land with all speed, lest thou fasten some heavier burden on my city!

ANTIGONE

Strangers of the reverent soul, since ye have not borne with mine aged father,—knowing, as ye do, the rumour of his unpurposed deeds,—pity, at least, my hapless self, I implore you, who supplicate you for my sire alone,—supplicate you with eyes that can still look on your own, even as though I were sprung from your own blood, that the sufferer may find compassion.

On you, as on a god, we depend in our misery. Nay, hear us! grant the boon for which we scarce dare hope. By everything sprung from you that ye hold dear, I implore you, yea, by child—by wife, or treasure, or god! Look well and thou wilt not find the mortal who, if a god should lead him on, could escape.

LEADER OF THE CHORUS

Nay, be thou sure, daughter of Oedipus, we pity thee and him alike for your fortune; but, dreading the judgment of the gods, we could not say aught beyond what hath now been said to thee.

OEDIPUS

What good comes, then, of repute or fair fame, if it ends in idle breath; seeing that Athens, as men say, has the perfect fear of Heaven, and the power, above all cities, to shelter the vexed stranger, and the power, above all, to succour him?

And where find I these things, when, after making me rise up from these rocky seats, ye then drive me from the land, afraid of my name alone? Not, surely, afraid of my person or of mine acts; since mine acts, at least, have been in suffering rather than doing—were it seemly that I should tell you the story of my mother or my sire, by reason whereof ye dread me—that know I full well.

And yet in *nature* how was I evil? I, who was but requiting a wrong, so that, had I been acting with knowledge, even then I could not be accounted wicked; but, as it was, all unknowing went I—whither I went—while they who wronged me knowingly sought my ruin.

Wherefore, strangers, I beseech you by the gods, even as ye made me leave my seat, so protect me, and do not, while ye honour the gods, refuse to give those gods their due; but rather deem that they look on the god-fearing among men, and on the godless, and that never yet hath escape been found for an impious mortal on the earth.

With the help of those gods, spare to cloud the bright fame of Athens by ministering to unholy deeds; but, as ye have received the suppliant under your pledge, rescue me and guard me to the end; nor scorn me when ye look on this face unlovely to behold: for I have come to you as one sacred, and pious, and fraught with comfort for this people. But when the master is come, whosoever he be that is your chief, then shall ye hear and know all; meanwhile in no wise show yourself false.

LEADER

The thoughts urged on thy part, old man, must needs move awe; they have been set forth in words not light; but I am content that the rulers of our country should judge in this cause.

.   .   .

THESEUS

What means this shout? What is the trouble? What fear can have moved you to stay my sacrifice at the altar unto the sea-god, the lord of your Colonus? Speak, that I may know all, since therefore have I sped hither with more than easeful speed of foot.

OEDIPUS

Ah, friend,—I know thy voice,—yon man, but now, hath done me foul wrong.

THESEUS

What is that wrong? And who hath wrought it? Speak!

OEDIPUS

Creon, whom thou seest there, hath torn away from me my two children,—mine all.

THESEUS

What dost thou tell me?

OEDIPUS

Thou hast heard my wrong.

THESEUS

Haste, one of you, to the altars yonder,—constrain the folk to leave

the sacrifice, and to speed—footmen,—horsemen all, with slack rein,—
to the region where the two highways meet, lest the maidens pass, and I
become a mockery to this stranger, as one spoiled by force. Away, I tell
thee—quick!—(*Some guards go out.*) As for yon man—if my wrath went
as far as he deserves—I would not have suffered him to go scatheless
from my hand. But now such law as he himself hath brought, and no
other, shall be the rule for his correction.—(*Addressing* CREON) Thou
shalt not quit this land until thou bring those maidens, and produce
them in my sight; for thy deed is a disgrace to me, and to thine own race,
and to thy country. Thou hast come unto a city that observes justice,
and sanctions nothing without law,—yet thou hast put her lawful powers
aside,—thou hast made this rude inroad,—thou art taking captives at
thy pleasure, and snatching prizes by violence, as in the belief that my
city was void of men, or manned by slaves, and I—a thing of nought.

Yet 'tis not by Theban training that thou art base; Thebes is not wont
to rear unrighteous sons; nor would she praise thee, if she learned that
thou art spoiling me,—yea, spoiling the gods, when by force thou leadest
off their hapless suppliants. Now, were my foot upon thy soil, never
would I wrest or plunder, without licence from the ruler of the land,
whoso he might be—no, though my claim were of all claims most just: I
should know how an alien ought to live among citizens. But thou art
shaming a city that deserves it not, even thine own; and the fulness of
thy years brings thee an old age bereft of wit.

I have said, then, and I say it once again—let the maidens be brought
hither with all speed, unless thou wouldst sojourn in this land by no
free choice;—and this I tell thee from my soul, as with my lips.

LEADER OF THE CHORUS

Seest thou thy plight, O stranger? Thou art deemed to come of a just
race; but thy deeds are found evil.

CREON

Not counting this city void of manhood, son of Aegeus, nor of counsel,
—as thou sayest,—have I wrought this deed; but because I judged that its
folk could never be so enamoured of my kinsfolk as to foster them against
my will. And I knew that this people would not receive a parricide,—a
polluted man,—a man with whom had been found the unholy bride of
her son. Such the wisdom, I knew, that dwells on the Mount of Ares in
their land; which suffers not such wanderers to dwell within this realm.
In that faith, I sought to take this prize. Nor had I done so, but that he
was calling down bitter curses on me, and on my race; when, being so
wronged, I deemed that I had warrant for this requital. For anger knows

no old age, till death come; the dead alone feel no smart.

Therefore thou shalt act as seems to thee good; for, though my cause is just, the lack of aid makes me weak: yet, old though I am, I will endeavour to meet deed with deed.

OEDIPUS

O shameless soul, where, thinkest thou, falls this thy taunt,—on my age, or on thine own? Bloodshed—incest—misery—all this thy lips have launched against me,—all this that I have borne, woe is me! by no choice of mine: for such was the pleasure of the gods, wroth, haply, with the race from of old. Take me alone, and thou couldst find no sin to upbraid me withal, in quittance whereof I was driven to sin thus against myself and against my kin. Tell me, now,—if, by voice of oracle, some divine doom was coming on my sire, that he should die by a son's hand, how couldst thou justly reproach me therewith, who was then unborn,—whom no sire had yet begotten, no mother's womb conceived? And if, when born to woe—as I was born—I met my sire in strife, and slew him, all ignorant what I was doing, and to whom,—how couldst thou justly blame the unknowing deed?

And my mother—wretch, hast thou no shame in forcing me to speak of her nuptials, when she was thy sister, and they such as I will now tell —for verily I will not be silent, when thou hast gone so far in impious speech. Yea, she was my mother,—oh, misery!—my mother,—I knew it not, nor she—and, for her shame, bare children to the son whom she had borne. But one thing, at least, I know,—that thy will consents thus to revile her and me; but not of my free will did I wed her and not of free will do I speak now.

Nay, not in this marriage shall I be called guilty, nor in that slaying of my sire which thou ever urgest against me with bitter reviling. Answer me but one thing that I ask thee. If, here and now, one should come up and seek to slay thee—thee, the righteous—wouldst thou ask if the murderer was thy father, or wouldst thou reckon with him straightway? I think, as thou lovest thy life, thou wouldst requite the culprit, nor look around thee for thy warrant. But such the plight into which *I* came, led by gods; and in this, could my sire come back to life, methinks he would not gainsay me.

Yet *thou,*—for thou art not a just man, but one who holds all things meet to utter, knowing no barrier betwixt speech and silence—*thou* tauntest me in such wise, before yon men. And thou findest it timely to flatter the renowned Theseus, and Athens, saying how well her State hath been ordered: yet, while giving such large praise, thou forgettest

25. Temple of Apollo, Delphi.

this,—that if any land knows how to worship the gods with due rites, this land excels therein; whence thou hadst planned to steal me, the suppliant, the old man, and didst seek to seize me, and hast already carried off my daughters. Wherefore I now call on yon goddesses, I supplicate them, I adjure them with prayers, to bring me help and to fight in my cause, that thou mayest learn well by what manner of men this realm is guarded.

LEADER

The stranger is a good man, O king; his fate hath been accurst; but 'tis worthy of our succour.

THESEUS

Enough of words:—the doers of deed are in flight, while we, the sufferers, stand still.

CREON

What, then, wouldst thou have a helpless man to do?

THESEUS

Show the way in their track,—while I escort thee,—that, if in these regions thou hast the maidens of our quest, thou thyself mayest discover them to me; but if thy men are fleeing with the spoil in their grasp, we may spare our trouble; the chase is for others, from whom they will never escape out of this land, to thank their gods.

Come,—forward! The spoiler hath been spoiled, I tell thee—Fate hath taken the hunter in the toils; gains got by wrongful arts are soon lost. And thou shalt have no ally in thine aim, for well wot I that not without accomplice or resource hast thou gone to such a length of violence in the daring mood which hath inspired thee here: no,—there was some one in whom thou wast trusting when thou didst essay these deeds. And to this I must look, nor make this city weaker than one man. Dost thou take my drift? Or seem these words as vain as seemed the warnings when thy deed was still a-planning?

CREON

Say what thou wilt while thou art here,—I will not cavil: but at home I, too, will know how to act.

THESEUS

For the present, threaten, but go forward.—Do thou, Oedipus, stay here in peace, I pray thee,—with my pledge that, unless I die before, I will not cease till I put thee in possession of thy children.

OEDIPUS

Heaven reward thee, Theseus, for thy nobleness, and thy loyal care in my behalf!

EURIPIDES

FROM MEDEA

. . .

MEDEA

On all sides sorrow pens me in. Who shall gainsay this? But all is not yet lost! think not so. Still are there troubles in store for the new bride, and for her bridegroom no light toil. Dost think I would ever have fawned on yonder man, unless to gain some end or form some scheme? Nay, I would not so much as have spoken to him or touched him with my hand. But he has in folly so far stepped in that, though he might have checked my plot by banishing me from the land, he hath allowed me to abide this day, in which I will lay low in death three of my enemies—a father and his daughter and my husband too. Now, though I have many ways to compass their death, I am not sure, friends, which I am to try first. Shall I set fire to the bridal mansion, or plunge the whetted sword through their hearts, softly stealing into the chamber where their couch is spread? One thing stands in my way. If I am caught making my way into the chamber, intent on my design, I shall be put to death and cause my foes to mock. 'Twere best to take the shortest way—the way we women are most skilled in—by poison to destroy them. Well, suppose them dead; what city will receive me? What friendly host will give me a shelter in his land, a home secure, and save my soul alive? None. So I will wait yet a little while in case some tower of defence rise up for me; then will I proceed to this bloody deed in crafty silence; but if some unexpected mischance drive me forth, I will with mine own hand seize the sword, e'en though I die for it, and slay them, and go forth on my bold path of daring. By that dread queen whom I revere before all others and have chosen to share my task, by Hecate who dwells within my inmost chamber, not one of them shall wound my heart and rue it not. Bitter and sad will I make their marriage for them; bitter shall be the wooing of it, bitter my exile from the land. Up, then, Medea, spare not the secrets of thy art in plotting and devising; on to the danger. Now comes a struggle needing courage. Dost see what thou art suffering? 'Tis not for thee to be a laughing-stock to the race of Sisyphus by reason of this wedding of Jason, sprung, as thou art, from a noble sire, and of the Sun-god's race. Thou hast cunning; and, more than this, we women, though by nature little apt for virtuous deeds, are most expert to fashion any mischief.

.   .   .

JASON

It is not now I first remark, but oft ere this, how unruly a pest is a harsh temper. For instance, thou, hadst thou but patiently endured the will of thy superiors, mightest have remained here in this land and house, but now for thy idle words wilt thou be banished. Thy words are naught to me. Cease not to call Jason basest of men; but for those words thou hast spoken against our rulers, count it all gain that exile is thy only punishment. I ever tried to check the outbursts of the angry monarch, and would have had thee stay, but thou wouldst not forego thy silly rage, always reviling our rulers, and so thou wilt be banished. Yet even after all this I weary not of my goodwill, but am come with thus much forethought, lady, that thou mayst not be destitute nor want for aught, when, with thy sons, thou art cast out. Many an evil doth exile bring in its train with it; for even though thou hatest me, never will I harbour hard thoughts of thee.

MEDEA

Thou craven villain (for that is the only name my tongue can find for thee, a foul reproach on thy unmanliness), comest thou to me, thou, most hated foe of gods, of me, and of all mankind? 'Tis no proof of courage or hardihood to confront thy friends after injuring them, but that worst of all human diseases—loss of shame. Yet hast thou done well to come; for I shall ease my soul by reviling thee, and thou wilt be vexed at my recital. I will begin at the very beginning. I saved thy life, as every Hellene knows who sailed with thee aboard the good ship Argo, when thou wert sent to tame and yoke fire-breathing bulls, and to sow the deadly tilth. Yea, and I slew the dragon which guarded the golden fleece, keeping sleepless watch o'er it with many a wreathed coil, and I raised for thee a beacon of deliverance. Father and home of my free will I left and came with thee to Iolcos, 'neath Pelion's hills, for my love was stronger than my prudence. Next I caused the death of Pelias by a doom most grievous, even by his own children's hand, beguiling them of all their fear. All this have I done for thee, thou traitor! and thou hast cast me over, taking to thyself another wife, though children have been born to us. Hadst thou been childless still, I could have pardoned thy desire for this new union. Gone is now the trust I put in oaths. I cannot even understand whether thou thinkest that the gods of old no longer rule, or that fresh decrees are now in vogue amongst mankind, for thy conscience must tell thee thou hast not kept faith with me. Ah! poor right hand, which thou didst often grasp. These knees thou didst embrace! All in vain, I suffered a traitor to touch me! How short of my hopes I am fallen! But come, I will deal with thee as though thou wert my friend. Yet what kindness can I expect from one so base as thee? But yet I will do it, for my questioning will show thee yet more base. Whither can I turn me now? to my father's house, to my own country, which I for thee deserted to come hither? to the hapless daughters of Pelias? A glad welcome, I trow, would they give me in their home, whose father's death I compassed! My case stands even thus: I am become the bitter foe to those of mine own home, and those whom I need ne'er have wronged I made mine enemies to pleasure thee. Wherefore to reward me for this thou hast made me doubly blest in the eyes of many a wife in Hellas; and in thee I own a peerless, trusty lord. O woe is me, if indeed I am to be cast forth an exile from the land, without one friend; one lone woman with her babes forlorn! Yea, a fine reproach to thee in thy bridal hour, that thy children and the wife who saved thy life are beggars and vagabonds! O Zeus! why hast thou granted unto man clear signs to know the sham in gold, while on man's brow no brand is stamped whereby to gauge the villain's heart?

LEADER OF THE CHORUS

There is a something terrible and past all cure, when quarrels arise 'twixt those who are near and dear.

JASON

Needs must I now, it seems, turn orator, and, like a good helmsman on a ship with close-reefed sails, weather that wearisome tongue of thine. Now, I believe, since thou wilt exaggerate thy favours, that to Cypris alone of gods or men I owe the safety of my voyage. Thou hast a subtle wit enough; yet were it a hateful thing for me to say that the Love-god constrained thee by his resistless shaft to save my life. However, I will not reckon this too nicely; 'twas kindly done, however thou didst serve me. Yet for my safety hast thou received more than ever thou gavest, as I will show. First, thou dwellest in Hellas, instead of thy barbarian land, and hast learnt what justice means and how to live by law, not by the dictates of brute force; and all the Hellenes recognized thy cleverness, and thou hast gained a name; whereas, if thou hadst dwelt upon the confines of the earth, no tongue had mentioned thee. Give me no gold within my halls, nor skill to sing a fairer strain than ever Orpheus sang, unless therewith my fame be spread abroad! So much I say to thee about my own toils, for 'twas thou didst challenge me to this retort. As for the taunts thou urgest against my marriage with the princess, I will prove to thee, first, that I am prudent herein, next chastened in my love, and last a powerful friend to thee and to thy sons; only hold thy peace. Since I have here withdrawn from Iolcos with many a hopeless trouble at my back, what happier device could I, an exile, frame than marriage with the daughter of the king? 'Tis not because I loathe thee for my wife —the thought that rankles in thy heart; 'tis not because I am smitten with desire for a new bride, nor yet that I am eager to vie with others in begetting many children, for those we have are quite enough, and I do not complain. Nay, 'tis that we—and this is most important—may dwell in comfort, instead of suffering want (for well I know that every whilom friend avoids the poor), and that I might rear my sons as doth befit my house; further, that I might be the father of brothers for the children thou hast borne, and raise these to the same high rank, uniting the family in one,—to my lasting bliss. Thou, indeed, hast no need of more children, but me it profits to help my present family by that which is to be. Have I miscarried here? Not even thou wouldest say so unless a rival's charms ranked in thy bosom. No, but you women have such strange ideas, that you think all is well so long as your married life runs smooth; but if some mischance occurs to ruffle your love, all that was good and lovely erst you reckon as your foes. Yea, men should have begotten children from some other source, no female race existing; thus would no evil ever have fallen on mankind.

LEADER

This speech, O Jason, hast thou with specious art arranged; but yet I think—albeit in speaking I am indiscreet—that thou hast sinned in thy betrayal of thy wife.

．　　　．　　　．

MEDEA

May that prosperity, whose end is woe, ne'er be mine, nor such wealth as would ever sting my heart!

JASON

Change that prayer as I will teach thee, and thou wilt show more wisdom. Never let happiness appear in sorrow's guise, nor, when thy fortune smiles, pretend she frowns! . . . At least I call the gods to witness, that I am ready in all things to serve thee and thy children, but thou dost scorn my favours and thrustest thy friends stubbornly away; wherefore thy lot will be more bitter still.

MEDEA

Away! By love for thy young bride entrapped, too long thou lingerest outside her chamber; go wed, for, if God will, thou shalt have such a marriage as thou wouldst fain refuse.

．　　　．　　　．

MEDEA

O Zeus, and Justice, child of Zeus, and Sun-god's light, now will I triumph o'er my foes, kind friends; on victory's road have I set forth; good hope have I of wreaking vengeance on those I hate. For where we were in most distress this stranger hath appeared, to be a haven in my counsels; to him will we make fast the cables of our ship when we come to the town and citadel of Pallas. But now will I explain to thee my

26. Erechtheum. Athens, Acropolis.

27. Temple of Apollo, Corinth.

plans in full; do not expect to hear a pleasant tale. A servant of mine will I to Jason send and crave an interview; then when he comes I will address him with soft words, say, "this pleases me," and, "that is well," even the marriage with the princess, which my treacherous lord is celebrating, and add "it suits us both, 'twas well thought out"; then will I entreat that here my children may abide, not that I mean to leave them in a hostile land for foes to flout, but that I may slay the king's daughter by guile. For I will send them with gifts in their hands, carrying them unto the bride to save them from banishment, a robe of finest woof and a chaplet of gold. And if these ornaments she take and put them on, miserably shall she die, and likewise everyone who touches her; with such fell poisons will I smear my gifts. And here I quit this theme; but I shudder at the deed I must do next; for I will slay the children I have borne; there is none shall take them from my toils; and when I have utterly confounded Jason's house I will leave the land, escaping punishment for my dear children's murder, after my most unholy deed. For I cannot endure the taunts of enemies, kind friends; enough! what gain is life to me? I have no country, home, or refuge left. O, I did wrong, that hour I left my father's home, persuaded by that Hellene's words, who now shall pay the penalty, so help me God. Never shall he see again alive the children I bore to him, nor from his new bride shall he beget issue, for she must die a hideous death, slain by my drugs. Let no one deem me a poor weak woman who sits with folded hands, but of another mould, dangerous to foes and well-disposed to friends; for they win the fairest fame who live their life like me.

.   .   .

JASON

I am come at thy bidding, for e'en though thy hate for me is bitter thou shalt not fail in this small boon, but I will hear what new request thou hast to make of me, lady.

MEDEA

Jason, I crave thy pardon for the words I spoke, and well thou mayest brook my burst of passion, for ere now we twain have shared much love. For I have reasoned with my soul and railed upon me thus, "Ah! poor heart! why am I thus distraught, why so angered 'gainst all good advice, why have I come to hate the rulers of the land, my husband too, who does the best for me he can, in wedding with a princess and rearing for my children noble brothers?" . . .

I yield and do confess that I was wrong then, but now have I come to a better mind. Come hither, my children, come, leave the house, step forth, and with me greet and bid farewell to your father, be reconciled from all past bitterness unto your friends, as now your mother is; for we have made a truce and anger is no more.

Take his right hand; ah me! my sad fate! when I reflect, as now, upon the hidden future. O my children, since there awaits you even thus a long, long life, stretch forth the hand to take a fond farewell. Ah me! how new to tears am I, how full of fear! For now that I have at last released me from my quarrel with your father, I let the tear-drops stream adown my tender cheek.

LEADER OF THE CHORUS

From my eyes too bursts forth the copious tear; O, may no greater ill than the present e'er befall!

JASON

Lady, I praise this conduct, not that I blame what is past; for it is but natural to the female sex to vent their spleen against a husband when he trafficks in other marriages besides his own. But thy heart is changed to wiser schemes and thou art determined on the better course, late though it be; this is acting like a woman of sober sense. . . .

.   .   .

MEDEA

. . . Since it is the pleasure of the rulers of the land to banish me, and well I know 'twere best for me to stand not in the way of thee or of the rulers by dwelling here, enemy as I am thought unto their house, forth from this land in exile am I going, but these children,—that they may know thy fostering hand, beg Creon to remit their banishment.

JASON

I doubt whether I can persuade him, yet must I attempt it.

MEDEA

At least do thou bid thy wife ask her sire this boon, to remit the exile of the children from this land.

JASON

Yea, that will I; and her methinks I shall persuade, since she is a woman like the rest.

MEDEA

I too will aid thee in this task, for by the children's hand I will send

288

to her gifts that far surpass in beauty, I well know, aught that now is seen 'mongst men, a robe of finest tissue and a chaplet of chased gold. But one of my attendants must haste and bring the ornaments hither. Happy shall she be not once alone but ten thousandfold, for in thee she wins the noblest soul to share her love, and gets these gifts as well which on a day my father's sire, the Sun-god, bestowed on his descendants. My children, take in your hands these wedding gifts, and bear them as an offering to the royal maid, the happy bride; for verily the gifts she shall receive are not to be scorned.

JASON

But why so rashly rob thyself of these gifts? Dost think a royal palace wants for robes or gold? Keep them, nor give them to another. For well I know that if my lady hold me in esteem, she will set my price above all wealth.

MEDEA

Say not so; 'tis said that gifts tempt even gods; and o'er men's minds gold holds more potent sway than countless words. Fortune smiles upon thy bride, and heaven now doth swell her triumph; youth is hers and princely power; yet to save my children from exile I would barter life, not dross alone. Children, when we are come to the rich palace, pray your father's new bride, my mistress, with suppliant voice to save you from exile, offering her these ornaments the while; for it is most needful that she receive the gifts in her own hand. Now go and linger not; may ye succeed and to your mother bring back the glad tidings she fain would hear!

.   .   .

(MEDEA *goes into the house with her children.*
Later she returns.)

MEDEA

Kind friends, long have I waited expectantly to know how things would at the palace chance. And lo! I see one of Jason's servants coming hither whose hurried gasps for breath proclaim him the bearer of some fresh tidings.

MESSENGER

Fly, fly, Medea! who hast wrought an awful deed, transgressing every law; nor leave behind or sea-borne bark or car that scours the plain.

MEDEA

Why, what hath chanced that calls for such a flight of mine?

MESSENGER

The princess is dead, a moment gone, and Creon too, her sire, slain by those drugs of thine.

MEDEA

Tidings most fair are thine! Henceforth shalt thou be ranked amongst my friends and benefactors.

MESSENGER

Ha! What? Art sane? Art not distraught, lady, who hearest with joy the outrage to our royal house done, and art not at the horrid tale afraid?

MEDEA

Somewhat have I, too, to say in answer to thy words. Be not so hasty, friend, but tell the manner of their death, for thou wouldst give me double joy, if so they perished miserably.

. . .

MESSENGER

. . . Not now for the first time I think this human life a shadow; yea, and without shrinking I will say that they amongst men who pretend to wisdom and expend deep thought on words do incur a serious charge of folly; for amongst mortals no man is happy; wealth may pour in and make one luckier than another, but none can happy be.

LEADER OF THE CHORUS

This day the deity, it seems, will mass on Jason, as he well deserves, a heavy load of evils. Woe is thee, daughter of Creon! We pity thy sad fate, gone as thou art to Hades' hall as the price of thy marriage with Jason.

MEDEA

My friends, I am resolved upon the deed; at once will I slay my children and then leave this land, without delaying long enough to hand them over to some more savage hand to butcher. Needs must they die in any case; and since they must, I will slay them—I, the mother that bare them. O heart of mine, steel thyself! Why do I hesitate to do the awful deed that must be done? Come, take the sword, thou wretched hand of mine! Take it, and advance to the post whence starts thy life of sorrow! Away with cowardice! Give not one thought to thy babes, how dear they are or how thou art their mother. This one brief day forget thy children dear, and after that lament; for though thou wilt slay them yet they were thy darlings still, and I am a lady of sorrows.

.   .   .

JASON

Ladies, stationed near this house, pray tell me is the author of these hideous deeds, Medea, still within, or hath she fled from hence? For she must hide beneath the earth or soar on wings towards heaven's vault, if she would avoid the vengeance of the royal house. Is she so sure she will escape herself unpunished from this house, when she hath slain the rulers of the land? But enough of this! I am forgetting her children. As for her, those whom she hath wronged will do the like by her; but I am come to save the children's life, lest the victim's kin visit their wrath on me, in vengeance for the murder foul, wrought by my children's mother.

LEADER OF THE CHORUS

Unhappy man, thou knowest not the full extent of thy misery, else had thou never said those words.

JASON

How now? Can she want to kill me too?

LEADER

Thy sons are dead; slain by their own mother's hand.

JASON

O God! what sayest thou? Woman, thou hast sealed my doom.

LEADER

Thy children are no more; be sure of this.

JASON

Where slew she them; within the palace or outside?

LEADER

Throw wide the doors and see thy children's murdered corpses.

JASON

Haste, ye slaves, loose the bolts, undo the fastenings, that I may see the sight of twofold woe, my murdered sons and her, whose blood in vengeance I will shed.

MEDEA

Why shake those doors and attempt to loose their bolts, in quest of the dead and me their murderess? From such toil desist. If thou wouldst aught with me, say on, if so thou wilt; but never shalt thou lay hand on me, so swift the steeds the sun, my father's sire, to me doth give to save me from the hand of my foes.

JASON

Accursed woman! by gods, by me and all mankind abhorred as never woman was, who hadst the heart to stab thy babes, thou their mother, leaving me undone and childless; this hast thou done and still dost gaze upon the sun and earth after this deed most impious. Curses on thee! I now perceive what then I missed in the day I brought thee, fraught with doom, from thy home in a barbarian land to dwell in Hellas, traitress to thy sire and to the land that nurtured thee. On me the gods have hurled the curse that dogged thy steps, for thou didst slay thy brother at his hearth ere thou cam'st aboard our fair ship, Argo. Such was the outset of thy life of crime; then didst thou wed with me, and having borne me sons to glut thy passion's lust, thou now hast slain them. Not one amongst the wives of Hellas e'er had dared this deed; yet before them all I chose thee for my wife, wedding a foe to be my doom, no woman, but a lioness fiercer than Tyrrhene Scylla in nature. But with reproaches heaped a thousandfold I cannot wound thee, so brazen is thy nature. Perish, vile sorceress, murderess of thy babes! Whilst I must mourn my luckless fate, for I shall ne'er enjoy my new-found bride, nor shall I have the children, whom I bred and reared, alive to say the last farewell to me; nay, I have lost them.

MEDEA

To this thy speech I could have made a long reply, but Father Zeus knows well all I have done for thee, and the treatment thou hast given me. Yet thou wert not ordained to scorn my love and lead a life of joy in mockery of me, nor was thy royal bride nor Creon, who gave thee a second wife, to thrust me from this land and rue it not. Wherefore, if thou wilt, call me e'en a lioness, and Scylla, whose home is in the Tyrrhene land; for I in turn have wrung thy heart, as well I might.

JASON

Thou, too, art grieved thyself, and sharest in my sorrow.

MEDEA

Be well assured I am; but it relieves my pain to know thou canst not mock at me.

JASON

O my children, how vile a mother ye have found!

MEDEA

My sons, your father's feeble lust has been your ruin!

JASON

'Twas not my hand, at any rate, that slew them.

MEDEA

No, but thy foul treatment of me, and thy new marriage.

JASON

Didst think that marriage cause enough to murder them?

MEDEA

Dost think a woman counts this a trifling injury?

JASON

So she be self-restrained; but in thy eyes all is evil.

MEDEA

Thy sons are dead and gone. That will stab thy heart.

JASON

They live, methinks, to bring a curse upon thy head.

MEDEA

The gods know, whoso of them began this troublous coil.

JASON

Indeed, they know that hateful heart of thine.

MEDEA

Thou art as hateful. I am aweary of thy bitter tongue.

JASON

And I likewise of thine. But parting is easy.

MEDEA

Say how; what am I to do? for I am fain as thou to go.

JASON

Give up to me those dead, to bury and lament.

MEDEA

No, never! I will bury them myself, bearing them to Hera's sacred field, who watches o'er the Cape, that none of their foes may insult them by pulling down their tombs; and in this land of Sisyphus I will ordain hereafter a solemn feast and mystic rites to atone for this impious murder. Myself will now to the land of Erechtheus, to dwell with Aegeus, Pandion's son. But thou, as well thou mayst, shalt die a caitiff's death, thy head crushed 'neath a shattered relic of Argo, when thou hast seen the bitter ending of my marriage.

.   .   .

2. The Responsibility of Men

In the following passage from Plato's last work, The Laws, the key problem is the conflict existing between passions, conceit of wisdom, and free will—conflict found in man's very soul and not in man's relation to moira (fate) and to the Gods above him. Freedom is not examined as such, but is clearly implied in the discussion on responsibility.

Although the interplay of fate and freedom is not mentioned in the following text, the often-quoted words of Plato, "May we not conceive each of us living beings to be a puppet of the gods?" (Laws, V), indicate that this interplay was still alive in Platonic thought.

In Aristotle's philosophy, on the contrary, fate yields the stage to freedom and the passage quoted below is devoted to a thematic analysis of the nature of freedom and of the difference between voluntary and involuntary actions.

PLATO

from THE LAWS

CLEINIAS. What you have said appears to me to be very reasonable, but will you favor me by stating a little more clearly the difference between hurt and injustice, and the various complications of the voluntary and involuntary which enter into them?

ATHENIAN. I will endeavour to do as you wish:—Concerning the soul, thus much would be generally said and allowed, that one element in her nature is passion, which may be described either as a state or a part of her, and is hard to be striven against and contended with, and by irrational force overturns many things.

CLEINIAS. Very true.

ATHENIAN. And pleasure is not the same with passion, but has an opposite power, working her will by persuasion and by the force of deceit in all things.

CLEINIAS. Quite true.

ATHENIAN. A man may truly say that ignorance is a third cause of crimes. Ignorance, however, may be conveniently divided by the legislator into two sorts: there is simple ignorance, which is the source of lighter of-

28. Acropolis, west view. Athens.

fences, and double ignorance, which is accompanied by a conceit of wisdom; and he who is under the influence of the latter fancies that he knows all about matters of which he knows nothing. This second kind of ignorance, when possessed of power and strength, will be held by the legislator to be the source of great and monstrous crimes, but when attended with weakness, will only result in the errors of children and old men; and these he will treat as errors, and will make laws accordingly for those who commit them, which will be the mildest and most merciful of all laws.

CLEINIAS. You are perfectly right.

ATHENIAN. We all of us remark of one man that he is superior to pleasure and passion, and of another that he is inferior to them; and this is true.

CLEINIAS. Certainly.

ATHENIAN. But no one was ever yet heard to say that one of us is superior and another inferior to ignorance.

CLEINIAS. Very true.

ATHENIAN. We are speaking of motives which incite men to the fulfillment of their will; although an individual may be often drawn by them in opposite directions at the same time.

29. Parthenon, façade. Athens, Acropolis.

CLEINIAS. Yes, often.

ATHENIAN. And now I can define to you clearly, and without ambiguity, what I mean by the just and unjust, according to my notion of them:— When anger and fear, and pleasure and pain, and jealousies and desires, tyrannize over the soul, whether they do any harm or not,—I call all this injustice. But when the opinion of the best, in whatever part of human nature states or individuals may suppose that to dwell, has dominion in the soul and orders the life of every man, even if it be sometimes mistaken, yet what is done in accordance therewith, and the principle in individuals which obeys this rule, and is best for the whole life of man, is to be called just; although the hurt done by mistake is thought by many to be involuntary injustice.

(from The Laws, Book IX)

ARISTOTLE

FREEDOM AND RESPONSIBILITY

Since virtue is concerned with passions and actions, and on voluntary passions and actions praise and blame are bestowed, on those that are involuntary pardon, and sometimes also pity, to distinguish the voluntary and involuntary is presumably necessary for those who are studying the nature of virtue, and useful also for legislators with a view to the assigning both of honours and of punishments.

Those things, then, are thought involuntary, which take place under compulsion or owing to ignorance; and that is compulsory of which the moving principle is outside, being a principle in which nothing is contributed by the person who is acting or is feeling the passion, e.g. if he were to be carried somewhere by a wind, or by men who had him in their power.

But with regard to the things that are done from fear of greater evils or for some noble object (e.g. if a tyrant were to order one to do something base, having one's parents and children in his power, and if one did the action they were to be saved, but otherwise would be put to death), it may be debated whether such actions are involuntary or voluntary. Something of the sort happens also with regard to the throwing of goods overboard in a storm; for in the abstract no one throws goods away voluntarily, but on condition of its securing the safety of himself and his crew any sensible man does so. Such actions, then, are mixed, but are more like voluntary actions; for they are worthy of choice at the time when they are done, and the end of an action is relative to the occasion. Both the terms, then, "voluntary" and "involuntary," must be used with reference to the moment of action. Now the man acts voluntarily; for the principle that moves the instrumental parts of the body in such actions is in him, and the things of which the moving principle is in a man himself are in his power to do or not to do. Such actions, therefore, are voluntary, but in the abstract perhaps involuntary; for no one would choose any such act in itself.

For such actions men are sometimes even praised, when they endure something base or painful in return for great and noble objects gained; in the opposite case they are blamed, since to endure the greatest indignities for no noble end or for a trifling end is the mark of an inferior person. On some actions praise indeed is not bestowed, but pardon is, when one does what he ought not under pressure which overstrains human nature and which no one could withstand. But some acts, perhaps, we cannot be forced to do, but ought rather to face death after the most fearful sufferings; for the things that "forced" Euripides' Alcmaeon to slay his mother seem absurd. It is difficult sometimes to determine what should be chosen at what cost, and what should be endured in return for what gain, and yet more difficult to abide by our decisions; for as a rule what is expected is painful, and what we are forced to do is base, whence praise and blame are bestowed on those who have been compelled or have not.

What sort of acts, then, should be called compulsory? We answer that without qualification actions are so when the cause is in the external circumstances and the agent contributes nothing. But the things that in themselves are involuntary, but now and in return for these gains are worthy of choice, and whose moving principle is in the agent, are in themselves involuntary, but now and in return for these gains voluntary. They are more like voluntary acts; for actions are in the class of particulars, and the particular acts here are voluntary. What sort of things are to be chosen, and in return for what, it is not easy to state; for there are many differences in the particular cases.

But if some one were to say that pleasant and noble objects have a compelling power, forcing us from without, all acts would be for him compulsory; for it is for these objects that all men do everything they do. And those who act under compulsion and unwillingly act with pain, but those who do acts for their pleasantness and nobility do them with pleasure; it is absurd to make external circumstances responsible, and not oneself, as being easily caught by such attractions, and to make oneself responsible for noble acts but the pleasant objects responsible for base acts. The compulsory, then, seems to be that whose moving principle is outside, the person compelled contributing nothing.

Everything that is done by reason of ignorance is *not* voluntary; it is only what produces pain and repentance that is *in*voluntary. For the man who has done something owing to ignorance, and feels not the least vexation at his action, has not acted voluntarily, since he did not know what he was doing, nor yet involuntarily, since he is not pained. Of people, then, who act by reason of ignorance he who repents is thought an involuntary agent, and the man who does not repent may, since he is different, be called a not voluntary agent; for, since he differs from the other, it is better that he should have a name of his own.

Acting by reason of ignorance seems also to be different from acting *in* ignorance; for the man who is drunk or in a rage is thought to act as a result not of ignorance but of one of the causes mentioned, yet not knowingly but in ignorance.

Now every wicked man is ignorant of what he ought to do and what he ought to abstain from, and it is by reason of error of this kind that men become unjust and in general bad; but the term "involuntary" tends to be used not if a man is ignorant of what is to his advantage— for it is not mistaken purpose that causes involuntary action (it leads rather to wickedness), nor ignorance of the universal (for *that* men are *blamed*), but ignorance of particulars, i.e. of the circumstances of the action and the objects with which it is concerned. For it is on these that both pity and pardon depend, since the person who is ignorant of any of these acts involuntarily.

Perhaps it is just as well, therefore, to determine their nature and number. A man may be ignorant, then, of who he is, what he is doing, what or whom he is acting on, and sometimes also what (e.g. what instrument) he is doing it with, and to what end (e.g. he may think his act will conduce to some one's safety), and how he is doing it (e.g. whether gently or violently). Now of all of these no one could be ignorant unless he were mad, and evidently also he could not be ignorant of the agent; for how could he not know himself? But of what he is doing a man might be ignorant, as for instance people say "it slipped out of their mouths as they were speaking," or "they did not know it was a secret," as Aeschylus said of the mysteries, or a man might say he "let it go off when he merely wanted to show its working," as the man did with the catapult. Again, one might think one's son was an enemy, as Merope did, or that a pointed spear had a button on it, or that a stone was pumice-stone; or one might give a man a draught to save him, and really kill him; or one might want to touch a man, as people do in sparring, and really wound him. The ignorance may relate, then, to any of these things, i.e. of the circumstances of the action, and the man who was ignorant of any of these is thought to have acted involuntarily, and especially if he was ignorant on the most important points; and these are thought to be the circumstances of the action and its end. Further, the doing of an act that is called involuntary in virtue of ignorance of this sort must be painful and involve repentance.

.   .   .

Both the voluntary and the involuntary having been delimited, we must next discuss choice; for it is thought to be most closely bound up with virtue and to discriminate characters better than actions do.

Choice, then, seems to be voluntary, but not the same thing as the voluntary; the latter extends more widely. For both children and the lower animals share in voluntary action, but not in choice, and acts done on the spur of the moment we describe as voluntary, but not as chosen.

Those who say it is appetite or anger or wish or a kind of opinion do not seem to be right. For choice is not common to irrational creatures as well, but appetite and anger are. Again, the incontinent man acts with appetite, but not with choice; while the continent man on the contrary acts with choice, but not with appetite. Again, appetite is contrary to choice, but not appetite to appetite. Again, appetite relates to the pleasant and the painful, choice neither to the painful nor to the pleasant.

Still less is it anger; for acts due to anger are thought to be less than any others objects of choice.

But neither is it wish, though it seems near to it; for choice cannot relate to impossibles, and if any one said he chose them he would be thought silly; but there may be a wish even for impossibles, e.g. for immortality. And wish may relate to things that could in no way be brought about by one's own efforts, e.g. that a particular actor or athlete should win in a competition; but no one chooses such things, but only the things that he thinks could be brought about by his own efforts. Again, wish relates rather to the end, choice to the means; for instance, we wish to be healthy, but we choose the acts which will make us healthy, and we wish to be happy and say we do, but we cannot well say we choose

30. Parthenon, view from inside. Athens, Acropolis.

31. Parthenon. Athens, Acropolis.

to be so; for, in general, choice seems to relate to the things that are in our power.

For this reason, too, it cannot be opinion; for opinion is thought to relate to all kinds of things, no less to eternal things and impossible things than to things in our own power; and it is distinguished by its falsity or truth, not by its badness or goodness, while choice is distinguished rather by these.

Now with opinion in general perhaps no one even says it is identical. But it is not identical even with any kind of opinion; for by choosing what is good or bad we are men of a certain character, which we are not by holding certain opinions. And we choose to get or avoid something good or bad, but we have opinions about what a thing is or whom it is good for or how it is good for him; we can hardly be said to opine to get or avoid anything. And choice is praised for being related to the right object rather than for being rightly related to it, opinion for being truly related to its object. And we choose what we best know to be good, but we opine what we do not quite know; and it is not the same people that are thought to make the best choices and to have the best opinions, but some are thought to have fairly good opinions, but by reason of vice to choose what they should not. If opinion precedes choice or accompanies it, that makes no difference; for it is not this that we are considering, but whether it is *identical* with some kind of opinion.

What, then, or what kind of thing is it, since it is none of the things we have mentioned? It seems to be voluntary, but not all that is voluntary to be an object of choice. Is it, then, what has been decided on by previous deliberation? At any rate choice involves a rational principle and thought. Even the name seems to suggest that it is what is chosen before other things.

Do we deliberate about everything, and is everything a possible subject of deliberation, or is deliberation impossible about some things? We ought presumably to call not what a fool or a madman would deliberate about, but what a sensible man would deliberate about, a subject of deliberation. Now about eternal things no one deliberates, e.g. about the material universe or the incommensurability of the diagonal and the side of a square. But no more do we deliberate about the things that involve movement but always happen in the same way, whether of necessity or by nature or from any other cause, e.g. the solstices and the risings of the stars; nor about things that happen now in one way, now in another, e.g. droughts and rains; nor about chance events, like the finding of treasure.

But we do not deliberate even about all human affairs; for instance, no Spartan deliberates about the best constitution for the Scythians. For none of these things can be brought about by our own efforts.

We deliberate about things that are in our power and can be done; and these are in fact what is left. For nature, necessity, and chance are thought to be causes, and also reason and everything that depends on man. Now every class of men deliberates about the things that can be done by their own efforts. And in the case of exact and self-contained sciences there is no deliberation, e.g. about the letters of the alphabet (for we have no doubt how they should be written); but the things that are brought about by our own efforts, but not always in the same way, are the things about which we deliberate, e.g. questions of medical treatment or of money-making. And we do so more in the case of the art of navigation than in that of gymnastics, inasmuch as it has been less exactly worked out, and again about other things in the same ratio, and more also in the case of the arts than in that of the sciences; for we have more doubt about the former. Deliberation is concerned with things that happen in a certain way for the most part, but in which the event is obscure, and with things in which it is indeterminate. We call in others to aid us in deliberation on important questions, distrusting ourselves as not being equal to deciding.

．　　．　　．

. . . Therefore virtue also is in our own power, and so too vice. For where it is in our power to act it is also in our power not to act, and *vice versa;* so that, if to act, where this is noble, is in our power, not to act, which will be base, will also be in our power, and if not to act, where this is noble, is in our power, to act, which will be base, will also be in our power. Now if it is in our power to do noble or base acts, and likewise in our power not to do them, and this was what being good or bad meant, then it is in our power to be virtuous or vicious.

The saying that "no one is voluntarily wicked nor involuntarily happy" seems to be partly false and partly true; for no one is involuntarily happy, but wickedness *is* voluntary. Or else we shall have to dispute what has just been said, at any rate, and deny that man is a moving principle or begetter of his actions as of children. But if these facts are evident and we cannot refer actions to moving principles other than those in ourselves, the acts whose moving principles are in us must themselves also be in our power and voluntary.

(from *Nicomachean Ethics,* Book III)

IV

Individual and Polis

But if all communities aim at some good,
the State aims at the highest good.

Aristotle, *Politics*

1. The Rise of the Polis

Jaeger tells us that the word "cosmos" originally signified "the right order in a state or other community" (Paideia, Vol. I, p. 110). This indicates simultaneously the element of order, lawfulness, in the city-state and the tremendous part it played in Greek life. Justice becomes the very core of morality. The high value the polis possessed for the Greeks is also evidenced in the fact that the state was not only the body organizing public life and the protector of Justice, but also the great educator of the people. "To establish a legal standard by written laws was for the Greeks an educational act." (Paideia, Vol. I, p. 109). Admirable as this achievement was, it might tempt one to overlook the primary importance of the individual's free will and overrate the moral efficaciousness of state laws. Moreover, this totalitarian danger comes to the fore in Plato's Republic, *where he advocates a community of wives and children. But in the same Plato we also find a completely different picture. In* Phaedo *and* Gorgias *he stresses both the value of the individual and the key importance of personal initiative and of knowledge in man's moral development; and knowledge is the very epitome of a personal, individual act. Greece is not only the country of the polis, it is also the country of the awakening to the importance of the individual person. Thus Jaeger could write: "Greek history appears to be the beginning of a new conception of the value of the individual." (Paideia, I, xix)*

SOLON

THE LAWGIVER'S BOAST

I gave the commons their sufficient meed
of strength, nor let them lack, nor yet exceed.
Those who were mighty and magnificent,
I bade them have their due and be content.
My strong shield guarded both sides equally
and gave to neither unjust victory.

(Translated by Gilbert Highet)

Although referring to events which took place in Persia, Herodotus' passage about democracy, oligarchy, and monarchy is a typical expression of the Greek mind in its clarity and impartial presentation of the advantages and disadvantages of these different forms of government. This text has a timeless interest.

HERODOTUS

THE FORMS OF GOVERNMENT

Five days later, when the excitement had died down, the conspirators met to discuss the situation in detail. At the meeting certain speeches were made—some of our own countrymen refuse to believe they were actually made at all; nevertheless—they were. The first speaker was Otanes, and his theme was to recommend the establishment in Persia of democratic government. "I think," he said, "that the time has passed for any one man amongst us to have absolute power. Monarchy is neither pleasant nor good. You know to what lengths the pride of power carried Cambyses, and you have personal experience of the effect of the same thing in the conduct of the Magus. How can one fit monarchy into any sound system of ethics, when it allows a man to do whatever he likes without any responsibility or control? Even the best of men raised to such a position would be bound to change for the worse—he could not possibly see things as he used to do. The typical vices of a monarch are envy and pride; envy, because it is a natural human weakness, and pride, because excessive wealth and power lead to the delusion that he is something more than a man. These two vices are the root cause of all wickedness: both

32. *Dionysus,* from the east pediment of the Parthenon.

lead to acts of savage and unnatural violence. Absolute power ought, by rights, to preclude envy on the principle that the man who possesses it has also at command everything he could wish for; but in fact it is not so, as the behaviour of kings to their subjects proves: they are jealous of the best of them merely for continuing to live, and take pleasure in the worst; and no one is readier than a king to listen to tale-bearers. A king, again, is the most inconsistent of men; show him reasonable respect, and he is angry because you do not abase yourself before his majesty; abase yourself, and he hates you for being a superserviceable rogue. But the worst of all remains to be said—he breaks up the structure of ancient tradition and law, forces women to serve his pleasure, and puts men to death without trial. Contrast with this the rule of the people: first, it has the finest of all names to describe it—*isonomy,* or equality before the law; and, secondly, the people in power do none of the things that monarchs do. Under a government of the people a magistrate is appointed by lot and is held responsible for his conduct in office, and all questions are put up for open debate. For these reasons I propose that we do away with the monarchy, and raise the people to power; for the state and the people are synonymous terms."

Otanes was followed by Megabyzus, who recommended the principle of oligarchy in the following words: "In so far as Otanes spoke in favour of abolishing monarchy, I agree with him; but he is wrong in asking us to transfer political power to the people. The masses are a feckless lot —nowhere will you find more ignorance or irresponsibility or violence. It would be an intolerable thing to escape the murderous caprice of a king, only to be caught by the equally wanton brutality of the rabble. A king does at least act consciously and deliberately; but the mob does not. Indeed how should it, when it has never been taught what is right and proper, and has no knowledge of its own about such things? The masses have not a thought in their heads; all they can do is to rush blindly into politics and sweep all before them like a river in flood. As for the people, then, let them govern Persia's enemies, not Persia; and let us ourselves choose a certain number of the best men in the country, and give *them* political power. We personally shall be amongst them, and it is only natural to suppose that the best men will produce the best policy."

Darius was the third to speak. "I support," he said, "all Megabyzus' remarks about the masses, but I do not agree with what he said of oligarchy. Take the three forms of government we are considering— democracy, oligarchy, and monarchy—and suppose each of them to be the best of its kind; I maintain that the third is greatly preferable to the other two. One ruler: it is impossible to improve upon that—provided he is the best man for the job. His judgement will be in keeping with his character; his control of the people will be beyond reproach; his measures against enemies and traitors will be kept secret more easily than under other forms of government. In an oligarchy, the fact that a number of men are competing for distinction in the public service cannot but lead to violent personal feuds; each of them wants to get to the top, and to see his own proposals carried; so they quarrel. Personal quarrels lead to open dissension, and then to bloodshed; and from that state of affairs the only way out is a return to monarchy—a clear proof that monarchy is best. Again, in a democracy, malpractices are bound to occur; in this case, how- ever, corrupt dealings in government services lead not to private feuds, but to close personal associations, the men responsible for them putting their heads together and mutually supporting one another. And so it goes on, until somebody or other comes forward as the people's champion and breaks up the cliques which are out for their own interests. This wins him the admiration of the mob, and as a result he soon finds himself entrusted with absolute power—all of which is another proof that the best form of government is monarchy. To sum up: where did we get our freedom from, and who gave it us? Is it the result of democracy, or of oligarchy, or of monarchy? We were set free by one man, and therefore I propose that we should preserve that form of government, and, further, that we should refrain from changing ancient laws, which have served us well in the past. To do so would lead only to disaster."

(from *The Histories*, Book III)

In reading the Funeral Speech of Pericles as related by Thu-cydides, we are drawn into the very atmosphere of the Athen-ian polis. In the passage on Pericles and his successors, the glory that Athens reached as city-state is impressively unfolded before one's eyes.

THUCYDIDES

THE GLORY OF ATHENS

THE FUNERAL SPEECH

Over the first who were buried, Pericles was chosen to speak. At the fitting moment he advanced from the sepulcher to a lofty stage, which had been erected in order that he might be heard as far away as possible by the crowd, and spoke somewhat as follows. . . .

.   .   .

"I will speak of our ancestors first, for it is right and seemly that on such an occasion as this we should also render this honor to their memory. Men of the same stock, ever dwelling in this land, in successive genera-tions to this very day, by their valor handed it down as a free land. They are worthy of praise, and still more are our fathers, who added to their inheritance, and after many a struggle bequeathed to us, their sons, the great empire we possess. Most of it those of our own number who are still in the settled time of life have strengthened further and have richly endowed our city in every way and made her most self-sufficient for both peace and war. Of the military exploits by which our various pos-sessions were acquired or of the energy with which we or our fathers resisted the onslaught of barbarians or Hellenes I will not speak, for the tale would be long and is familiar to you. But before I praise the dead, I shall first proceed to show by what kind of practices we attained to our position, and under what kind of institutions and manner of life our empire became great. For I conceive that it would not be unsuited to the occasion that this should be told, and that this whole assembly of citizens and foreigners may profitably listen to it.

"Our institutions do not emulate the laws of others. We do not copy our neighbors: rather, we are an example to them. Our system is called a democracy, for it respects the majority and not the few; but while the law secures equality to all alike in their private disputes, the claim of excellence is also recognized; and when a citizen is in any way distinguished, he is generally preferred to the public service, not in rotation, but for merit. Nor again is there any bar in poverty and obscurity of rank to a man who can do the state some service. It is as free men that we conduct our public life, and in our daily occupations we avoid mutual suspicions; we are not angry with our neighbor if he does what he likes; we do not put on sour looks at him which, though harmless, are not pleasant. While we give no offense in our private intercourse, in our public acts we are prevented from doing wrong by fear; we respect the authorities and the laws, especially those which are ordained for the protection of the injured as well as those unwritten laws which bring upon the transgressor admitted dishonor.

"Furthermore, none have provided more relaxation for the spirit from toil; we have regular games and sacrifices throughout the year; our homes are furnished with elegance; and the delight which we daily feel in all these things banishes melancholy. Because of the greatness of our city, the fruits of the whole earth flow in upon us so that we enjoy the goods of other countries as freely as our own.

"Then, again, in military training we are superior to our adversaries, as I shall show. Our city is thrown open to the world, and we never expel a foreigner or prevent him from seeing or learning anything which, if not concealed, it might profit an enemy to see. We rely not so much upon preparations or stratagems, as upon our own courage in action. And in the matter of education, whereas from early youth they are always undergoing laborious exercises which are to make them brave, we live at ease and yet are equally ready to face perils to which our strength is equal. And here is the evidence. The Lacedaemonians march against our land not by themselves, but with all their allies: we invade a neighbor's country alone; and although our opponents are fighting for their homes and we are on foreign soil, we seldom have any difficulty in overcoming them. Our enemies have never yet felt our strength in full; the care of a navy divides our attention, and on land we are obliged to send our own citizens to many parts. But if they meet and defeat some part of our army, they boast of having routed us all, and when defeated, of having been vanquished by our whole force.

"If then we prefer to meet danger with a light heart but without laborious training and with a courage which is instilled by habit more than by laws, we are the gainers; we do not anticipate the pain, although, when the hour comes, we show ourselves no less bold than those who never allow themselves to rest. Nor is this the only cause for marveling at our city. We are lovers of beauty without extravagance and of learning without loss of vigor. Wealth we employ less for talk and ostentation than when there is a real use for it. To avow poverty with us is no disgrace: the true disgrace is in doing nothing to avoid it. The same persons attend at once to the concerns of their households and of the city, and men of diverse employments have a very fair idea of politics. If a man takes no interest in public affairs, we alone do not commend him as quiet but condemn him as useless; and if few of us are originators, we are all sound judges of a policy. In our opinion action does not suffer from discussion but, rather, from the want of that instruction which is gained by discussion preparatory to the action required. For we have an exceptional gift of acting with audacity after calculating the prospects of our enterprises, whereas other men are bold from ignorance but hesitate upon reflection. But it would be right to esteem those men bravest in spirit who have the clearest understanding of the pains and pleasures of life and do not on that account shrink from danger. In doing good, again we are unlike others; we make our friends by conferring, not by receiving favors. Now a man who confers a favor is the firmer friend because he would keep alive the memory of an obligation by kindness to the recipient; the man who owes an obligation is colder in his feelings because he knows that in requiting the service, he will not be winning gratitude but only paying a debt. We alone do good to our neighbors, not so much upon a calculation of interest, but in the fearless confidence of freedom.

"To sum up, I say that the whole city is an education for Hellas and that each individual in our society would seem to be capable of the greatest self-reliance and of the utmost dexterity and grace in the widest range of activities. This is no passing boast in a speech, but truth and fact, and verified by the actual power of the city which we have won by this way of life. For when put to the test, Athens alone among her contemporaries is superior to report. No enemy who comes against her is indignant at the reverses which he sustains at the hands of such men; no subject complains that his masters do not deserve to rule. And we shall assuredly not be without witnesses; there are mighty monuments of our power which will make us the wonder of this and of succeeding ages; we shall not need the praises of Homer or of any other whose poetry will please for the moment, but whose reconstruction of the facts the truth will damage. For we have compelled every land and sea to open a path to our daring and have everywhere planted eternal memorials of our triumphs and misfortunes. Such is the city these men fought and died for and nobly disdained to lose, and every one of us who survive would naturally wear himself out in her service.

"This is why I have dwelt upon the greatness of Athens, showing you that we are contending for a higher prize than those who enjoy no like advantages, and establishing by manifest proof the merit of those men whom I am now commemorating. Their loftiest praise has been already spoken; for in descanting on the city, I have honored the qualities which earned renown for them and for men such as they. And of how few Hellenes can it be said as of them, that their deeds matched their fame! In my belief an end such as theirs proves a man's worth; it is at once its first revelation and final seal. For even those who come short in other ways may justly plead the valor with which they have fought for their country; they have blotted out evil with good, and their public services have outweighed the harm they have done in their private actions. None of these men were enervated by wealth or hesitated to resign the pleasures of life; none of them put off the evil day in the hope, natural to poverty, that a man, though poor, may yet become rich. But deeming that vengeance on their enemies was sweeter than any of these things and that they could hazard their lives in no nobler cause, they accepted the risk and resolved on revenge in preference to every other aim. They resigned to hope the obscure chance of success, but in the danger already visible they thought it right to act in reliance upon themselves alone. And when the moment for fighting came, they held it nobler to suffer death than to yield and save their lives; it was the report of dishonor from which they fled, but on the battlefield their feet stood fast; and while for a moment they were in the hands of fortune, at the height, less of terror than of glory, they departed.

"Such was the conduct of these men; they were worthy of Athens. The rest of us must pray for a safer issue to our courage and yet disdain to show any less daring towards our enemies. We must not consider only what words can be uttered on the utility of such a spirit. Anyone might discourse to you at length on all the advantages of resisting the enemy bravely, but you know them just as well yourselves. It is better that you should actually gaze day by day on the power of the city until you are filled with the love of her; and when you are convinced of her greatness, reflect that it was acquired by men of daring who knew their duty and feared dishonor in the hour of action, men who if they ever failed in an enterprise, even then disdained to deprive the city of their prowess but offered themselves up as the finest contribution to the common cause. All alike gave their lives and received praise which grows not old and the most conspicuous of sepulchers—I speak not so much of that in which their remains are laid as of that in which their glory survives to be remembered forever, on every fitting occasion in word and deed. For every land is a sepulcher for famous men; not only are they commemorated by inscriptions on monuments in their own country, but even in foreign lands there dwells an unwritten memorial of them, graven not so much on stone as in the hearts of men. Make them your examples now; and, esteeming courage to be freedom and freedom to be happiness, do not weigh too nicely the perils of war. It is not the unfortunate men with no hope of blessing, who would with best reason be unsparing of their lives, but the prosperous, who, if they survive, are always in danger of a change for the worse, and whose situation would be most transformed by any reverse. To a man of spirit it is more painful to be oppressed like a weakling than in the consciousness of strength and common hopes to meet a death that comes unfelt."

PERICLES AND HIS SUCCESSORS

After the second Peloponnesian invasion, now that Attica had been once more ravaged, and war and plague together oppressed the Athenians, a change came over their spirit. They blamed Pericles because he had persuaded them to go to war, declaring that he was the author of their troubles; and they were anxious to come to terms with the Lacedaemonians. Accordingly, envoys were dispatched to Sparta, but they met with no success. Completely at their wits' end, they turned upon Pericles. He saw that they were exasperated by their situation and were behaving just as he had always anticipated that they would. As he was still general, he called an assembly, wanting to encourage them and to convert their angry feelings into a gentler and less fearful mood. At this assembly he came forward and spoke somewhat as follows:

315

33. *Demeter, Triptolemus and Persephone.*

"I was expecting this outburst of anger against me, for I can see its causes. And I have summoned an assembly to remind you of your resolutions and reprove you if you are wrong to display anger against me and want of tenacity in misfortune. In my judgment it is better for individuals themselves that the citizens should suffer and the state as a whole flourish than that the citizens should prosper singly and the state communally decline. A private man who thrives in his own business is involved in the common ruin of his country; but if he is unsuccessful in a prosperous city he is much more likely to be saved in the end. Seeing then that states can bear the misfortunes of individuals, but that no individual can bear the misfortunes of his state, let us all stand by our country and not do what you are doing now. Because you are stunned by your domestic calamities, you are abandoning the safety of the commonwealth and blaming not only me who advised the war but yourselves who consented to it. And yet what sort of man am I to provoke your anger? I believe that I am second to none in devising and explaining a sound policy, a lover of my country, and incorruptible. Now a man may have a policy which he does not clearly expound, and then he might as well have none at all; or he may possess both qualities but be disloyal to his country, and then he would not be so apt to speak in her interest; or again, though loyal, he may be unable to resist a bribe, and then all his other good qualities would be sold for money. If, when you determined to go to war, you even half-believed me to have somewhat more of the qualities required than others, it is not fair that I should now be charged with doing wrong.

"I allow that for men who are fortunate in other respects and free to choose it is great folly to make war. But when it is necessary either to yield and at once take orders from others or to hold out at the cost of danger, it is more blameworthy to shun the danger than to meet it. For my own part, I am unchanged and stand where I did. It is you who are changed; you repent in suffering of decisions you made when unhurt, and you think that my advice was wrong because your own judgment is impaired. The pain is present and comes home to each of you, but the good is as yet not manifest to any one; and your minds have not the strength to persevere in your resolution, now that a great vicissitude has overtaken you unawares. Anything which is sudden and unexpected and utterly beyond calculation enthralls the spirit of a man. This is your condition, especially as the plague has come upon other hardships. Nevertheless, as the citizens of a great city, educated in a temper of greatness, you should not succumb even to the greatest calamities nor darken the luster of your fame. For men think it equally right to hate the presumption of those who claim a reputation to which they have no title and to condemn the faintheartedness of those who fall below the glory which is their own. You should put away your private sorrows and hold fast to the deliverance of the commonwealth.

.   .   .

"It is reasonable for you to support the imperial dignity of your city in which you all take pride; you should not covet glory unless you will make exertions. And do not imagine that you are fighting about a simple issue, freedom or slavery; you have an empire to lose, and there is the danger to which the hatred of your imperial rule has exposed you. Neither can you any longer resign your power if, at this crisis, any timorous spirit is for playing the peace lover and the honest man. For by this time your empire has become a despotism, which it is thought unjust to acquire but unsafe to surrender. The men of whom I was speaking, if they could find followers, would soon ruin a city, and if they were to go and found a state of their own, would equally ruin that. The love of peace is secure only in association with the spirit of action; in an imperial city it is of no use, but it is suited to subjects who enjoy safety in servitude."

.   .   .

By such words Pericles endeavored to appease the anger of the Athenians against himself, and to divert their minds from their terrible situation. In the conduct of public affairs they took his advice and sent no more embassies to Sparta but turned instead to prosecuting the war. Yet as individuals they felt their sufferings keenly.

(from *The Peloponnesian Wars,* Book II)

The victory of the intellect in Greece manifests itself again in Aristotle's Politics *for it was written while the glory of the polis was waning and while Greek independence was menaced. It is a remarkable fact that the Greek conception of the state in all its grandeur and limitation should find its most perfect theoretical elaboration at the very moment of its decline. Aristotle's treatment of women and of slavery reflect the shortcomings of his epoch; but his sober and detailed analysis of*

the nature of the state and of the relationships existing be-
tween individuals is a piece of work that has kept all its value
and actuality. His approach to the various sociological phe-
nomena is so existential and immediate that one is tempted
to call it "phenomenological." Yet Aristotle's work not only
embodies the Greek conception of the polis; he also surpasses
it insofar as in him emerges for the first time the ideal of a
nation-state—so alien to the Greeks—when he stresses that if
the Greeks were united they could rule the world. (Politics,
7.7.1327 B32).

ARISTOTLE

FROM POLITICS

Every state is a community of some kind, and every community is
established with a view to some good; for mankind always act in order
that which they think good. But, if all communities aim at some good, the
state or political community, which is the highest of all, and which embraces all the rest, aims at good in a greater degree than any other, and
at the highest good.

.   .   .

He who thus considers things in their first growth and origin, whether
a state or anything else, will obtain the clearest view of them. In the
first place there must be a union of those who cannot exist without each
other; namely, of male and female, that the race may continue (and this
is a union which is formed, not of deliberate purpose, but because, in
common with other animals and with plants, mankind have a natural desire to leave behind them an image of themselves), and of natural ruler
and subject, that both may be preserved. For that which can foresee by
the exercise of mind is by nature intended to be lord and master, and
that which can with its body give effect to such foresight is a subject,
and by nature a slave; hence master and slave have the same interest.
Now nature has distinguished between the female and the slave. For
she is not niggardly, like the smith who fashions the Delphian knife for
many uses; she makes each thing for a single use, and every instrument
is best made when intended for one and not for many uses. But among
barbarians no distinction is made between women and slaves, because

319

there is no natural ruler among them: they are a community of slaves, male and female. Wherefore the poets say—

It is meet that Hellenes should rule over barbarians;

as if they thought that the barbarian and the slave were by nature one.

Out of these two relationships between man and woman, master and slave, the first thing to arise is the family, and Hesiod is right when he says—

First house and wife and an ox for the plough,

for the ox is the poor man's slave. The family is the association established by nature for the supply of men's everyday wants, and the members of it are called by Charondas "companions of the cupboard," and by Epimenides the Cretan, "companions of the manger." But when several families are united, and the association aims at something more than the supply of daily needs, the first society to be formed is the village. And the most natural form of the village appears to be that of a colony from the family, composed of the children and grandchildren, who are said to be "suckled with the same milk." . . .

When several villages are united in a single complete community, large enough to be nearly or quite self-sufficing, the state comes into existence, originating in the bare needs of life, and continuing in existence for the sake of a good life. And therefore, if the earlier forms of society are natural, so is the state, for it is the end of them, and the nature of a thing is its end.

.   .   .

Now, that man is more of a political animal than bees or any other gregarious animals is evident. Nature, as we often say, makes nothing in vain, and man is the only animal whom she has endowed with the gift of speech. And whereas mere voice is but an indication of pleasure or pain, and is therefore found in other animals (for their nature attains to the perception of pleasure and pain and the intimation of them to one another, and no further), the power of speech is intended to set forth the expedient and inexpedient, and therefore likewise the just and the unjust. And it is a characteristic of man that he alone has any sense of good and evil, of just and unjust, and the like, and the association of living beings who have this sense makes a family and a state.

Further, the state is by nature clearly prior to the family and to the individual, since the whole is of necessity prior to the part; for example, if the whole body be destroyed, there will be no foot or hand, except in an equivocal sense, as we might speak of a stone hand; for when destroyed the hand will be no better than that. But things are defined by their working and power; and we ought not to say that they are the same when they no longer have their proper quality, but only that they have the same name. The proof that the state is a creation of nature and prior to the individual is that the individual, when isolated, is not self-sufficing; and therefore he is like a part in relation to the whole. But he who is unable to live in society, or who has no need because he is sufficient for himself, must be either a beast or a god: he is no part of a state. A social instinct is implanted in all men by nature, and yet he who first founded the state was the greatest of benefactors. For man, when perfected, is the best of animals, but, when separated from law and justice, he is the worst of all; since armed injustice is the more dangerous, and he is equipped at birth with arms, meant to be used by intelligence and virtue, which he may use for the worst ends. Wherefore, if he have not virtue, he is the most unholy and the most savage of animals, and the most full of lust and gluttony. But justice is the bond of men in states, for the administration of justice, which is the determination of what is just, is the principle of order in political society.

．　　　．　　　．

Let us first speak of master and slave, looking to the needs of practical life and also seeking to attain some better theory of their relation than exists at present. . . . The master is only the master of the slave; he does not belong to him, whereas the slave is not only the slave of his master, but wholly belongs to him. Hence we see what is the nature and office of a slave; he who is by nature not his own but another's man, is by nature a slave; and he may be said to be another's man who, being a human being, is also a possession. And a possession may be defined as an instrument of action, separable from the possessor.

But is there any one thus intended by nature to be a slave, and for whom such a condition is expedient and right, or rather is not all slavery a violation of nature?

There is no difficulty in answering this question, on grounds both of reason and of fact. For that some should rule and others be ruled is a thing not only necessary, but expedient; from the hour of their birth, some are marked out for subjection, others for rule.

34. *Leader of the sacrificial cattle,* from the north frieze of the Parthenon.

35. *Hydria-bearers,* from the north frieze of the Parthenon.

. . . We will therefore restrict ourselves to the living creature, which, in the first place, consists of soul and body: and of these two, the one is by nature the ruler, and the other the subject. But then we must look for the intentions of nature in things which retain their nature, and not in things which are corrupted. And therefore we must study the man who is in the most perfect state both of body and soul, for in him we shall see the true relation of the two; although in bad or corrupted natures the body will often appear to rule over the soul, because they are in an evil and unnatural condition. At all events we may firstly observe in living creatures both a despotical and a constitutional rule; for the soul rules the body with a despotical rule, whereas the equality of the two or the rule of the inferior is always hurtful. The same holds good of animals in relation to men; for tame animals have a better nature than wild, and all tame animals are better off when they are ruled by man; for then they are preserved. Again, the male is by nature superior, and the female inferior; and the one rules, and the other is ruled; this principle, of necessity, extends to all mankind. Where then there is such a difference as that between soul and body, or between men and animals (as in the case of those whose business is to use their body, and who can do nothing better), the lower sort are by nature slaves and it is better for them as for all inferiors that they should be under the rule of a master. For he who can be, and therefore is, another's, and he who participates in rational principle enough to apprehend, but not to have, such a principle, is a slave by nature. . . .

But that those who take the opposite view have in a certain way right on their side, may be easily seen. For the words slavery and slave are used in two senses. There is a slave or slavery by law as well as by nature. The law of which I speak is a sort of convention—the law by which whatever is taken in war is supposed to belong to the victors. But this right many jurists impeach, as they would an orator who brought forward an unconstitutional measure: they detest the notion that, because one man has the power of doing violence and is superior in brute strength, another shall be his slave and subject. Even among philosophers there is a difference of opinion. The origin of the dispute, and what makes the views invade each other's territory, is as follows: in some sense virtue, when furnished with means, has actually the greatest power of exercising force: and as superior power is only found where there is superior excellence of some kind, power seems to imply virtue, and the dispute to be simply one about justice (for it is due to one party identifying justice with goodwill, while the other identifies it with the mere rule of the stronger). If these views are thus set out separately, the other views have no force or plausibility against the view that the superior in virtue ought to rule, or be master. Others, clinging, as they think, simply to a principle of justice (for law and custom are a sort of justice), assume that slavery in accordance with the custom of war is justified by law, but at the same moment they deny this. For what if the cause of the war is unjust? And again, no one would ever say that he is a slave who is unworthy to be a slave. Were this the case, men of the highest rank would be slaves and the children of slaves if they or their parents chance to have been taken captive and sold. Wherefore Hellenes do not like to call Hellenes slaves, but confine the term to barbarians. Yet, in using this language, they really mean the natural slave of whom we spoke at first; for it must be admitted that some are slaves everywhere, others nowhere. The same principle applies to nobility. Hellenes regard themselves as noble everywhere, and not only in their own country, but they deem the barbarians noble only when at home, thereby implying that there are two sorts of nobility and freedom, the one absolute, the other relative. The Helen of Theodectes says:

> Who would presume to call me servant who am on both sides
> sprung from the stem of the Gods?

What does this mean but that they distinguish freedom and slavery, noble and humble birth, by the two principles of good and evil? They think that as men and animals beget men and animals, so from good men a good man springs. But this is what nature, though she may intend it, cannot always accomplish.

We see then that there is some foundation for this difference of opinion, and that all are not either slaves by nature or freemen by nature, and also that there is in some cases a marked distinction between the two classes, rendering it expedient and right for the one to be slaves and the others to be masters: the one practising obedience, the others exercising the authority and lordship which nature intended them to have. The abuse of this authority is injurious to both; for the interests of part and whole, of body and soul, are the same, and the slave is a part of the master, a living but separated part of his bodily frame. Hence, where the relation of master and slave between them is natural they are friends and have a common interest, but where it rests merely on law and force the reverse is true.

. . .

Having determined these points, we have next to consider how many forms of government there are, and what they are; and in the first place what are the true forms, for when they are determined the perversions of them will at once be apparent. The words constitution and government have the same meaning, and the government, which is the supreme authority in states, must be in the hands of one, or of a few, or of the many. The true forms of government, therefore, are those in which the one, or the few, or the many, govern with a view to the common interest; but governments which rule with a view to the private interest, whether of the one, or of the few, or of the many, are perversions. For the members of a state, if they are truly citizens, ought to participate in its advantages. Of forms of government in which one rules, we call that which regards the common interests, kingship or royalty; that in which more than one, but not many, rule, aristocracy; and it is so called, either because the rulers are the best men, or because they have at heart the best interests of the state and of the citizens. But when the citizens at large administer the state for the common interest, the government is called by the generic name—a constitution. And there is a reason for this use of language. One man or a few may excel in virtue; but as the number increases it becomes more difficult for them to attain perfection in every kind of virtue, though they may in military virtue, for this is found in the masses. Hence in a constitutional government the fighting-men have the supreme power, and those who possess arms are the citizens.

Of the above-mentioned forms, the perversions are as follows:—of royalty, tyranny; of aristocracy, oligarchy; of constitutional government, democracy. For tyranny is a kind of monarchy which has in view the interest of the monarch only; oligarchy has in view the interest of the wealthy; democracy, of the needy: none of them the common good of all.

.   .   .

There is also a doubt as to what is to be the supreme power in the state:—Is it the multitude? Or the wealthy? Or the good? Or the one best man? Or a tyrant? Any of these alternatives seems to involve disagreeable consequences. If the poor, for example, because they are more in number, divide among themselves the property of the rich—is not this unjust? No, by heaven (will be the reply), for the supreme authority justly willed it. But if this is not injustice, pray what is? Again, when in the first division all has been taken, and the majority divide anew the property of the minority, is it not evident, if this goes on, that they will ruin the state?

Yet surely, virtue is not the ruin of those who possess her, nor is justice destructive of a state; and therefore this law of confiscation clearly cannot be just. If it were, all the acts of a tyrant must of necessity be just; for he only coerces other men by superior power, just as the multitude coerce the rich. But is it just then that the few and the wealthy should be the rulers? And what if they, in like manner, rob and plunder the people— is this just? If so, the other case will likewise be just. But there can be no doubt that all these things are wrong and unjust.

Then ought the good to rule and have supreme power? But in that case everybody else, being excluded from power, will be dishonoured. For the offices of a state are posts of honour; and if one set of men always hold them, the rest must be deprived of them. Then will it be well that the one best man should rule? Nay, that is still more oligarchical, for the number of those who are dishonoured is thereby increased. Some one may say that it is bad in any case for a man, subject as he is to all the accidents of human passion, to have the supreme power, rather than the law. But what if the law itself be democratical or oligarchical, how will that help us out of our difficulties? Not at all; the same consequences will follow.

(from Politics, Books I and III)

*After periods of political and social upheavals, the Athenians'
sense of the primordial value of the city-state was reawakened
in Demosthenes (384-322), the last great patriot before Athens'
collapse. In the hour of greatest danger for the survival of
Greek independence, seeing the blindness of the leading ap-
peasers, Demosthenes understood that "the people must be
educated to a new mentality for politicians always said what
the public wanted to hear anyhow." The following pages
sketch the nature of his program.*

DEMOSTHENES

FROM THE FIRST PHILIPPIC

"First I say, you must not despond, Athenians, under your present circumstances, wretched as they are; for that which is worst in them as regards the past, is best for the future. What do I mean? That your affairs are amiss, men of Athens, because you do nothing which is need-

ful; if, notwithstanding you performed your duties, it were the same, there would be no hope of amendment.

"Consider next, what you know by report, and men of experience remember; how vast a power the Lacedaemonians had not long ago, yet how nobly and becomingly you consulted the dignity of Athens, and undertook the war against them for the rights of Greece. Why do I mention this? To show and convince you, Athenians, that nothing, if you take precaution, is to be feared, nothing, if you are negligent, goes as you desire. Take for examples the strength of the Lacedaemonians then, which you overcame by attention to your duties, and the insolence of this man now, by which through neglect of our interests we are confounded. But if any among you, Athenians, deem Philip hard to be conquered, looking at the magnitude of his existing power, and the loss by us of all our strongholds, they reason rightly, but should reflect, that once we held Pydna and Potidaea and Methone and all the region round about as our own, and many of the nations now leagued with him were independent and free, and preferred our friendship to his. Had Philip then taken it into his head, that it was difficult to contend with Athens, when she had so many fortresses to infest his country, and he was destitute of allies, nothing that he has accomplished would he have undertaken, and never would he have acquired so large a dominion. But he saw well, Athenians, that all these places are the open prizes of war, that the possessions of the absent naturally belong to the present, those of the remiss to them that will venture and toil. Acting on such principle, he has won everything and keeps it, either by way of conquest, or by friendly attachment and alliance, for all men will side with and respect those whom they see prepared and willing to make proper exertion. If you, Athenians, will adopt this principle now, though you did not before, and every man, where he can and ought to give his service to the state, be ready to give it without excuse, the wealthy to contribute, the able-bodied to enlist; in a word, plainly, if you will become your own masters, and cease each expecting to do nothing himself, while his neighbour does everything for him, you shall then with heaven's permission recover your own, and get back what has been frittered away, and chastise Philip. Do not imagine that his empire is everlastingly secured to him as a god. There are those who hate and fear and envy him, Athenians, even among those that seem most friendly; and all feelings that are in other men belong, we may assume, to his confederates. But now they are all cowed, having no refuge through your tardiness and indolence, which I say you must abandon forthwith. For you see, Athenians, the case, to what

36. *Battle between Greeks and Trojans,* from the east frieze of the Siphnian Treasury.

pitch of arrogance the man has advanced who leaves you not even the choice of action or inaction, but threatens and uses (they say) outrageous language, and, unable to rest in possession of his conquests, continually widens their circle, and, whilst we dally and delay, throws his net all around us. When then, Athenians, when will ye act as becomes you? In what event? In that of necessity, I suppose. And how should we regard the events happening now? Methinks, to freemen the strongest necessity is the disgrace of their condition. Or tell me, do ye like walking about and asking one another:—Is there any news? Why, could there be greater news than a man of Macedonia subduing Athenians, and directing the affairs of Greece? Is Philip dead? No, but he is sick. And what matters it to you? Should anything befall this man, you will soon create another Philip, if you attend to business thus. For even he has been exalted not so much by his own strength as by our negligence. And again; should anything happen to him; should fortune, which still takes better care of us than we of ourselves, be good enough to accomplish this; observe that, being on the spot, you would step in while things were in confusion, and manage them as you pleased; but as you now are, though occasion offered Amphipolis, you would not be in a position to accept it, with neither forces nor counsels at hand.

"However, as to the importance of a general zeal in the discharge of duty, believing you are convinced and satisfied, I say no more.

"As to the kind of force which I think may extricate you from your difficulties, the amount, the supplies of money, the best and speediest method (in my judgment) of providing all the necessaries, I shall endeavour to inform you forthwith, making only one request, men of Athens. When you have heard all, determine; prejudge not before. And let none think I delay our operations, because I recommend an entirely new force. Not those that cry, quickly! to-day! speak most to the purpose (for what has already happened we shall not be able to prevent by our present armament); but he that shows what and how great and whence procured must be the force capable of enduring, till either we have advisedly terminated the war, or overcome our enemies: for so shall we escape annoyance in future. This I think I am able to show, without offence to any other man who has a plan to offer. My promise indeed is large; it shall be tested by the performance; and you shall be my judges."

2. Man and His Conscience

> But I shall obey God rather than you.
>
> Plato, *Apology*

Diametrically different from the part played by the city-state, but equally important, is the discovery of the absolute primacy of morality by Socrates, who embodies a matchless emphasis on the importance and dignity of the individual person.

In Sophocles' Antigone we witness an absolute refusal to submit man's conscience to the raison d'état *and simultaneously the most radical rejection of statolatry.*

PLATO

FROM APOLOGY

How you, O Athenians, have been affected by my accusers, I cannot tell; but I know that they almost made me forget who I was—so persuasively did they speak; and yet they have hardly uttered a word of truth. But of the many falsehoods told by them, there was one which quite amazed me;—I mean when they said that you should be upon your guard and not allow yourselves to be deceived by the force of my eloquence. To say this, when they were certain to be detected as soon as I opened my lips and proved myself to be anything but a great speaker, did indeed appear to me most shameless—unless by the force of eloquence they mean the force of truth; for if such is their meaning, I admit that I am eloquent.

. . .

. . . Now I regard this as a fair challenge, and I will endeavour to explain to you the reason why I am called wise and have such an evil fame. Please to attend then. And although some of you may think that I am joking, I declare that I will tell you the entire truth. Men of Athens, this reputation of mine has come of a certain sort of wisdom which I possess. If you ask me what kind of wisdom, I reply, wisdom such as may perhaps be attained by man, for to that extent I am inclined to believe that I am wise; whereas the persons of whom I was speaking have a super-human wisdom, which I may fail to describe, because I have it not myself; and he who says that I have, speaks falsely, and is taking away my character. And here, O men of Athens, I must beg you not to interrupt me, even if I seem to say something extravagant. For the word which I will speak is not mine. I will refer you to a witness who is worthy of credit; that witness shall be the God of Delphi—he will tell you about my wisdom, if I have any, and of what sort it is. You must have known Chaerephon; he was early a friend of mine, and also a friend of yours, for he shared in the recent exile of the people, and returned with you. Well, Chaerephon, as you know, was very impetuous in all his doings, and he went to Delphi and boldly asked the oracle to tell him whether—as I was saying, I must beg you not to interrupt—he asked the oracle to tell him whether any one was wiser than I was, and the Pythian prophetess answered, that there was no man wiser. Chaerephon is dead himself; but his brother, who is in court, will confirm the truth of what I am saying.

Why do I mention this? Because I am going to explain to you why I have such an evil name. When I heard the answer, I said to myself, What can the God mean? and what is the interpretation of his riddle? for I know that I have no wisdom, small or great. What then can he mean when he says that I am the wisest of men? And yet he is a God, and cannot lie; that would be against his nature. After long consideration, I thought of a method of trying the question. I reflected that if I could only find a man wiser than myself, then I might go to the God with a refutation in my hand. I should say to him, "Here is a man who is wiser than I am; but you said that I was the wisest." Accordingly I went to one who had the reputation of wisdom, and observed him—his name I need not mention; he was a politician whom I selected for examination—and the result was as follows: When I began to talk with him, I could not help thinking that he was not really wise, although he was thought wise by many, and still wiser by himself; and thereupon I tried to explain to him that he thought himself wise, but was not really wise; and the consequence was that he hated me, and his enmity was shared by several who were present and heard me. So I left him, saying to myself, as I went away: Well, although I do not suppose that either of us knows anything really beautiful and good, I am better off than he is,—for he knows nothing, and thinks that he knows; I neither know nor think that I know. . . .

.   .   .

At last I went to the artisans, for I was conscious that I knew nothing at all, as I may say, and I was sure that they knew many fine things; and here I was not mistaken, for they did know many things of which I was ignorant, and in this they certainly were wiser than I was. But I observed that even the good artisans fell into the same error as the poets;—because they were good workmen they thought that they also knew all sorts of high matters, and this defect in them overshadowed their wisdom; and therefore I asked myself on behalf of the oracle, whether I would like to be as I was, neither having their knowledge nor their ignorance, or like them in both; and I made answer to myself and to the oracle that I was better off as I was.

This inquisition has led to my having many enemies of the worst and most dangerous kind, and has given occasion also to many calumnies. And I am called wise, for my hearers always imagine that I myself possess the wisdom which I find wanting in others: but the truth is, O men of Athens, that God only is wise; and by his answer he intends to show that wisdom of men is worth little or nothing; he is not speaking of Socrates, he is only using my name by way of illustration, as if he said, He, O men, is the wisest, who, like Socrates, knows that his wisdom is in truth worth nothing. And so I go about the world, obedient to the God, and search and make enquiry into the wisdom of any one, whether citizen or stranger, who appears to be wise; and if he is not wise, then in vindication of the oracle I show him that he is not wise; and my occupation quite absorbs me, and I have no time to give either to any public matter of interest or to any concern of my own, but I am in utter poverty by reason of my devotion to the God.

.   .   .

I have said enough in answer to the charge of Meletus: any elaborate defence is unnecessary; but I know only too well how many are the enmities which I have incurred, and this is what will be my destruction if I am destroyed;—not Meletus, nor yet Anytus, but the envy and detraction of the world, which has been the death of many good men, and will probably be the death of many more; there is no danger of my being the last of them.

Some one will say: And are you not ashamed, Socrates, of a course of life which is likely to bring you to an untimely end? To him I may fairly answer: There you are mistaken: a man who is good for anything ought not to calculate the chance of living or dying; he ought only to consider whether in doing anything he is doing right or wrong—acting the part of a good man or of a bad. . . .

Strange, indeed, would be my conduct, O men of Athens, if I who, when I was ordered by the generals whom you chose to command me at Potidaea and Amphipolis and Delium, remained where they placed me, like any other man, facing death—if now, when, as I conceive and imagine, God orders me to fulfil the philosopher's mission of searching into myself and other men, I were to desert my post through fear of death, or any other fear; that would indeed be strange, and I might justly be arraigned in court for denying the existence of the gods, if I disobeyed the oracle because I was afraid of death, fancying that I was wise when I was not wise. For the fear of death is indeed the pretence of wisdom, and not real wisdom, being a pretence of knowing the unknown; and no one knows whether death, which men in their fear apprehend to be the greatest evil, may not be the greatest good. Is not this ignorance of a disgraceful sort, the ignorance which is the conceit that man knows what he does not know? And in this respect only I believe myself to differ from men in general, and may perhaps claim to be wiser than they are:—that whereas I know but little of the world below, I do not suppose that I know: but I do know that injustice and disobedience to a better, whether God or man, is evil and dishonourable, and I will never fear or avoid a possible good rather than a certain evil. And therefore if you let me go now, and are now convinced by Anytus, who said that since I had been prosecuted, I must be put to death (or if not that I ought never to have been prosecuted at all); and that if I escape now, your sons will all be utterly ruined by listening to my words—if you say to me, Socrates, this time we will not mind Anytus, and you shall be let off, but upon one condition, that you are not to enquire and speculate in this way any more, and that if you are caught doing so again you shall die;—if this was the condition on which you let me go, I should reply: Men of Athens, I honour and love you; but I shall obey God rather than you, and while I have life and strength I shall never cease from the practice and teaching of philosophy, exhorting any one whom I meet and saying to him after my manner: You, my friend,—a citizen of the great and mighty and wise city of Athens,—are you not ashamed of heaping up the greatest amount of money and honour and reputation, and caring so little about wisdom and truth and the greatest improvement of the soul, which you never regard or heed at all? And if the person with whom I am arguing, says: Yes, but I do care; then I do not leave him or let him go at once; but I proceed to interrogate and examine and cross-examine him, and if I think that he has no virtue in him, but only says that he has, I reproach him with undervaluing the greater, and overvaluing the less. And I shall repeat the same words to every one whom I meet, young and old, citizen and alien, but especially to the citizens, inasmuch as they are my brethren. For know that this is the command of God; and I believe that no greater good has ever happened in the state than my service to the God. For I do nothing but go about persuading you all, old and young alike, not to take thought for your persons or your properties, but first and chiefly to care about the greatest improvement of the soul. I tell you that virtue is not given by money, but that from virtue comes money and every other good of man, public as well as private. This is my teaching, and if this is the doctrine which corrupts the youth, I am a mischievous person. But if any one says that this is not my teaching, he is speaking an untruth. Wherefore, O men of Athens, I say to you, do as Anytus bids or not as Anytus bids, and either acquit me or not; but whichever you do, understand that I shall never alter my ways, not even if I have to die many times.

Men of Athens, do not interrupt, but hear me; there was an understanding between us that you should hear me to the end: I have something more to say, at which you may be inclined to cry out; but I believe that to hear me will be good for you, and therefore I beg that you will not cry out. I would have you know, that if you kill such an one as I am, you will injure yourselves more than you will injure me. Nothing will injure me, not Meletus nor yet Anytus—they cannot, for a bad man is not permitted to injure a better than himself. I do not deny that Anytus may, perhaps, kill him, or drive him into exile, or deprive him of civil rights; and he may imagine, and others may imagine, that he is inflicting a great injury upon him: but there I do not agree. For the evil of doing as he is doing—the evil of unjustly taking away the life of another—is greater far.

And now, Athenians, I am not going to argue for my own sake, as you may think, but for yours, that you may not sin against the God by condemning me, who am his gift to you. For if you kill me you will not easily find a successor to me, who, if I may use such a ludicrous figure of speech, am a sort of gadfly, given to the state by God; and the state is a great and noble steed who is tardy in his motions owing to his very size, and requires to be stirred into life. I am that gadfly which God has attached to the state, and all day long and in all places am always fastening upon you, arousing and persuading and reproaching you. You will not easily find another like me, and therefore I would advise you to spare me. I dare say that you may feel out of temper (like a person who is suddenly awakened from sleep), and you think that you might easily strike me dead as Anytus advises, and then you would sleep on for the remainder of your lives, unless God in his care of you sent you another gadfly. When I say that I am given to you by God, the proof of my mission is this:—if I had been like other men, I should not have neglected all my own concerns or patiently seen the neglect of them during all these years, and have been doing yours, coming to you individually like a father or elder brother, exhorting you to regard virtue; such conduct, I say, would be unlike human nature. If I had gained anything, or if my exhortations had been paid, there would have been some sense in my doing so; but now, as you will perceive, not even the impudence of my accusers dares to say that I have ever exacted or sought pay of any one; of that they have no witness. And I have a sufficient witness to the truth of what I say—my poverty.

Some one may wonder why I go about in private giving advice and busying myself with the concerns of others, but do not venture to come forward in public and advise the state. I will tell you why. You have heard me speak at sundry times and in divers places of an oracle or sign which comes to me, and is the divinity which Meletus ridicules in the indictment. This sign, which is a kind of voice, first began to come to me when I was a child; it always forbids but never commands me to do anything which I am going to do. This is what deters me from being a politician. And rightly, as I think. For I am certain, O men of Athens, that if I had engaged in politics, I should have perished long ago, and done no good either to you or to myself. And do not be offended at my telling you the truth: for the truth is, that no man who goes to war with you or any other multitude, honestly striving against the many lawless and unrighteous deeds which are done in a state, will save his life; he who will fight for the right, if he would live even for a brief space, must have a private station and not a public one.

. . . .

But, setting aside the question of public opinion, there seems to be something wrong in asking a favour of a judge, and thus procuring an acquittal, instead of informing and convincing him. For his duty is, not to make a present of justice, but to give judgment; and he has sworn that he will judge according to the laws, and not according to his own good pleasure; and we ought not to encourage you, nor should you allow yourself to be encouraged, in this habit of perjury—there can be no piety in that. Do not then require me to do what I consider dishonourable and impious and wrong, especially now, when I am being tried for impiety on the indictment of Meletus. For if, O men of Athens, by force of persuasion and entreaty I could overpower your oaths, then I should be teaching you to believe that there are no gods, and in defending should simply convict myself of the charge of not believing in them. But that is not so—far otherwise. For I do believe that there are gods, and in a sense higher than that in which any of my accusers believe in them. And to you and to God I commit my cause, to be determined by you as is best for you and me.

.   .   .

. . . The difficulty, my friends, is not to avoid death, but to avoid unrighteousness; for that runs faster than death. I am old and move slowly, and the slower runner has overtaken me, and my accusers are keen and quick, and the faster runner, who is unrighteousness, has overtaken them. And now I depart hence condemned by you to suffer the penalty of death,—they too go their ways condemned by the truth to suffer the penalty of villainy and wrong; and I must abide by my award—let them abide by theirs. I suppose that these things may be regarded as fated,—and I think that they are well.

And now, O men who have condemned me, I would fain prophesy to you; for I am about to die, and in the hour of death men are gifted with prophetic power. And I prophesy to you who are my murderers, that immediately after my departure punishment far heavier than you have inflicted on me will surely await you. Me you have killed because you wanted to escape the accuser, and not to give an account of your lives. But that will not be as you suppose: far otherwise. For I say that there will be more accusers of you than there are now; accusers whom hitherto I have restrained: and as they are younger they will be more inconsiderate with you, and you will be more offended at them. If you think that by killing men you can prevent some one from censuring your evil lives, you are mistaken; that is not a way of escape which is either possible or honourable; the easiest and the noblest way is not to be disabling others, but to be improving yourselves. This is the prophecy which I utter before my departure to the judges who have condemned me.

Friends, who would have acquitted me, I would like also to talk with you about the thing which has come to pass, while the magistrates are busy, and before I go to the place at which I must die.

.　　　.　　　.

. . . But if death is the journey to another place, and there, as men say, all the dead abide, what good, O my friends and judges, can be greater than this? If indeed when the pilgrim arrives in the world below, he is delivered from the professors of justice in this world, and finds the true judges who are said to give judgment there, Minos and Rhadamanthus and Aeacus and Triptolemus, and other sons of God who were righteous in their own life, that pilgrimage will be worth making. What would not a man give if he might converse with Orpheus and Musaeus and Hesiod and Homer? Nay, if this be true, let me die again and again. I myself, too, shall have a wonderful interest in there meeting and conversing with Palamedes, and Ajax the son of Telamon, and any other ancient hero who has suffered death through an unjust judgment; and there will be no small pleasure, as I think, in comparing my own sufferings with theirs. Above all, I shall then be able to continue my search into true and false knowledge; as in this world, so also in the next; and I shall find out who is wise, and who pretends to be wise, and is not. What would not a man give, O judges, to be able to examine the leader of the great Trojan expedition; or Odysseus or Sisyphus, or numberless others, men and women too! What infinite delight would there be in conversing with them and asking them questions! In another world they do not put a man to death for asking questions: assuredly not. For besides being happier than we are, they will be immortal, if what is said is true.

Wherefore, O judges, be of good cheer about death, and know of a certainty, that no evil can happen to a good man, either in life or after death. He and his are not neglected by the gods; nor has my own approaching end happened by mere chance. But I see clearly that the time had arrived when it was better for me to die and be released from trouble; wherefore the oracle gave no sign. For which reason, also, I am not angry with my condemners, or with my accusers; they have done me no harm, although they did not mean to do me any good; and for this I may gently blame them.

37. Man dying during a race. Grave stele.

Still I have a favour to ask of them. When my sons are grown up, I would ask you, O my friends, to punish them; and I would have you trouble them, as I have troubled you, if they seem to care about riches, or anything, more than about virtue; or if they pretend to be something when they are really nothing,—then reprove them, as I have reproved you, for not caring about that for which they ought to care, and thinking that they are something when they are really nothing. And if you do this, both I and my sons will have received justice at your hands.

The hour of departure has arrived, and we go our ways—I to die, and you to live. Which is better God only knows.

SOPHOCLES

FROM ANTIGONE

ANTIGONE

Ismene, sister, mine own dear sister, knowest thou what ill there is, of all bequeathed by Oedipus, that Zeus fulfils not for us twain while we live? Nothing painful is there, nothing fraught with ruin, no shame, no dishonour, that I have not seen in thy woes and mine.

And now what new edict is this of which they tell, that our Captain hath just published to all Thebes? Knowest thou aught? Hast thou heard? Or is it hidden from thee that our friends are threatened with the doom of our foes?

ISMENE

No word of friends, Antigone, gladsome or painful, hath come to me, since we two sisters were bereft of brothers twain, killed in one day by a twofold blow; and since in this last night the Argive host hath fled, I know no more, whether my fortune be brighter, or more grievous.

ANTIGONE

I knew it well, and therefore sought to bring thee beyond the gates of the court, that thou mightest hear alone.

ISMENE

What is it? 'Tis plain that thou art brooding on some dark tidings.

ANTIGONE

What, hath not Creon destined our brothers, the one to honoured burial, the other to unburied shame? Eteocles, they say, with due observance of right and custom, he hath laid in the earth, for his honour among the dead below. But the hapless corpse of Polyneices—as rumour saith, it hath been published to the town that none shall entomb him or mourn, but leave unwept, unsepulchred, a welcome store for the birds, as they espy him, to feast on at will.

Such, 'tis said, is the edict that the good Creon hath set forth for thee and for me,—yes, for *me,*—and is coming hither to proclaim it clearly to those who know it not; nor counts the matter light, but, whoso disobeys in aught, his doom is death by stoning before all the folk. Thou knowest it now; and thou wilt soon show whether thou art nobly bred, or the base daughter of a noble line.

ISMENE

Poor sister,—and if things stand thus, what could I help to do or undo?

ANTIGONE

Consider if thou wilt share the toil and the deed.

ISMENE

In what venture? What can be thy meaning?

ANTIGONE

Wilt thou aid this hand to lift the dead?

ISMENE

Thou wouldst bury him,—when 'tis forbidden to Thebes?

ANTIGONE

I will do my part,—and thine, if thou wilt not,—to a brother. False to him will I never be found.

ISMENE

Ah, over-bold! when Creon hath forbidden?

ANTIGONE

Nay, he hath no right to keep me from mine own.

.   .   .

ISMENE

I do them no dishonour; but to defy the State,—I have no strength for that.

ANTIGONE

Such be thy plea:—I, then, will go to heap the earth above the brother whom I love.

ISMENE

Alas, unhappy one! How I fear for thee!

ANTIGONE

Fear not for me: guide thine own fate aright.

. . .

(ANTIGONE *and* ISMENE *depart. A* GUARD *and* CREON *enter.*)

GUARD

My liege, I will not say that I come breathless from speed, or that I have plied a nimble foot; for often did my thoughts make me pause, and wheel round in my path, to return. My mind was holding large discourse with me. . . .

CREON

And what is it that disquiets thee thus?

GUARD

I wish to tell thee first about myself—I did not do the deed—I did not see the doer—it were not right that I should come to any harm.

CREON

Thou hast a shrewd eye for thy mark; well dost thou fence thyself round against the blame; clearly thou hast some strange thing to tell.

GUARD

Aye, truly; dread news makes one pause long.

CREON

Then tell it, wilt thou, and so get thee gone?

GUARD

Well, this is it.—The corpse—some one hath just given it burial, and gone away,—after sprinkling thirsty dust on the flesh, with such other rites as piety enjoins.

CREON

What sayest thou? What living man hath dared this deed?

GUARD

I know not; no stroke of pickaxe was seen there, no earth thrown up by mattock; the ground was hard and dry, unbroken, without track of wheels; the doer was one who had left no trace. And when the first day-watchman showed it to us, sore wonder fell on all. The dead man was veiled from us; not shut within a tomb, but lightly strewn with dust, as by the hand of one who shunned a curse. And no sign meet the eye as though any beast of prey or any dog had come night to him, or torn him.

. . .

Creon

. . . Now, as Zeus still hath my reverence, know this—I tell it thee on my oath:—If ye find not the very author of this burial, and produce him before mine eyes, death alone shall not be enough for you, till first, hung up alive, ye have revealed this outrage,—that henceforth ye may thieve with better knowledge whence lucre should be won, and learn that it is not well to love gain from every source. For thou wilt find that ill-gotten pelf brings more men to ruin than to weal.

. . .

(Creon *goes into the palace*.)

Chorus

Wonders are many, and none is more wonderful than man; the power that crosses the white sea, driven by the stormy south-wind, makes a path under surges that threaten to engulf him; and Earth, the eldest of the gods, the immortal, the unwearied, doth he wear, turning the soil with the offspring of horses, as the ploughs go to and fro from year to year.

And the light-hearted race of birds, and the tribes of savage beasts, and the sea-brood of the deep, he snares in the meshes of his woven toils, he leads captive, man excellent in wit. And he masters by his arts the beast whose lair is in the wilds, who roams the hills; he tames the horse of shaggy mane, he puts the yoke upon its neck, he tames the tireless mountain bull.

And speech, and wind-swift thought, and all the moods that mould a state, hath he taught himself; and how to flee the arrows of the frost, when 'tis hard lodging under the clear sky, and the arrows of the rushing rain; yea, he hath resource for all; without resource he meets nothing that must come: only against Death shall he call for aid in vain; but from baffling maladies he hath devised escapes.

Cunning beyond fancy's dream is the fertile skill which brings him, now to evil, now to good. When he honours the laws of the land, and that justice which he hath sworn by the gods to uphold, proudly stands his city: no city hath he who, for his rashness, dwells with sin. Never may he share my hearth, never think my thoughts, who doth these things!

(*The* Guard *enters, leading in* Antigone.)

Leader of the Chorus

What portent from the gods is this?—my soul is amazed. I know her—how can I deny that yon maiden is Antigone?

38. *The birth of Aphrodite out of sea foam, aided by two maidens.*

O hapless, and child of hapless sire,—of Oedipus! What means this? Thou brought a prisoner?—thou, disloyal to the king's laws, and taken in folly?

GUARD

Here she is, the doer of the deed:—we caught this girl burying him: —but where is Creon?

LEADER

Lo, he comes forth again from the house, at our need.

CREON

What is it? What hath chanced, that makes my coming timely? . . . And thy prisoner here—how and whence hast thou taken her?

GUARD

She was burying the man; thou knowest all.

CREON

Dost thou mean what thou sayest? Dost thou speak aright?

GUARD

I saw her burying the corpse that thou hadst forbidden to bury. Is that plain and clear?

342

CREON

And how was she seen? how taken in the act?

GUARD

It befell on this wise. When we had come to the place,—with those dread menaces of thine upon us,—we swept away all the dust that covered the corpse, and bared the dank body well; and then sat us down on the brow of the hill, to windward, heedful that the smell from him should not strike us; every man was wide awake, and kept his neighbour alert with torrents of threats, if anyone should be careless of this task.

.   .   .

And when, after a long while, this storm had passed, the maid was seen; and she cried aloud with the sharp cry of a bird in its bitterness,—even as when, within the empty nest, it sees the bed stripped of its nestlings. So she also, when she saw the corpse bare, lifted up a voice of wailing, and called down curses on the doers of that deed. And straightway she brought thirsty dust in her hands; and from a shapely ewer of bronze, held high, with thrice-poured drink-offering she crowned the dead.

We rushed forward when we saw it, and at once closed upon our quarry, who was in no wise dismayed. Then we taxed her with her past and present doings; and she stood not on denial of aught,—at once to my joy and to my pain. . . .

CREON

Thou—thou whose face is bent to earth—dost thou avow, or disavow this deed?

ANTIGONE

I avow it; I make no denial.

CREON (*to* **GUARD**)

Thou canst betake thee whither thou wilt, free and clear of a grave charge.

(*The* **GUARD** *leaves.*)

Now, tell me thou—not in many words, but briefly—knewest thou that an edict had forbidden this?

ANTIGONE

I knew it: could I help it? It was public.

CREON

And thou didst indeed dare to transgress that law?

343

ANTIGONE

Yes; for it was not Zeus that had published me that edict; not such are the laws set among men by the Justice who dwells with the gods below; nor deemed I that thy decrees were of such force, that a mortal could override the unwritten and unfailing statutes of heaven. For their life is not of to-day or yesterday, but from all time, and no man knows when they were first put forth.

Not through dread of any human pride could I answer to the gods for breaking *these*. . . .

CREON

. . . This girl was already versed in insolence when she transgressed the laws that had been set forth; and, that done, lo, a second insult,—to vaunt of this, and exult in her deed.

Now verily I am no man, she is the man, if this victory shall rest with her, and bring no penalty. No! be she sister's child, or nearer to me in blood than any that worships Zeus at the altar of our house,—she and her kinsfolk shall not avoid a doom most dire; for indeed I charge that other with a like share in the plotting of this burial.

And summon her—for I saw her e'en now within,—raving, and not mistress of her wits. So oft, before the deed, the mind stands self-convicted in its treason, when folks are plotting mischief in the dark. But verily this, too, is hateful,—when one who hath been caught in wickedness then seeks to make the crime a glory.

ANTIGONE

Wouldst thou do more than take and slay me?

CREON

No more, indeed; having that, I have all.

ANTIGONE

Why then dost thou delay? In thy discourse there is nought that pleases me,—never may there be!—and so my words must needs be unpleasing to thee. And yet, for glory—whence could I have won a nobler, than by giving burial to mine own brother? All here would own that they thought it well, were not their lips sealed by fear. But royalty, blest in so much besides, hath the power to do and say what it will.

CREON

Thou differest from all these Thebans in that view.

ANTIGONE

These also share it; but they curb their tongues for thee.

344

CREON

And art thou not ashamed to act apart from them?

ANTIGONE

No; there is nothing shameful in piety to a brother.

CREON

Was it not a brother, too, that died in the opposite cause?

ANTIGONE

Brother by the same mother and the same sire.

CREON

Why, then, dost thou render a grace that is impious in his sight?

ANTIGONE

The dead man will not say that he so deems it.

CREON

Yea, if thou makest him but equal in honour with the wicked.

ANTIGONE

It was his brother, not his slave, that perished.

CREON

Wasting this land; while *he* fell as its champion.

ANTIGONE

Nevertheless, Hades desires these rites.

CREON

But the good desires not a like portion with the evil.

ANTIGONE

Who knows but this seems blameless in the world below?

CREON

A foe is never a friend—not even in death.

ANTIGONE

'Tis not my nature to join in hating, but in loving.

CREON

Pass, then, to the world of the dead, and, if thou must needs love, love them. While I live, no woman shall rule me.

(ANTIGONE *is led away*.)

.   .   .

LEADER OF THE CHORUS

But lo, Haemon, the last of thy sons;—comes he grieving for the doom

345

of his promised bride, Antigone, and bitter for the baffled hope of his marriage?

CREON

We shall know soon, better than seers could tell us.—My son, hearing the fixed doom of thy betrothed, art thou come in rage against thy father? Or have I thy good will, act how I may?

HAEMON

Father, I am thine; and thou, in thy wisdom, tracest for me rules which I shall follow. No marriage shall be deemed by me a greater gain than thy good guidance.

CREON

Yea, this, my son, should be thy heart's fixed law,—in all things to obey thy father's will. 'Tis for this that men pray to see dutiful children grow up around them in their homes,—that such may requite their father's foe with evil, and honour, as their father doth, his friend. But he who begets unprofitable children—what shall we say that he hath sown, but troubles for himself, and much triumph for his foes? Then do not thou, my son, at pleasure's beck, dethrone thy reason for a woman's sake; knowing that this is a joy that soon grows cold in clasping arms,— an evil woman to share thy bed and thy home. For what wound could strike deeper than a false friend? Nay, with loathing, and as if she were thine enemy, let this girl go to find a husband in the house of Hades. For since I have taken her, alone of all the city, in open disobedience, I will not make myself a liar to my people—I will slay her.

.   .   .

But disobedience is the worst of evils. This it is that ruins cities; this makes homes desolate; by this, the ranks of allies are broken into head-long rout; but, of the lives whose course is fair, the greater part owes safety to obedience. Therefore we must support the cause of order, and in no wise suffer a woman to worst us. Better to fall from power, if we must, by a man's hand; then we should not be called weaker than a woman.

LEADER

To us, unless our years have stolen our wit, thou seemest to say wisely what thou sayest.

HAEMON

Father, the gods implant reason in men, the highest of all things that we call our own. Not mine the skill—far from me be the quest!—to say wherein thou speakest not aright; and yet another man, too, might have some useful thought. At least, it is my natural office to watch, on thy behalf, all that men say, or do, or find to blame. For the dread of thy frown forbids the citizen to speak such words as would offend thine ear; but I can hear these murmurs in the dark, these moanings of the city for this maiden; "no woman," they say, "ever merited her doom less,—none ever was to die so shamelessly for deeds so glorious as hers; who, when her own brother had fallen in bloody strife, would not leave him unburied, to be devoured by carrion dogs, or by any bird:—deserves not *she* the meed of golden honour?"

Such is the darkling rumour that spreads in secret. For me, my father, no treasure is so precious as thy welfare. What, indeed, is a nobler ornament for children than a prospering sire's fair fame, or for sire than son's? Wear not, then, one mood only in thyself; think not that thy word, and thine alone, must be right. For if any man thinks that he alone is wise,—that in speech, or in mind, he hath no peer,—such a soul, when laid open, is ever found empty.

No, though a man be wise, 'tis no shame for him to learn many things, and to bend in season. Seest thou, beside the wintry torrent's course, how the trees that yield to it save every twig, while the stiff-necked perish root and branch? And even thus he who keeps the sheet of his sail taut, and never slackens it, upsets his boat, and finishes his voyage with keel uppermost.

Nay, forego thy wrath; permit thyself to change. For if I, a younger man, may offer my thought, it were far best, I ween, that men should be all-wise by nature; but, otherwise—and oft the scale inclines not so— 'tis good also to learn from those who speak aright.

LEADER
Sire, 'tis meet that thou shouldest profit by his words, if he speaks aught in season, and thou, Haemon, by thy father's; for on both parts there hath been wise speech.

CREON
Men of my age—are we indeed to be schooled, then, by men of his?

HAEMON
In nothing that is not right; but if I am young, thou shouldest look to my merits, not to my years.

CREON
Is it a merit to honour the unruly?

347

HAEMON

I could wish no one to show respect for evil-doers.

CREON

Then is not she tainted with that malady?

HAEMON

Our Theban folk, with one voice, denies it.

CREON

Shall Thebes prescribe to me how I must rule?

HAEMON

See, there thou hast spoken like a youth indeed.

CREON

Am I to rule this land by other judgment than mine own?

HAEMON

That is no city which belongs to one man.

CREON

Is not the city held to be the ruler's?

HAEMON

Thou wouldst make a good monarch of a desert.

CREON

This boy, it seems, is the woman's champion.

HAEMON

If thou art a woman; indeed, my care is for thee.

CREON

Shameless, at open feud with thy father!

HAEMON

Nay, I see thee offending against justice.

CREON

Do I offend, when I respect mine own prerogatives?

HAEMON

Thou dost not respect them, when thou tramplest on the gods' honours.

CREON

O dastard nature, yielding place to woman!

HAEMON

Thou wilt never find me yield to baseness.

CREON

All thy words, at least, plead for that girl.

HAEMON

And for thee, and for me, and for the gods below.

CREON

Thou canst never marry her, on this side the grave.

HAEMON

Then she must die, and in death destroy another.

CREON

How! doth thy boldness run to open threats?

HAEMON

What threat is it, to combat vain resolves?

CREON

Thou shalt rue thy witless teaching of wisdom.

HAEMON

Wert thou not my father, I would have called thee unwise.

CREON

Thou woman's slave, use not wheedling speech with me.

HAEMON

Thou wouldest speak, and then hear no reply?

CREON

Sayest thou so? Now, by the heaven above us—be sure of it—thou shalt smart for taunting me in this opprobrious strain. Bring forth that hated thing, that she may die forthwith in his presence—before his eyes—at her bridegroom's side!

HAEMON

No, not at my side—never think it—shall she perish; nor shalt thou ever set eyes more upon my face:—rave, then, with such friends as can endure thee.

(*Exit* HAEMON. CREON *goes into the palace.*)

.   .   .

CHORUS

Love, unconquered in the fight, Love, who makest havoc of wealth, who keepest thy vigil on the soft cheek of a maiden; thou roamest over the sea, and among the homes of dwellers in the wilds; no immortal can escape thee, nor any among men whose life is for a day; and he to whom thou hast come is mad.

.   .   .

ANTIGONE

See me, citizens of my fatherland, setting forth on my last way, looking my last on the sunlight that is for me no more; no, Hades who gives sleep to all leads me living to Acheron's shore; who have had no portion in the chant that brings the bride, nor hath any song been mine for the crowning of bridals; whom the lord of the Dark Lake shall wed.

CHORUS

Glorious, therefore, and with praise, thou departest to that deep place of the dead: wasting sickness hath not smitten thee; thou hast not found the wages of the sword; no, mistress of thine own fate, and still alive, thou shalt pass to Hades, as no other of mortal kind hath passed.

.   .   .

ANTIGONE

Unwept, unfriended, without marriage-song, I am led forth in my sorrow on this journey that can be delayed no more. No longer, hapless one, may I behold yon day-star's sacred eye; but for my fate no tear is shed, no friend makes moan.

CREON

Know ye not that songs and wailings before death would never cease, if it profited to utter them? Away with her—away! And when ye have enclosed her, according to my word, in her vaulted grave, leave her alone, forlorn—whether she wishes to die, or to live a buried life in such a home. Our hands are clean as touching this maiden. But this is certain —she shall be deprived of her sojourn in the light.

ANTIGONE

Tomb, bridal-chamber, eternal prison in the caverned rock, whither I go to find mine own, those many who have perished, and whom Persephone hath received among the dead! Last of all shall I pass thither, and far most miserably of all, before the term of my life is spent. But I cherish good hope that my coming will be welcome to my father, and pleasant to thee, my mother, and welcome, brother, to thee; for, when ye died, with mine own hands I washed and dressed you, and poured drink-offerings at your graves; and now, Polyneices, 'tis for tending thy corpse that I win such recompense as this.

.   .   .

And what law of heaven have I transgressed? Why, hapless one, should

39. and 40. *Battle of the Gods and Giants,* from the north frieze of the Siphnian Treasury.

I look to the gods any more,—what ally should I invoke,—when by piety I have earned the name of impious? Nay, then, if these things are pleasing to the gods, when I have suffered my doom, I shall come to know my sin; but if the sin is with my judges, I could wish them no fuller measure of evil than they, on their part, mete wrongfully to me.

CHORUS

Still the same tempest of the soul vexes this maiden with the same fierce gusts.

CREON

Then for this shall her guards have cause to rue their slowness.

ANTIGONE

Ah me! that word hath come very near to death.

CREON

I can cheer thee with no hope that this doom is not thus to be fulfilled.

ANTIGONE

O city of my fathers in the land of Thebes! O ye gods, eldest of our race!—they lead me hence—now, now—they tarry not! Behold me, princes of Thebes, the last daughter of the house of your kings,—see what I suffer, and from whom, because I feared to cast away the fear of Heaven!

(ANTIGONE is led away by the guards.)

.   .   .

Teiresias comes to counsel and forewarn Creon about the folly of his edict and the punishment of Antigone, but Creon is committed to his course and distrusts the prophet.

LEADER OF THE CHORUS

The man hath gone, O King, with dread prophecies. And, since the hair on this head, once dark, hath been white, I know that he hath never been a false prophet to our city.

CREON

I, too, know it well, and am troubled in soul. 'Tis dire to yield; but, by resistance, to smite my pride with ruin—this, too, is a dire choice.

LEADER

Son of Menoeceus, it behoves thee to take wise counsel.

CREON

What should I do, then? Speak, and I will obey.

LEADER

Go thou, and free the maiden from her rocky chamber, and make a tomb for the unburied dead.

CREON

And this is thy counsel? Thou wouldst have me yield?

LEADER

Yea, King, and with all speed; for swift harms from the gods cut short the folly of men.

CREON

Ah me, 'tis hard, but I resign my cherished resolve,—I obey. We must not wage a vain war with destiny.

LEADER

Go, thou, and do these things; leave them not to others.

CREON

Even as I am I'll go:—on, on, my servants, each and all of you,—take axes in your hands, and hasten to the ground that ye see yonder! Since our judgment hath taken this turn, I will be present to unloose her, as I myself bound her. My heart misgives me, 'tis best to keep the established laws, even to life's end.

(CREON *and his servants leave.*)

.　　.　　.

(EURYDICE, CREON'S *wife, comes in.*)

EURYDICE

People of Thebes, I heard your words as I was going forth, to salute the goddess Pallas with my prayers. Even as I was loosing the fastenings of the gate, to open it, the message of a household woe smote on mine ear: I sank back, terror-stricken, into the arms of my handmaids, and my senses fled. But say again what the tidings were; I shall hear them as one who is no stranger to sorrow.

MESSENGER

Dear lady, I will witness of what I saw, and will leave no word of the truth untold. Why, indeed, should I soothe thee with words in which I must presently be found false? Truth is ever best.—I attended thy lord as his guide to the furthest part of the plain, where the body of Polyneices, torn by dogs, still lay unpitied. We prayed the goddess of the roads, and Pluto, in mercy to restrain their wrath; we washed the dead with holy washing; and with freshly-plucked boughs we solemnly burned such relics as there were. We raised a high mound of his native earth; and then we turned away to enter the maiden's nuptial chamber with rocky couch, the caverned mansion of the bride of Death. And, from afar off, one of us heard a voice of loud wailing at that bride's unhallowed bower; and came to tell our master Creon.

And as the king drew nearer, doubtful sounds of a bitter cry floated around him; he groaned, and said in accents of anguish, "Wretched that I am, can my foreboding be true? Am I going on the wofullest way that ever I went? My son's voice greets me.—Go, my servants,—haste ye nearer, and when ye have reached the tomb, pass through the gap, where the stones have been wrenched away, to the cell's very mouth,—and look, and see if 'tis Haemon's voice that I know, or if mine ear is cheated by the gods."

This search, at our despairing master's word, we went to make; and in the furthest part of the tomb we descried *her* hanging by the neck, slung by a thread-wrought halter of fine linen: while *he* was embracing her with arms thrown around her waist,—bewailing the loss of his bride who is with the dead, and his father's deeds, and his own ill-starred love.

But his father, when he saw him, cried aloud with a dread cry and went in, and called to him with a voice of wailing:—"Unhappy, what a deed hast thou done! What thought hath come to thee? What manner of mischance hath marred thy reason? Come forth, my child! I pray thee —I implore!" But the boy glared at him with fierce eyes, spat in his face, and without a word of answer, drew his cross-hilted sword:—as his father rushed forth in flight, he missed his aim;—then, hapless one, wroth with himself, he straightway leaned with all his weight against his sword, and drove it, half its length, into his side; and, while sense lingered, he clasped the maiden to his faint embrace, and, as he gasped, sent forth on her pale cheek the swift stream of the oozing blood.

Corpse enfolding corpse he lies; he hath won his nuptial rites, poor youth, not here, yet in the halls of Death; and he hath witnessed to mankind that, of all curses which cleave to man, ill counsel is the sovereign curse.

(EURYDICE *returns to the house.*)

LEADER

What wouldst thou augur from this? The lady hath turned back, and is gone, without a word, good or evil.

MESSENGER

I, too, am startled; yet I nourish the hope that, at these sore tidings of her son, she cannot deign to give her sorrow public vent, but in the privacy of the house will set her handmaids to mourn the household grief. For she is not untaught of discretion, that she should err.

LEADER

I know not; but to me, at least, a strained silence seems to portend peril, no less than vain abundance of lament.

MESSENGER

Well, I will enter the house, and learn whether indeed she is not hiding some repressed purpose in the depth of a passionate heart. Yea, thou sayest well: excess of silence, too, may have a perilous meaning.

(CREON enters with attendants carrying the body of HAEMON on a bier.)

CHORUS

Lo, yonder the king himself draws near, bearing that which tells too clear a tale,—the work of no stranger's madness,—if we may say it,—but of his own misdeeds.

CREON

Woe for the sins of a darkened soul, stubborn sins, fraught with death! Ah, ye behold us, the sire who hath slain, the son who hath perished! Woe is me, for the wretched blindness of my counsels! Alas, my son, thou hast died in thy youth, by a timeless doom, woe is me!—thy spirit hath fled,—not by thy folly, but by mine own!

CHORUS

Ah me, how all too late thou seemest to see the right!

CREON

Ah me, I have learned the bitter lesson! But then, methinks, oh then, some god smote me from above with crushing weight, and hurled me into ways of cruelty, woe is me,—overthrowing and trampling on my joy! Woe, woe, for the troublous toils of men!

MESSENGER

Sire, thou hast come, methinks, as one whose hands are not empty, but who hath store laid up besides; thou bearest yonder burden with thee: and thou art soon to look upon the woes within thy house.

CREON

And what worse ill is yet to follow upon ills?

MESSENGER

Thy queen hath died, true mother of yon corpse—ah, hapless lady!— by blows newly dealt.

CREON

Oh Hades, all-receiving, whom no sacrifice can appease! Hast thou, then, no mercy for me? O thou herald of evil, bitter tidings, what word dost thou utter? Alas, I was already as dead, and thou hast smitten me anew! What sayest thou, my son? What is this new message that thou bringest—woe, woe is me!—of a wife's doom—of slaughter heaped on slaughter?

CHORUS

Thou canst behold: 'tis no longer hidden within.

CREON

Ah me,—yonder I behold a new, a second woe! What destiny, ah what, can yet await me? I have but now raised my son in my arms,—and there, again, I see a corpse before me! Alas, alas, unhappy mother! Alas, my child!

MESSENGER

There, at the altar, self-stabbed with a keen knife, she suffered her darkening eyes to close, when she had wailed for the noble fate of Megareus who died before, and then for his fate who lies there,—and when, with her last breath, she had invoked evil fortunes upon thee, the slayer of thy sons.

CREON

Woe, woe! I thrill with dread. Is there none to strike me to the heart with two-edged sword?—O miserable that I am, and steeped in miserable anguish!

MESSENGER

Yea, both this son's doom, and that other's, were laid to thy charge by her whose corpse thou seest.

.   .   .

CREON

Lead me away, I pray you; a rash, foolish man; who have slain thee, ah my son, unwittingly, and thee, too, my wife—unhappy that I am! I know not which way I should bend my gaze, or where I should seek support; for all is amiss with that which is in my hands,—and yonder, again, a crushing fate hath leapt upon my head.

LEADER

Wisdom is the supreme part of happiness; and reverence towards the gods must be inviolate. Great words of prideful men are ever punished with great blows, and, in old age, teach the chastened to be wise.

3. Love and Friendship

Love is the greatest of heaven's blessings.

Plato, *Phaedrus*

The "roundness" of the Greek mind manifests itself anew when we examine the place held by communion between individual persons. We saw earlier the Greek emphasis on the state. We also saw how the Greeks broke through to the importance of the individual person, to the kingdom of the individual soul and the primacy of conscience. Now we shall turn to the glorious documentation on love and friendship offered in Greek writings. These partly typify a poetic expression of a concrete love, partly a philosophical prise de conscience of the nature of this central experience in man's life, "that stirs the soul to its very depth." (Jaeger, Paideia, Vol. I, 134)

HOMER

HECTOR AND ANDROMACHE

. . .

Hector this heard, return'd without delay;
Swift through the town he trod his former way,
Through streets of palaces, and walks of state;
And met the mourner at the Scaean gate.
With haste to meet him sprung the joyful fair,
His blameless wife, Aëtion's wealthy heir:
(Cilician Thebè great Aëtion sway'd,
And Hippoplacus' wide extended shade:)
The nurse stood near, in whose embraces press'd,
His only hope hung smiling at her breast,
Whom each soft charm and early grace adorn,
Fair as the new-born star that gilds the morn.
To this loved infant Hector gave the name
Scamandrius, from Scamander's honour'd stream;
Astyanax the Trojans call'd the boy,
From his great father, the defence of Troy.

Silent the warrior smiled, and pleased resign'd
To tender passions all his mighty mind;
His beauteous princess cast a mournful look,
Hung on his hand, and then dejected spoke;
Her bosom labour'd with a boding sigh,
And the big tear stood trembling in her eye.
    "Too daring prince! ah, whither dost thou run?
Ah, too forgetful of thy wife and son!
And think'st thou not how wretched we shall be,
A widow I, a helpless orphan he?
For sure such courage length of life denies,
And thou must fall, thy virtue's sacrifice.
Greece in her single heroes strove in vain;
Now hosts oppose thee, and thou must be slain.
Oh grant me, gods, ere Hector meets his doom,
All I can ask of heaven, an early tomb!
So shall my days in one sad tenor run,
And end with sorrows as they first begun.
No parent now remains my griefs to share,
No father's aid, no mother's tender care.
The fierce Achilles wrapt our walls in fire!
Laid Thebè waste, and slew my warlike sire!
His fate compassion in the victor bred;
Stern as he was, he yet revered the dead,
His radiant arms preserved from hostile spoil,
And laid him decent on the funeral pile;
Then raised a mountain where his bones were burn'd;
The mountain-nymphs the rural tomb adorn'd,
Jove's sylvan daughters bade their elms bestow
A barren shade, and in his honour grow.
    "By the same arm my seven brave brothers fell;
In one sad day beheld the gates of hell;
While the fat herds and snowy flocks they fed,
Amid their fields the hapless heroes bled!
My mother lived to wear the victor's bands,
The queen of Hippoplacia's sylvan lands:
Redeem'd too late, she scarce beheld again
Her pleasing empire and her native plain,
When ah! oppress'd by life-consuming woe,
She fell a victim to Diana's bow.

"Yet while my Hector still survives, I see
My father, mother, brethren, all, in thee:
Alas! my parents, brothers, kindred, all
Once more will perish, if my Hector fall,
Thy wife, thy infant, in thy danger share:
Oh, prove a husband's and a father's care!
That quarter most the skilful Greeks annoy,
Where yon wild fig-trees join the wall of Troy;
Thou, from this tower defend the important post;
There Agamemnon points his dreadful host,
That pass Tydides, Ajax, strive to gain,
And there the vengeful Spartan fires his train.
Thrice our bold foes the fierce attack have given,
Or led by hopes, or dictated from heaven.
Let others in the field their arms employ,
But stay my Hector here, and guard his Troy."
The chief replied: "That post shall be my care,
Not that alone, but all the works of war.
How would the sons of Troy, in arms renown'd,
And Troy's proud dames, whose garments sweep the ground,
Attaint the lustre of my former name,
Should Hector basely quit the field of fame?
My early youth was bred to martial pains,
My soul impels me to the embattled plains!
Let me be foremost to defend the throne,
And guard my father's glories, and my own.
"Yet come it will, the day decreed by fates!
(How my heart trembles while my tongue relates!)
The day when thou, imperial Troy! must bend,
And see thy warriors fall, thy glories end.
And yet no dire presage so wounds my mind,
My mother's death, the ruin of my kind,
Not Priam's hoary hairs defiled with gore,
Not all my brothers gasping on the shore;
As thine, Andromache! Thy griefs I dread:
I see thee trembling, weeping, captive led!
In Argive looms our battles to design,
And woes, of which so large a part was thine!
To bear the victor's hard commands, or bring
The weight of waters from Hyperia's spring.

There while you groan beneath the load of life,
They cry, 'Behold the mighty Hector's wife!'
Some haughty Greek, who lives thy tears to see,
Imbitters all thy woes, by naming me.
The thoughts of glory past, and present shame,
A thousand griefs shall waken at the name!
May I lie cold before that dreadful day,
Press'd with a load of monumental clay!
Thy Hector, wrapt in everlasting sleep,
Shall neither hear thee sigh, nor see thee weep."

 Thus having spoke, the illustrious chief of Troy
Stretch'd his fond arms to clasp the lovely boy.
The babe clung crying to his nurse's breast,
Scared at the dazzling helm, and nodding crest.
With secret pleasure each fond parent smiled,
And Hector hasted to relieve his child,
The glittering terrors from his brows unbound,
And placed the beaming helmet on the ground;
Then kiss'd the child, and, lifting high in air,
Thus to the gods preferr'd a father's prayer:

 "O thou! whose glory fills the ethereal throne,
And all ye deathless powers! protect my son!
Grant him, like me, to purchase just renown,
To guard the Trojans, to defend the crown,
Against his country's foes the war to wage,
And rise the Hector of the future age!
So when triumphant from successful toils
Of heroes slain he bears the reeking spoils,
Whole hosts may hail him with deserved acclaim,
And say, 'This chief transcends his father's fame.'
While pleased amidst the general shouts of Troy,
His mother's conscious heart o'erflows with joy."

 He spoke, and fondly gazing on her charms,
Restored the pleasing burden to her arms;
Soft on her fragrant breast the babe she laid,
Hush'd to repose, and with a smile survey'd.
The troubled pleasure soon chastised by fear,
She mingled with a smile a tender tear.
The soften'd chief with kind compassion view'd,
And dried the falling drops, and thus pursued:

41. *Nike* from the balustrade of the Temple of Athena Nike.

"Andromache! my soul's far better part,
Why with untimely sorrows heaves thy heart?
No hostile hand can antedate my doom,
Till fate condemns me to the silent tomb.
Fix'd is the term to all the race of earth;
And such the hard condition of our birth:
No force can then resist, no flight can save,
All sink alike, the fearful and the brave.
No more—but hasten to thy tasks at home,
There guide the spindle, and direct the loom:
Me glory summons to the martial scene,
The field of combat is the sphere for men.
Where heroes war, the foremost place I claim,
The first in danger as the first in fame."

Thus having said, the glorious chief resumes
His towery helmet, black with shading plumes.
His princess parts with a prophetic sigh,
Unwilling parts, and oft reverts her eye
That stream'd at every look; then, moving slow,
Sought her own palace, and indulged her woe.
There, while her tears deplored the godlike man,
Through all her train the soft infection ran;
The pious maids their mingled sorrows shed,
And mourn the living Hector, as the dead.

(from *The Iliad,* Book VI)

THEOCRITUS

SERENADE

O beautiful Amaryllis, why no longer from your cave
Do you peep forth to greet me, your beloved? Do you hate me
    then?
Can it be I appear snub-nosed, dear nymph, when seen from
    close?
A jutting-bearded satyr? You will make me hang myself.
See here ten apples I have brought you, fetched down from
    the tree
From which you bade me fetch them. I will bring ten more
    to-morrow.

Look on my heart-tormenting grief. Would that I might be-
    come
Yon booming bee, and enter to your cavern, steering through
The ivy and the feathery fern, wherein you lie embowered.
Now I know Love. A cruel god is he: a she-lion's breasts
He sucked, and in a forest his mother nurtured him,
Since with slow fire he burns me thus, smiting me to the bone.
O beautifully glancing—but all stone! O dark-browed Nymph!
Around me, your own goatherd, fling your arms, that I may
    kiss you.
Even in empty kisses there is a sweet delight.
Soon you will make me tear this garland into little shreds,
This ivy wreath, dear Amaryllis, that I keep for you,
Twining it with rose-buds and sweet-smelling parsley-leaves.
Oh misery! What will be my fate, poor wretch! Will you not
    answer?
I'll strip my cloak off and leap down to the waves from yonder
    cliff,
Whence Olpis, the fisherman, watches for tunny shoals:
And if I perish—well, at least that will be sweet to you.

                (Translated by R. C. Trevelyan)

ANACREON

TO DIONYSUS

Roving god, whose playfellows
Over the mountains' airy brows
    In happy chase are led;
Where Love, who breaks the heart of pride,
Or nymphs amuse thee, violet-eyed,
Or Aphrodîtê keeps thy side,
    The goddess rosy-red—
Lord Dionyse, I kneel to thee;
Stoop to me of thy charity
    And this my prayer receive:
Dear Lord, thy best persuasion use,
Bid Cleobûlus not refuse
    The gift of love I give.

            (Translated by T. F. Higham)

SAPPHO

LOVE

Love has unbound my limbs and set me shaking,
A monster bitter-sweet and my unmaking.

(Translated by C. M. Bowra)

PARTING

Truly I want to die.
Such was her weeping when she said Good-bye.

These words she said to me:
"What sad calamity!
Sappho, I leave you most unwillingly."

To her I made reply:
"Go with good heart, but try
Not to forget our love in days gone by.

"Else let me call to mind,
If your heart proves unkind,
The soft delightful ways you leave behind.

"Many a coronet
Of rose and violet,
Crocus and dill upon your brow you set:

"Many a necklace too
Round your soft throat you threw,
Woven with me from buds of ravishing hue,

"And often balm you spread
Of myrrh upon my head,
And royal ointment on my hair you shed."

(Translated by C. M. Bowra)

TO A BRIDE

Blest beyond earth's bliss, with heaven I deem him
Blest, the man that in thy presence near thee
Face to face may sit, and while thou speakest,

Listening may hear thee,

And thy sweet-voiced laughter:—In my bosom
 The rapt heart so troubleth, wildly stirred:
Let me see thee, but a glimpse—and straightway
 Utterance of word

Fails me; no voice comes; my tongue is palsied;
 Thrilling fire through all my flesh hath run;
Mine eyes cannot see, mine ears make dinning
 Noises that stun;

The sweat streameth down,—my whole frame seized with
 Shivering,—and wan paleness o'er me spread,
Greener than the grass; I seem with faintness
 Almost as dead.

(Translated by Walter Headlam)

EURIPIDES

FROM THE TROJAN WOMEN

. . .

HECUBA (*to herself*)
 O the foul sin of it!
The wickedness! My child. My child! Again
I cry to thee. How cruelly art thou slain!

ANDROMACHE
She hath died her death, and how so dark it be,
Her death is sweeter than my misery.

HECUBA
Death cannot be what Life is, Child; the cup
Of Death is empty, and Life hath always hope.

ANDROMACHE
O Mother, having ears, hear thou this word
Fear-conquering, till thy heart as mine be stirred
With joy. To die is only not to be;
And better to be dead than grievously
Living. They have no pain, they ponder not

Their own wrong. But the living that is brought
From joy to heaviness, his soul doth roam,
As in a desert, lost, from its old home.

.   .   .

ANDROMACHE (*to the child*)
Go, die, my best-beloved, my cherished one,
In fierce men's hands, leaving me here alone.
Thy father was too valiant; that is why
They slay thee! Other children, like to die,
Might have been spared for that. But on thy head
His good is turned to evil.

PLATO

THE WINGS OF THE SOUL

SOCRATES. I mean to say that as I was about to cross the stream the usual sign was given to me,—that sign which always forbids, but never bids, me to do anything which I am going to do; and I thought that I heard a voice saying in my ear that I had been guilty of impiety, and that I must not go away until I had made an atonement. Now I am a diviner, though not a very good one, but I have enough religion for my own use, as you might say of a bad writer—his writing is good enough for him; and I am beginning to see that I was in error. O my friend, how prophetic is the human soul! At the time I had a sort of misgiving, and, like Ibycus, "I was troubled; I feared that I might be buying honour from men at the price of sinning against the gods." Now I recognize my error. . . . [as Stesichorus says] "I told a lie when I said" that the beloved ought to accept the non-lover when he might have the lover, because the one is sane, and the other mad. It might be so if madness were simply an evil; but there is also a madness which is a divine gift, and the source of the chiefest blessings granted to men. For prophecy is a madness, and the prophetess at Delphi and the priestesses at Dodona when out of their senses have conferred great benefits on Hellas, both in public and private life, but when in their senses few or none. And I might also tell you how the Sibyl and other inspired persons have given to many an one many an intimation of the future which has saved them from falling. But it would be tedious to speak of what every one knows.

.   .   .

I might tell of many other noble deeds which have sprung from inspired madness. And therefore, let no one frighten or flutter us by saying that the temperate friend is to be chosen rather than the inspired, but let him further show that love is not sent by the gods for any good to lover or beloved; if he can do so we will allow him to carry off the palm. And we, on our part, will prove in answer to him that the madness of love is the greatest of heaven's blessings, and the proof shall be one which the wise will receive, and the witling disbelieve. But first of all, let us view the affections and actions of the soul divine and human, and try to ascertain the truth about them.

·   ·   ·

Of the nature of the soul, though her true form be ever a theme of large and more than mortal discourse, let me speak briefly, and in a figure. And let the figure be composite—a pair of winged horses and a charioteer. Now the winged horses and the charioteers of the gods are all of them noble and of noble descent, but those of other races are mixed; the human charioteer drives his in a pair; and one of them is noble and of noble breed, and the other is ignoble and of ignoble breed; and the driving of them of necessity gives a great deal of trouble to him. I will endeavour to explain to you in what way the mortal differs from the immortal creature. The soul in her totality has the care of inanimate being everywhere, and traverses the whole heaven in divers forms appearing:—when perfect and fully winged she soars upward, and orders the whole world; whereas the imperfect soul, losing her wings and drooping in her flight at last settles on the solid ground—there, finding a home, she receives an earthly frame which appears to be self-moved, but is really moved by her power; and this composition of soul and body is called a living and mortal creature. For immortal no such union can be reasonably believed to be; although fancy, not having seen nor surely known the nature of God, may imagine an immortal creature having both a body and also a soul which are united throughout all time. Let that, however, be as God wills, and be spoken of acceptably to him. And now let us ask the reason why the soul loses her wings!

The wing is the corporeal element which is most akin to the divine, and which by nature tends to soar aloft and carry that which gravitates downwards into the upper region, which is the habitation of the gods. The divine is beauty, wisdom, goodness, and the like; and by these the wing of the soul is nourished, and grows apace; but when fed upon evil and foulness and the opposite of good, wastes and falls away. . . . The chariots of the gods in even poise, obeying the rein, glide rapidly; but the others labour, for the vicious steed goes heavily, weighing down the charioteer to the earth when his steed has not been thoroughly trained:— and this is the hour of agony and extremest conflict for the soul. For the immortals, when they are at the end of their course, go forth and stand upon the outside of heaven, and the revolution of the spheres carries them round, and they behold the things beyond. But of the heaven which is above the heavens, what earthly poet ever did or ever will sing worthily? It is such as I will describe; for I must dare to speak the truth, when truth is my theme. There abides the very being with which true knowledge is concerned; the colourless, formless, intangible essence, visible only in mind, the pilot of the soul. The divine intelligence, being nurtured upon mind and pure knowledge, and the intelligence of every soul which is capable of receiving the food proper to it, rejoices at beholding reality, and once more gazing upon truth, is replenished and made glad, until the revolution of the worlds brings her round again to the same place. In the revolution she holds justice, and temperance, and knowledge absolute, not in the form of generation or of relation, which men call existence, but knowledge absolute in existence absolute; and beholding the other true existences in like manner, and feasting upon them, she passes down into the interior of the heavens and returns home; and there the charioteer putting up his horses at the stall, gives them ambrosia to eat and nectar to drink.

Such is the life of the gods; but of other souls, that which follows God best and is likest to him lifts the head of the charioteer into the outer world, and is carried round in the revolution, troubled indeed by the steeds, and with difficulty beholding true being; while another only rises and falls, and sees, and again fails to see by reason of the unruliness of the steeds. The rest of the souls are also longing after the upper world and they all follow, but not being strong enough they are carried round below the surface, plunging, treading on one another, each striving to be first; and there is confusion and perspiration and the extremity of effort; and many of them are lamed or have their wings broken through the ill-driving of the charioteers; and all of them after a fruitless toil, not having attained to the mysteries of true being, go away, and feed upon opinion. . . . And therefore the mind of the philosopher alone has wings; and this is just, for he is always, according to the measure of his abilities, clinging in recollection to those things in which God abides, and in beholding which He is what He is. And he who employs aright these memories is ever being initiated into perfect mysteries and alone becomes truly perfect. But, as he forgets earthly interests and is rapt in the divine, the vulgar deem him mad, and rebuke him; they do not see that he is inspired.

.   .   .

But of beauty, I repeat again that we saw her there shining in company with the celestial forms; and coming to earth we find her here too, shining in clearness through the clearest aperture of sense. For sight is the most piercing of our bodily senses; though not by that is wisdom seen; her loveliness would have been transporting if there had been a visible image of her, and the other ideas, if they had visible counterparts, would be equally lovely. But this is the privilege of beauty, that being the loveliest she is also the most palpable to sight. Now he who is not newly initiated or who has become corrupted, does not easily rise out of this world to the sight of true beauty in the other; he looks only at her earthly namesake, and instead of being awed at the sight of her, he is given over to pleasure, and like a brutish beast he rushes on to enjoy and beget; he consorts with wantonness, and is not afraid or ashamed of pursuing pleasure in violation of nature. But he whose initiation is recent, and who has been the spectator of many glories in the other world, is amazed when he sees any one having a godlike face or form, which is the expression of divine beauty; and at first a shudder runs through him, and again the old awe steals over him; then looking upon the face of his beloved as of a god he reverences him, and if he were not afraid of being thought a downright madman, he would sacrifice to his beloved as to the image of a god; then while he gazes on him there is a sort of reaction, and the shudder passes into an unusual heat and perspiration; for, as he receives the effluence of beauty through the eyes, the wing moistens and he warms. And as he warms, the parts out of which the wing grew, and which had been hitherto closed and rigid, and had prevented the wing from shooting forth, are melted, and as nourishment streams upon him, the lower end of the wings begins to swell and grow from the root upwards; and the growth extends under the whole soul—for once the whole was winged. . . . [This] is the reason why the soul of the lover will never forsake his beautiful one, whom he esteems above all; he has forgotten mother and brethren and companions, and he thinks nothing of the neglect and loss of his property; the rules and proprieties of life, on which he formerly prided himself, he now despises, and is ready to sleep like a servant, wherever he is allowed, as near as he can to his desired one, who is the object of his worship, and the physician who can alone assuage the greatness of his pain. And this state, my dear imaginary youth to whom I am talking, is by men called love, and among the gods has a name at which you, in your simplicity, may be inclined to mock. . . .

.   .   .

As I said at the beginning of this tale, I divided each soul into three —two horses and a charioteer; and one of the horses was good and the other bad: the division may remain, but I have not yet explained in what the goodness or badness of either consists, and to that I will proceed. The right-hand horse is upright and cleanly made; he has a lofty neck and an aquiline nose; his colour is white, and his eyes dark; he is a lover of honour and modesty and temperance, and the follower of true glory; he needs no touch of the whip, but is guided by word and admonition only. The other is a crooked lumbering animal, put together anyhow; he has a short thick neck; he is flat-faced and of a dark colour, with grey eyes and blood-red complexion; the mate of insolence and pride, shag-eared and deaf, hardly yielding to whip and spur. Now when the charioteer beholds the vision of love, and has his whole soul warmed through sense, and is full of the prickings and ticklings of desire, the obedient steed, then as always under the government of shame, refrains from leaping on the beloved; but the other, heedless of the pricks and of the blows of the whip, plunges and runs away, giving all manner of trouble to his companion and the charioteer, whom he forces to approach the beloved and to remember the joys of love. They at first indignantly oppose him and will not be urged on to do terrible and unlawful deeds; but at last, when he persists in plaguing them, they yield and agree to do as he bids them. And now they are at the spot and behold the flashing beauty of the beloved; which when the charioteer sees, his memory is carried to the true beauty, whom he beholds in company with Modesty like an image placed upon a holy pedestal. He sees her, but he is afraid and falls backwards in adoration, and by his fall is compelled to pull back the reins with such violence as to bring both the steeds on their haunches, the one willing and unresisting, the unruly one very unwilling; and when they have gone back a little, the one is overcome with shame and wonder, and his whole soul is bathed in perspiration; the other, when the pain is over which the bridle and the fall had given him, having with difficulty taken breath, is full of wrath and reproaches, which he

371

43. *Team of horses,* from the west frieze of the Siphnian Treasury.

heaps upon the charioteer and his fellow-steed, for want of courage and manhood, declaring that they have been false to their agreement and guilty of desertion. Again they refuse, and again he urges them on, and will scarce yield to their prayer that he would wait until another time. When the appointed hour comes, they make as if they had forgotten, and he reminds them, fighting and neighing and dragging them on, until at length he, on the same thoughts intent, forces them to draw near again. And when they are near, he stoops his head and puts up his tail, and takes the bit in his teeth and pulls shamelessly. Then the charioteer is worse off than ever; he falls back like a racer at the barrier, and with a still more violent wrench drags the bit out of the teeth of the wild steed and covers his abusive tongue and jaws with blood, and forces his legs and haunches to the ground and punishes him sorely. And when this has happened several times and the villain has ceased from his wanton way, he is tamed and humbled, and follows the will of the charioteer, and when he sees the beautiful one he is ready to die of fear. And from that time forward the soul of the lover follows the beloved in modesty and holy fear.

.   .   .

Thus great are the heavenly blessings which the friendship of a lover will confer upon you, my youth. Whereas the attachment of the non-lover, which is alloyed with a worldly prudence and has worldly and niggardly ways of doling out benefits, will breed in your soul those vulgar qualities which the populace applaud. . . .

(from *Phaedrus*)

ARISTOTLE

ON FRIENDSHIP

After what we have said, a discussion of friendship would naturally follow, since it is a virtue or implies virtue, and is besides most necessary with a view to living. For without friends no one would choose to live, though he had all other goods; even rich men and those in possession of office and of dominating power are thought to need friends most of all; for what is the use of such prosperity without the opportunity of beneficence, which is exercised chiefly and in its most laudable form towards friends? Or how can prosperity be guarded and preserved without friends? The greater it is, the more exposed is it to risk. And in poverty and in other misfortunes men think friends are the only refuge. It helps the young, too, to keep from error; it aids older people by ministering to their needs and supplementing the activities that are failing from weakness; those in the prime of life it stimulates to noble actions—"two going together"—for with friends men are more able both to think and to act. Again, parent seems by nature to feel it for offspring and offspring for parent, not only among men but among birds and among most animals; it is felt mutually by members of the same race, and especially by men, whence we praise lovers of their fellowmen. We may see even in our travels how near and dear every man is to every other. Friendship seems too to hold states together, and law-givers to care more for it than for justice; for unanimity seems to be something like friendship, and this they aim at most of all, and expel faction as their worst enemy; and when men are friends they have no need of justice, while when they are just they need friendship as well, and the truest form of justice is thought to be a friendly quality.

But it is not only necessary but also noble; for we praise those who love their friends, and it is thought to be a fine thing to have many friends; and again we think it is the same people that are good men and are friends.

.   .   .

The kinds of friendship may perhaps be cleared up if we first come to know the object of love. For not everything seems to be loved but only the lovable, and this is good, pleasant, or useful; but it would seem to be that by which some good or pleasure is produced that is useful, so that it is the good and the useful that are lovable as ends. Do men love, then, *the* good, or what is good for *them?* These sometimes clash. So too with regard to the pleasant. Now it is thought that each loves what is good for himself, and that the good is without qualification lovable, and what is good for each man is lovable for him; but each man loves not what is good for him but what seems good. This however will make no difference; we shall just have to say that this is "that which seems lovable." Now there are three grounds on which people love; of the love of lifeless objects we do not use the word "friendship"; for it is not mutual love, nor is there a wishing of good to the other (for it would surely be ridiculous to wish wine well; if one wishes anything for it, it is that it may keep, so that one may have it oneself); but to a friend we say we ought to wish what is good for his sake. But to those who thus wish good we ascribe only goodwill, if the wish is not reciprocated; goodwill when it *is* reciprocal being friendship. Or must we add "when it is recognized"? For many people have goodwill to those whom they have not seen but judge to be good or useful; and one of these might return this feeling. These people seem to bear goodwill to each other; but how could one call them friends when they do not know their mutual feelings? To be friends, then, they must be mutually recognized as bearing goodwill and wishing well to each other for one of the aforesaid reasons.

Now these reasons differ from each other in kind; so, therefore, do the corresponding forms of love and friendship. There are therefore three kinds of friendship, equal in number to the things that are lovable; for with respect to each there is a mutual and recognized love, and those who love each other wish well to each other in that respect in which they love one another. Now those who love each other for their utility do not love each other for themselves but in virtue of some good which they get from each other. So too with those who love for the sake of pleasure; it is not for their character that men love ready-witted people, but because they find them pleasant. Therefore, those who love for the sake of utility love for the sake of what is good for *themselves,* and those who love for the sake of pleasure do so for the sake of what is pleasant to *themselves,* and not in so far as the other is the person loved but in so

44. *Hermes, Orfeo and Eurydice.*

far as he is useful or pleasant. And thus these friendships are only incidental; for it is not as being the man he is that the loved person is loved, but as providing some good or pleasure. Such friendships, then, are easily dissolved, if the parties do not remain like themselves; for if the one party is no longer pleasant or useful the other ceases to love him.

Now the useful is not permanent but is always changing. Thus when the motive of the friendship is done away, the friendship is dissolved, inasmuch as it existed only for the ends in question. This kind of friendship seems to exist chiefly between old people (for at that age people pursue not the pleasant but the useful) and, of those who are in their prime or young, between those who pursue utility. And such people do not live much with each other either; for sometimes they do not even find each other pleasant; therefore they do not need such companionship unless they are useful to each other; for they are pleasant to each other only in so far as they rouse in each other hopes of something good to come. Among such friendships people also class the friendship of host and guest. On the other hand the friendship of young people seems to aim at pleasure; for they live under the guidance of emotion, and pursue above all what is pleasant to themselves and what is immediately before them; but with increasing age their pleasures become different. This is why they quickly become friends and quickly cease to be so; their friendship changes with the object that is found pleasant, and such pleasure alters quickly.

Young people are amorous too; for the greater part of the friendship of love depends on emotion and aims at pleasure; this is why they fall in love and quickly fall out of love, changing often within a single day. But these people do wish to spend their days and lives together; for it is thus that they attain the purpose of their friendship.

Perfect friendship is the friendship of men who are good, and alike in virtue; for these wish well alike to each other *qua* good, and they are good in themselves. Now those who wish well to their friends for their sake are most truly friends; for they do this by reason of their own nature and not incidentally; therefore their friendship lasts as long as they are good—and goodness is an enduring thing. And each is good without qualification and to his friend, for the good are both good without qualification and useful to each other. So too they are pleasant; for the good are pleasant both without qualification and to each other, since to each his own activities and others like them are pleasurable, and the actions of the good *are* the same or like. And such a friendship is as might be expected permanent, since there meet in it all the qualities that friends should have. For all friendship is for the sake of good or of pleasure—good or pleasure either in the abstract or such as will be enjoyed by him who has the friendly feeling—and is based on a certain resemblance; and to a friendship of good men all the qualities we have named belong in virtue of the nature of the friends themselves; for in the case of this kind of friendship the other qualities also are alike in both friends, and that which is good without qualification is also without qualification pleasant, and these are the most lovable qualities. Love and friendship therefore are found most and in their best form between such men.

But it is natural that such friendships should be infrequent; for such men are rare. Further, such friendship requires time and familiarity; as the proverb says, men cannot know each other till they have "eaten salt together"; nor can they admit each other to friendship or be friends till each has been found lovable and been trusted by each. Those who quickly show the marks of friendship to each other wish to be friends, but are not friends unless they both are lovable and know the fact; for a wish for friendship may arise quickly, but friendship does not.

This kind of friendship, then, is perfect both in respect of duration and in all other respects, and in it each gets from each in all respects the same as, or something like what, he gives; which is what ought to happen between friends. Friendship for the sake of pleasure bears a resemblance to this kind; for good people too *are* pleasant to each other. So too does friendship for the sake of utility; for the good are also useful to each other. Among men of these inferior sorts too, friendships are most permanent when the friends get the same thing from each other (e.g. pleasure), and not only that but also from the same source, as happens between ready-witted people, not as happens between lover and beloved. For these do not take pleasure in the same things, but the one in seeing the beloved and the other in receiving attentions from his lover; and when the bloom of youth is passing the friendship sometimes passes too (for the one finds no pleasure in the sight of the other, and the other gets no attentions from the first); but many lovers on the other hand are constant, if familiarity has led them to love each other's characters, these being alike. But those who exchange not pleasure but utility in their amour are both less truly friends and less constant. Those who are friends for the sake of utility part when the advantage is at an end; for they were lovers not of each other but of profit.

.   .   .

But there is another kind of friendship, viz. that which involves an inequality between the parties, e.g. that of father to son and in general of elder to younger, that of man to wife and in general that of ruler to subject. And these friendships differ also from each other; for it is not the same that exists between parents and children and between rulers and subjects, nor is even that of father to son the same as that of son to father, nor that of husband to wife the same as that of wife to husband. For the virtue and the function of each of these is different, and so are the reasons for which they love; the love and the friendship are therefore different also. Each party, then, neither gets the same from the other, nor ought to seek it; but when children render to parents what they ought to render to those who brought them into the world, and parents render what they should to their children, the friendship of such persons will be abiding and excellent. In all friendships implying inequality the love also should be proportional, i.e. the better should be more loved than he loves, and so should the more useful, and similarly in each of the other cases; for when the love is in proportion to the merit of the parties, then in a sense arises equality, which is certainly held to be characteristic of friendship.

.   .   .

Most people seem, owing to ambition, to wish to be loved rather than to love; which is why most men love flattery; for the flatterer is a friend in an inferior position, or pretends to be such and to love more than he is loved; and being loved seems to be akin to being honoured, and this is what most people aim at. But it seems to be not for its own sake that people choose honour, but incidentally. For most people enjoy being honoured by those in positions of authority because of their hopes (for they think that if they want anything they will get it from them; and therefore they delight in honour as a token of favour to come); while those who desire honour from good men, and men who know, are aiming at confirming their own opinion of themselves; they delight in honour, therefore, because they believe in their own goodness on the strength of the judgement of those who speak about them. In being loved, on the other hand, people delight for its own sake; whence it would seem to be better than being honoured, and friendship to be desirable in itself. But it seems to lie in loving rather than in being loved, as is indicated by the delight mothers take in loving; for some mothers hand over their children to be brought up, and so long as they know their fate they love them and do not seek to be loved in return (if they cannot have both), but seem to be satisfied if they see them prospering; and they themselves love their children even if these owing to their ignorance give them nothing of a mother's due. Now since friendship depends more on loving, and it is those who love their friends that are praised, loving seems to be the characteristic virtue of friends, so that it is only those in whom this is found in due measure that are lasting friends, and only their friendship that endures.

.   .   .

Another question that arises is whether friendships should or should not be broken off when the other party does not remain the same. Perhaps we may say that there is nothing strange in breaking off a friendship based on utility or pleasure, when our friends no longer have these attributes. For it was of these attributes that we were the friends; and when these have failed it is reasonable to love no longer. But one might complain of another if, when he loved us for our usefulness or pleasantness, he pretended to love us for our character. For, as we said at the outset, most differences arise between friends when they are not friends in the spirit in which they think they are. So when a man has deceived himself and has thought he was being loved for his character, when the other person was doing nothing of the kind, he must blame himself; but when he has been deceived by the pretences of the other person, it is just that he should complain against his deceiver; he will complain with more justice than one does against people who counterfeit the currency, inasmuch as the wrongdoing is concerned with something more valuable.

But if one accepts another man as good, and he turns out badly and is seen to do so, must one still love him? Surely it is impossible, since not everything can be loved, but only what is good. What is evil neither can nor should be loved; for it is not one's duty to be a lover of evil, nor to become like what is bad; and we have said that like is dear to like. Must the friendship, then, be forthwith broken off? Or is this not so in all cases, but only when one's friends are incurable in their wickedness? If they are capable of being reformed one should rather come to the assistance of their character or their property, inasmuch as this is better and more characteristic of friendship. But a man who breaks off such

45. *Hetaera playing the flute.* Side relief of Throne of Ludovisi.

a friendship would seem to be doing nothing strange; for it was not to a man of this sort that he was a friend; when his friend has changed, therefore, and he is unable to save him, he gives him up.

. . .

Benefactors are thought to love those they have benefited, more than those who have been well treated love those that have treated them well, and this is discussed as though it were paradoxical. Most people think it is because the latter are in the position of debtors and the former of creditors; and therefore as, in the case of loans, debtors wish their creditors did not exist, while creditors actually take care of the safety of their debtors, so it is thought that benefactors wish the objects of their action to exist since they will then get their gratitude, while the beneficiaries take no interest in making this return. Epicharmus would perhaps declare that they say this because they "look at things on their bad side," but it is quite like human nature; for most people are forgetful, and are more anxious to be well treated than to treat others well. . . .

. . .

Should we, then, make as many friends as possible, or—as in the case of hospitality it is thought to be suitable advice, that one should be "neither a man of many guests nor a man of none"—will that apply to friendship as well; should a man neither be friendless nor have an excessive number of friends?

To friends made with a view to *utility* this saying would seem thoroughly applicable; for to do service to many people in return is a laborious task and life is not long enough for its performance. Therefore friends in excess of those who are sufficient for our own life are superfluous, and hindrances to the noble life; so that we have no need of them. Of friends made with a view to *pleasure*, also, few are enough, as a little seasoning in food is enough.

But as regards *good* friends, should we have as many as possible, or is there a limit to the number of one's friends, as there is to the size of a city? You cannot make a city of ten men, and if there are a hundred thousand it is a city no longer. But the proper number is presumably not a single number, but anything that falls between certain fixed points. So for friends too there is a fixed number—perhaps the largest number with whom one can live together (for that, we found, is thought to be very characteristic of friendship); and that one cannot live with many people and divide oneself up among them is plain. Further, they too must be friends of one another, if they are all to spend their days together; and it is a hard business for this condition to be fulfilled with a large number. It is found difficult, too, to rejoice and to grieve in an intimate way with many people, for it may likely happen that one has at once to be happy with one friend and to mourn with another. Presumably, then, it is well not to seek to have as many friends as possible, but as many as are enough for the purpose of living together; for it would seem actually impossible to be a great friend to many people. This is why one cannot love several people; love is ideally a sort of excess of friendship, and that can only be felt towards one person; therefore great friendship too can only be felt towards a few people. This seems to be confirmed in practice; for we do not find many people who are friends in the comradely way of friendship, and the famous friendships of this sort are always between two people. Those who have many friends and mix intimately with them all are thought to be no one's friend, except in the way proper to fellow-citizens, and such people are also called obsequious. In the way proper to fellow-citizens, indeed, it is possible to be the friend of many and yet not be obsequious but a genuinely good man; but one cannot have with many people the friendship based on virtue and on the character of our friends themselves, and we must be content if we find even a few such.

(from *Nicomachean Ethics,* Books VIII, IX)